PROJECTILE POINT TECHNOLOGY AND ECONOMY
A Case Study from Paiján, North Coastal Peru

THE CENTER FOR THE STUDY OF THE FIRST AMERICANS

The Center for the Study of the First Americans (CSFA) is a unit of the Department of Anthropology, College of Liberal Arts, Texas A&M University, College Station, TX. The CSFA was established in July 1981 by a seed grant from Mr. William Bingham's Trust for Charity (renamed Bingham Trust). The mission of the Center is the promotion of interdisciplinary scholarly dialogue and the stimulation of public interest on the subject of the peopling of the Americas through research, education, and outreach. Toward these goals:

- CSFA designs and implements programs of study and research involving the physical, biological, and cultural sciences;
- CSFA provides leadership and coordination to scholars world wide on the subject of the First Americans;
- CSFA promotes an open dialogue between government, business, avocation archaeologists, and the Native American community on the preservation of cultural and biological resources, and other issues relating to the study of the First Americans;
- CSFA disseminates the product of this synergism through education programs reaching a broad range of groups, including school children, the general public, and international scholars.

The mission of the Center's staff and Advisory Board is to further the goals and programs of the CSFA, which has a membership of over 1400 individuals. The Center's office and research laboratories are located in the Anthropology Building on the TAMU campus. The Center's faculty and associates include:

Robson Bonnichsen	Director and General Editor e-mail: rbonnichsen@tamu.edu
Michael R. Waters	Associate Director e-mail: mwaters@tamu.edu
Ted Goebel	Editor, *CRP* e-mail: goebel@unr.edu
Laurie Lind	Office Manager e-mail: csfa@tamu.edu
James M. Chandler	Editor, Mammoth Trumpet e-mail: wordsmiths@acadia.net
Ruth Gruhn	Series Editor of CSFA books

The Center's Peopling of the Americas publication program focuses on the earliest Americans and their environments. The Center solicits high-quality original manuscripts in English. For information write to: Robson Bonnichsen, Center for the Study of the First Americans, Department of Anthropology, Texas A&M University, 4352 TAMU, College Station, TX 77843-4352. *Current Research in the Pleistocene* presents note-length articles about current research in the interdisciplinary field of Quaternary studies as it relates to the peopling of the Americas. The submission deadline is February 15 of each calendar year. In addition, the Center publishes a quarterly newsmagazine, the *Mammoth Trumpet,* written for both general and professional audiences. Subscription to the *Mammoth Trumpet* is by membership in the Center. Contact Laurie Lind, CSFA, Department of Anthropology, Texas A&M University, 4352 TAMU, College Station, TX 77843-4352; phone (979) 845-4046, fax (979) 845-4070 for more information about the CSFA, its programs, and membership in the Center. The CSFA is a non-profit organization that depends on gifts and grants for its support. To learn about America's earliest cultural and biological heritage, join the Center today. For more information check our Web site **www.CenterFirstAmericans.org**

Projectile Point Technology and Economy
A Case Study from Paiján, North Coastal Peru

Claude Chauchat and Jacques Pelegrin
Cesar Galvez Mora, Rosario Becerra Urteaga, and Rocio Esquerre Alva

Appendix by Cesar Galvez Mora, Hélène Martin, and Philippe Pannoux

Foreword by Jacques Tixier

Translated by Magen O'Farrell

A Peopling of the Americas Publication
Robson Bonnichsen, General Editor
Ruth Gruhn, Series Editor

PROJECTILE POINT TECHNOLOGY AND ECONOMY
A Case Study from Paiján, North Coastal Peru

©2004 Center for the Study of the First Americans. All rights reserved. No part of this book may be reproduced, projected, stored in a retrieval system, or transmitted, for whatever purpose, in any form or by any means, whether electronic, mechanical, magnetic, photographic, laser, or otherwise, without the prior written permission of the Center for the Study of the First Americans, Department of Anthropology, Texas A&M University, College Station, TX 77843-4352.

Design and typesetting by C & C Wordsmiths, Blue Hill, ME.
Cover design by Ann Ahearn of Downeast Graphics & Printing, Inc, Ellsworth, ME.
Printed in the United States of America by Thomson-Shore, Inc., Dexter, MI.

Distributed by the Texas A&M University Press, College Station, TX.
This book is printed on 100% acid-free paper.

ISBN 1-58544-365-4

Contents

Foreword	vii
Introduction	ix
Methods	ix
Vocabulary	x
Chapter 1 The Paiján Complex, or Paijánense	1
Paiján Projectile Point Technology	7
Chivateros Bifaces and Foliate Pieces	7
Projectile Points	9
Chapter 2 Research Strategy and Experimentation	13
The Research Strategy	13
Experimentation	15
Qualitative Results: The Phases of the *Chaîne Opératoire*	15
Phase 1	16
Phase 2	17
Phase 3	18
Phase 4	20
Evaluating Constraints	20
Quantitative Results and Principles of Application	22
Recognizing Blanks	22
Principles of Quantitative Evaluation	23
Conclusions	25
Chapter 3 Return to the Archaeological Record	29
Pampa de los Fósiles 14, Unit 1	29
Methodology	30
Post-Occupational Formation Processes	35
The Collected Material	37
Bifacial Knapping Activity	41
Chapter 4 The Raw Material Varieties	59
Pale Rhyolite Varieties	59
Varieties Present in Several Concentrations	59
Varieties Restricted to Concentration D	72
Varieties Restricted to Concentration B	73
Other Observations	77
Conclusions on Pale Rhyolite Bifacial Knapping	80

    Green Tuff 80
    Minor Rejections of Flakes 84
    Other Bifacially Knapped Materials 86
    Conclusions on Bifacial Knapping Activities 88
    Point Fabrication at Pampa de los Fósiles 14, Unit 1 92
    Qualitative Aspects: Skill Levels 94
    Spatial Distribution of Knapping Activities 98
    Duration of Occupation and Number of Knappers 99

Chapter 5   Other Observations 103
    Unifaces 103
    Methods of Analysis 103
    Description 103
    Conclusions 109
    Rare Materials 110

Chapter 6   Conclusions 113
    Methodology 113
    Results of Knapping Activities 114
    Occupation Duration and Group Composition 115
    Circulation and Territory 115
    Acknowledgments 117

Appendix   Faunal Remains Found in the Pit near Concentration D 119

References Cited 121

Index 125

Foreword

CAN WE IMAGINE the daily behavior of prehistoric people? Of course it is possible to let our suppositions run free, or even to describe our fantasies in detail, in a form of science-fiction, since the moment has not yet arrived (will it ever?) when a time machine will allow us the benefits of direct observation. . . . However, a supposition is not an hypothesis.

Is it possible then, to *scientifically* evoke a part of the daily life of a prehistoric ethnic group, a part that is linked to a certain projectile point? I think so; that is, as long as we adhere to a scientific procedure that consists of testing hypotheses through rigorous, demonstrative reasoning which, when possible, is supported by experimentation that also is rigorous.

It can't always be done. First, it is necessary to have access to adequate field data that has been exploited according to a well thought and efficient procedure.

Next, it is necessary to locate the outcrops of the different stone raw materials exploited by the prehistoric people; then to experiment with these same materials in order to estimate their experimental pieces will act as a verification of the proposed hypotheses.

Finally, it is necessary to evaluate the mobility patterns, task durations, group composition and skill levels of the prehistoric people as well as environmental data. All these factors lead, in conclusion, to hypotheses concerning territories.

These studies must be carried out by confirmed specialists. Such an accumulation of integrated factors is certainly unusual but it exists here in this work.

However, I remind you that, as exceptional and developed as this study is, it still concerns one type of knapped object. All this work and energy devoted to one, single tool type? Indeed, since we have here one of the rare cases in which a single artifact type is sufficient to represent the presence of a human group. The "Paiján" point is a true paleo-ethnological marker. With its well-delimited geographic territory, elegant complexity, and obviously skilled artisans, it certainly deserves this attention.

To all of this, is added the excellent and innovative work accomplished by the authors of this monograph, a work which itself should clearly be considered as an example to follow.

The Paiján people are no longer here to contradict us; but in the pages that follow, their lives are evoked with reason and conviction, and thus with respect.

—*Jacques Tixier*
Directeur de recherche Honoraire
CNRS

Introduction

THE EXCLUSIVE FOCUS on projectile points as prehistoric cultural markers in the Americas has often been criticized, owing to the partial nature of information that is obtained, compared with what can be gathered from the ensemble of artifacts collected by archaeologists. The quantitative definition of assemblages of non-selected stone tools is an approach that yields a greater amount of information concerning the activities in which these tools participated, as well as providing a basis for chronocultural attributions. Moreover, the excessive explanation of lithic tools in exclusively cultural terms was justifiably criticized several times and in several ways by L. and S. Binford. They remarked that lithic tools are first utilitarian objects, manufactured with the goal of being utilized, before they are cultural markers (Binford 1972, 1977; Binford and Binford 1966; see also S. Binford 1968).

At the same time, and sometimes even very early in the development of prehistoric archaeology, questions of "how" were addressed to lithic tools concerning their techniques of manufacture. Answers were sought through ethnographic observations and/or experimentation. This approach led to the development of the concept of *chaîne opératoire* by Leroi-Gourhan (1965:35), which was then most actively promoted by J. Tixier (1967). From this perspective, a lithic assemblage is no longer considered only as a series of objects to be described, but as the remains of a succession of technical actions beginning at the moment of raw material acquisition and continuing through the manufacture, utilization, and abandonment of tools. Recognizing these different actions, in the order of the technical processes of production and use, implies analyzing and classifying all lithic remains, including the waste products, finished tools, and used and abandoned or broken tools. This goal is achieved through a technological reading of each object. Next, the different stages or sequences thus distinguished can be studied in qualitative and quantitative terms. Studying the phases of the manufacture of tools also better reveals the complexity of the mental processes necessary to obtain a finished product, which are not so clearly or immediately revealed by the tool morphology alone. Since the great majority of stone knappers have definitively disappeared, experimental replication is the only method by which we can build the modern reference bases necessary for this method of defining and quantifying the activities of the ancient artisans based on the artifacts they have left behind.

We have applied the *chaîne opératoire* approach in our study of lithic technology at the Peruvian site of Pampa de los Fósiles 14, unit 1. This methodological approach to surface sites in arid zones, and particularly combining lithic technology and spatial analysis, was directly inspired by the seminal work of J. Tixier at the open-air camp of Bordj Mellala in the Algerian Sahara (Tixier et al. 1976). Tixier himself was influenced by the publications of the Magdalenian site of Pincevent (Leroi-Gourhan and Brézillon 1966, 1972).

Methods

This monograph presents a project of lithic technological analysis in which a series of experiments were conducted and documented in strict relation to a precise archaeological context, whose results we then applied to the study of a site of this same archaeological context. This research thus returns to the knapped-stone projectile points, which are the objects of long and complex manufacture sequences. However, the projectile point is seen not only as a cultural marker, even if by all evidence it is one, but rather as a functional object whose manufacture needs both a certain degree of expertise and a certain quantity of work. These are elements that can allow us to understand better the prehistoric economy and society of which these objects are the product.

In this study, we will analyze a biface manufacture chipping floor or workshop situated in a desert area of the north coast of Peru called Cupisnique, where the first inhabitants made bifacial projectile points using an elaborate *chaîne opératoire* adapted at the same time to the available raw materials and to functional and cultural constraints. Such workshops, clearly visible on the naked surface of the desert, are numerous in this region. In a research project with explicit regional objectives that began in the '70s we were able to assign to the same complex several types of surface sites that were spatially separated in the better-known zone of Pampa de los Fósiles, but were sometimes mingled in other areas of the same region (Ascope, Quebrada de Cupisnique) as well as in other regions (Moche and Casma valleys to the south). Clearly the specialized workshops for knapping bifacial projectile points are not the only sites of this culture, and as should be expected, short-duration—or seasonal—living sites exist in the vicinity. Of course, their lithic equipment is quite different, since a projectile point is a very specialized implement and subsistence activities will need other types of tools, but the careful researcher will soon identify in those other sites rare fragments of used or discarded projectile points as well as traces of short or aborted episodes of knapping. Where rockshelter deposits and stratigraphy are lacking and all the material is on the surface, pro and con arguments of contemporaneity and association must be drawn from contextual analysis. Any small seasonal site such as those that exist in the Peruvian desert never contains in itself all the data necessary to understand it. A regional long-term research strategy is a prerequisite to understanding the complexity of relations between seemingly very different sites whose elements were actually intimately intermingled in the life of prehistoric people responsible for their making. Systematic analysis by surface collection, followed by excavating more than 20 sites and cursorily examining countless others, led to conclusions that are mainly valid within the region of Cupisnique and for the Paiján culture. Conditions can be different elsewhere, although we can surmise that, in nearby regions, the same cultural complex could be present, perhaps with settlement systems adapted to different geographical conditions. This report is not the place to undertake a regional synthesis of the early prehistory of northern Peru; that is certainly needed but will be done in another study.

Our main objective here is to estimate what kind of information can be acquired by studying waste products of bifacial manufacture. The first phase of this program was devoted to documenting the replicating of this special kind of projectile point, the "Paiján point," by a modern expert knapper. After summarizing the major aims of this first phase and its results, we will return to an actual archaeological workshop and study its material to see what interpretations can be made at the same time about the discarded pieces—broken or defective bifaces or points—and the waste products of successful manufacture of projectile points that have disappeared, for they were taken away to fulfill their function.

But, as with any archaeological site, this one has its peculiarities. A kind of multipurpose scraper that is generally scarce in this area is present here in some number, mixed with the remains of bifacial knapping. Also present are flake or unifacial tools ("common tools") that are typical of the living sites of this area. At the same time, the kind of shallow excavation that we systematically dug to retrieve material apparently buried by the trampling of the prehistoric people themselves led to the discovery of a refuse pit containing remnants of animals that were consumed during the stay of the knappers at the site. Describing these elements can be deemed external to the aims of a study devoted to projectile points, but an archaeological site is a whole, and all its elements can and must contribute to understanding the prehistoric way of life.

Vocabulary

Any research program develops it own vocabulary to deal with newly found realities or ones that are special to the explored research area. This is even more the case for a project of more than 20 years' duration, and this situation can lead to a significant semantic drift from other research on nearby areas. A careful assessment of this specialized, sometimes provisional, vocabulary is thus necessary. The research program on the Paiján complex first took its technical vocabulary from the French school of lithic analysis, the result of more than a century of research on that matter. The works by F. Bordes and A. Leroi-Gourhan are the most prominent in that realm, but the more recent syntheses on lithic technology were published by J. Tixier's team; an English version is available (Inizan et al. 1999). In the chapter dealing with lithic technology we will explain at greater length the various terms used here that may not be familiar to English-speaking specialists, as well as terms that arose by necessity from our study.

But a regional research program carries with it other constraints when it deals with numerous sites. A typology of various kinds of localities found on the field is essential to such a study. In that case we followed and adapted practices of the Chanchan-Moche Valley Project of Harvard University in northern Peru (M. Moseley, pers. comm. 1970) by assembling under the heading of sites spatial clusters of smaller elements, called units. What we call "site" here is often a group of small localities, which themselves generally consist of artifacts clusters visible on the surface. These small localities, which we called "units," are thus actually the real units of study. The boundaries of larger sites are sometimes determined by natural features such as rocky hills, terraces, bluffs, and dry washes, most often by a clear difference in distance between intra-site units compared with outside units. But, of course there is often a certain degree of arbitrariness in their exact placement. A good example of spatial distribution of sites and units is given in Figure 4; others can be found in Chauchat et al. 1998:22, 46, 95, 114. It must be understood that the above-mentioned number of sites is just the number of these groups. The actual number of units has not been calculated, but it must be several hundreds. Most often these units have a rather small extension, from 50 to 300 m^2, although there are some estimated at larger than several thousand square meters. It must be stressed that the term "unit" is used in comparison with larger sites. We have sometimes used "site" as a more common term for the spatial units of our study when the context is unequivocal.

At the same time, features within these sites must be defined. Considering one kind of site, the biface knapping workshop, especially Pampa de los Fósiles 14, unit 1, we recognized on the surface spots of great density of soft-hammer flakes that we have called concentrations (A, B, C, D). Actually, after examining plans showing the spatial distributions of these flakes, we were able to distinguish smaller spots of greater density of flakes that we called knapping localities. In some instances, concentrations of flakes

Introduction

driven under the surface as the result of trampling by prehistoric people led to the same result. Knapping localities, for instance, are numbered B1, B2, B3, etc. This distinction of two superimposed types of flake concentrations is an analytic device created in order to isolate the original place of knapping, given that experimental knapping localities are much smaller than the concentrations in this workshop, which themselves have probably been blurred after very long exposure on the surface (see below, "Post-Occupational Processes").

Chapter 1
The Paiján Complex, or Paijánense

THE PAIJÁN COMPLEX is known from numerous open-air sites and one rockshelter occupation distributed over nearly 1,000 km of Peruvian coastal desert (Bird 1948; Bonavia 1979, 1982; Chauchat 1976, 1988; Chauchat et al. 1992; Chauchat and Bonavia 1990; Lanning 1963; Lanning and Hammel 1961; Larco Hoyle 1948; Ossa 1973; Ossa and Moseley 1972; Patterson 1966; Uceda 1986, 1992). The best-known region, where we have been working for the last 25 years, is the desert zone of Cupisnique, located to the north of the modern city of Trujillo, at 7° 30' south, between the Chicama and Jequetepeque valleys (Figures 1, 2, and 3).

Within the Cupisnique region, the Pampa de los Fósiles zone is a depression, or dry valley, situated in the upper part of the coastal plain, there about 15 km wide, at the foot of the Cerro Tres Puntas massif (around 800 m altitude) and on its north and northwest flanks. This zone contains numerous Paiján archaeological sites, Ceramic-period sites, and even paleontological sites. Pampa de los Fósiles was originally a paleontological site, located on the coastal plain about 15 km to the northwest. The same name was applied to the archaeological sites, despite the distance, by Peruvian archaeologist R. Larco Hoyle (1948); it is thus necessary to distinguish these two localities. The sites distributed around site 14 are indicated on the map in Figure 4. Site 12, the first subject of our research starting in 1972 (Chauchat 1976, 1979), which includes two large quarries, is located to the southwest just beyond the limits of this map.

During a systematic survey of the whole region that began in 1972 and was completed in 1997 (Chauchat et al. 1998), 196 Paiján sites were discovered and located on the map. The fact that they are all open-air sites, that very few material boundaries exist locally to restrict their extension—as would be the case under a rockshelter, for instance—has very important consequences for their interpretation. The first interpretation is that these small sites or units represent short-duration occupations by small groups. Figures are difficult to estimate but they could well be in the order of several days to several weeks, perhaps a few months at most, with numbers of occupants consistent with a nuclear family. The second interpretation is that one can estimate a very low probability that two chronologically distant occupations would take place at exactly the same spot and that each spatial cluster of artifacts (unit) thus represents a culturally homogeneous assemblage. Of course this interpretation does not dismiss the possibility of intrusive isolated pieces, but they would probably be only isolated, very rare pieces.

The most evident, but not the only, cultural marker of the Paiján complex is a stemmed bifacial point of relatively large dimensions, examples of which are described below. These points are mainly found on surface chipping floors (workshops), which are themselves traceable by the raw materials to quarries found on nearby outcrops of high-quality stone. This point type has been named the Paiján point after a nearby village.

Recognizing localities with an abundance of stone-knapped irregular bifaces, associated with their by-products and located on outcrops of the same material, as quarry sites devoted to producing blanks for Paiján projectile points (Chauchat 1977), helped us to solve the apparent mystery of the so-called *Chivateros* complex discovered by Patterson (1966) and assigned by Lanning (1970) to a supposed Andean horizon of bifaces. The radiocarbon date obtained by Patterson on wood from the Cerro Chivateros site near Lima is perfectly consistent with the northern Paiján dates yielded by the Cupisnique sites. Projectile points very similar to the Paiján points (the so-called Luz complex) had been discovered in the same region as the Cerro Chivateros site (Lanning 1963) but were not related to it, mainly because the spatial as well as raw-material relationships were not so clear as in the northern Peruvian case. Another cause is that radiocarbon assays from material associated with this Luz complex gave much later dates, probably because of lack of awareness about possible contamination by modern carbon in a superficial site with very thin archaeological deposit (we had the same

Figure 1. Map of Peru; main modern coastal cities (squares) and Paiján archaeological sites (dots).

problem at the beginning of our research in Cupisnique).

From the beginning we also recognized other localities generally grouped with the Paiján points workshops but spatially distinct, which were in most instances completely without Paiján points. However, in a few cases one or two bifacial fragments, or fragments definitely assignable to Paiján points, and sometimes remains of bifacial knapping (soft-hammer flakes), could be found in these localities. These varied remains stood out very clearly in the material because the stone varieties knapped for Paiján points were quite different from those found in the debitage. The tool assemblage associated with these localities consists mostly of utilized flakes, denticulates, and a few pebble tools. Endscrapers and burins are absent. This large class of what we call "common tools" has been described in detail by Chauchat et al. (1992). Also weakly represented are ovate sidescrapers, of which certain forms are identical to Mousterian *limaces* (Bordes 1961). Limaces (slugs) had already been recognized by Paul Ossa in the site of La Cumbre as associated with Paiján points (Ossa 1973; Ossa and Moseley 1972). At this time we began to call them unifaces, to differentiate them from the true Mousterian limaces, because we found that their range of variation was considerably greater, even though the word has a different significance for some English-speaking lithic specialists. Some examples of these tools appear in our descriptions, although most of this monograph is devoted to bifacial tools and thus to projectile points.

Since the quarry sites and the workshops for Paiján points are all specialized sites where, judging by their remains, few if any subsistence activities were carried out, it was natural to look for a kind of living site in the vicinity. We found that the abovementioned localities were an obvious candidate. This seemed at the moment the more parsimonious hypothesis given the data at hand, and preferable to assigning sites dogmatically to different traditions every time different lithic assemblages are found. So we concluded that the *Chivateros* biface localities, the Paiján point chipping floors, and the localities seemingly without projectile

The Paiján Complex, or Paijánense

points (or with very few) but with a wealth of flake tools and debitage are all part of the same settlement system, i.e., were produced by human groups with only one material culture during the same period (Chauchat 1977:18–20). At no time since the '70s have we found data to the contrary in our surveys and studies of the hundreds of sites in the Cupisnique region.

All these data and the reasoning that led to these conclusions were exposed at length in several articles and three books (Chauchat 1976, 1977, 1978, 1979, 1987, 1988, 1990, 1991; Chauchat and Bonavia 1998; Chauchat and Pelegrin 1994; Chauchat et al. 1992, 1998).

The Paiján complex seems to constitute a local adaptation to exploiting marine resources by Paleoindian hunter-gatherers who made fluted or unfluted fishtail points (El Inga–Fell's Cave lithic complex). This transformation was recently revealed at a manufacture workshop of these points situated in the interior of the Cupisnique region at the foot of the Andes (Briceño 1994, 1997; Chauchat 1990; Chauchat and Briceño 1998; Hall 1995). In this open-air workshop, which represents a short-term occupation, fishtail points of the El Inga–Fell's Cave style are associated with Paiján points. The latter are relatively short but already show their distinctive characteristics; morphologically intermediate forms are lacking. At this time the discovery of two different point types, both made of the same local lithic material in the same workshop, could indicate that the transition from one form to another was rapid. This transformation may have appeared when the group added a new type (the Paiján point) to their technical equipment and shortly thereafter abandoned the older type (the fishtail point). The absence of any intermediate form in a region so intensively explored (Chauchat et al. 1998) also suggests that this transformation could have resulted from a conscious decision that led almost instanta-

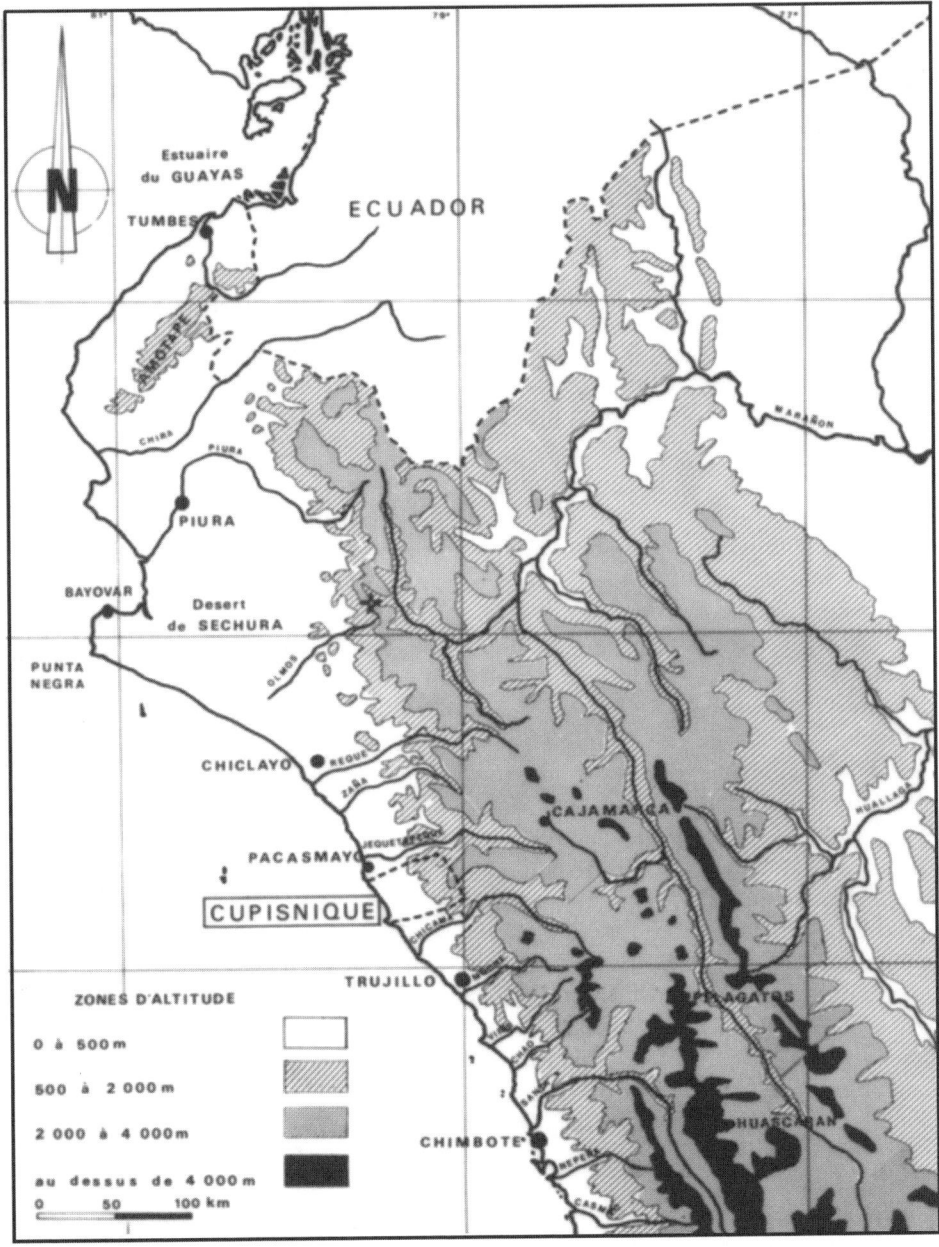

Figure 2. Northern Peru: relief of the Andes mountains and location of the Cupisnique region (from Chauchat et al. 1992: 13).

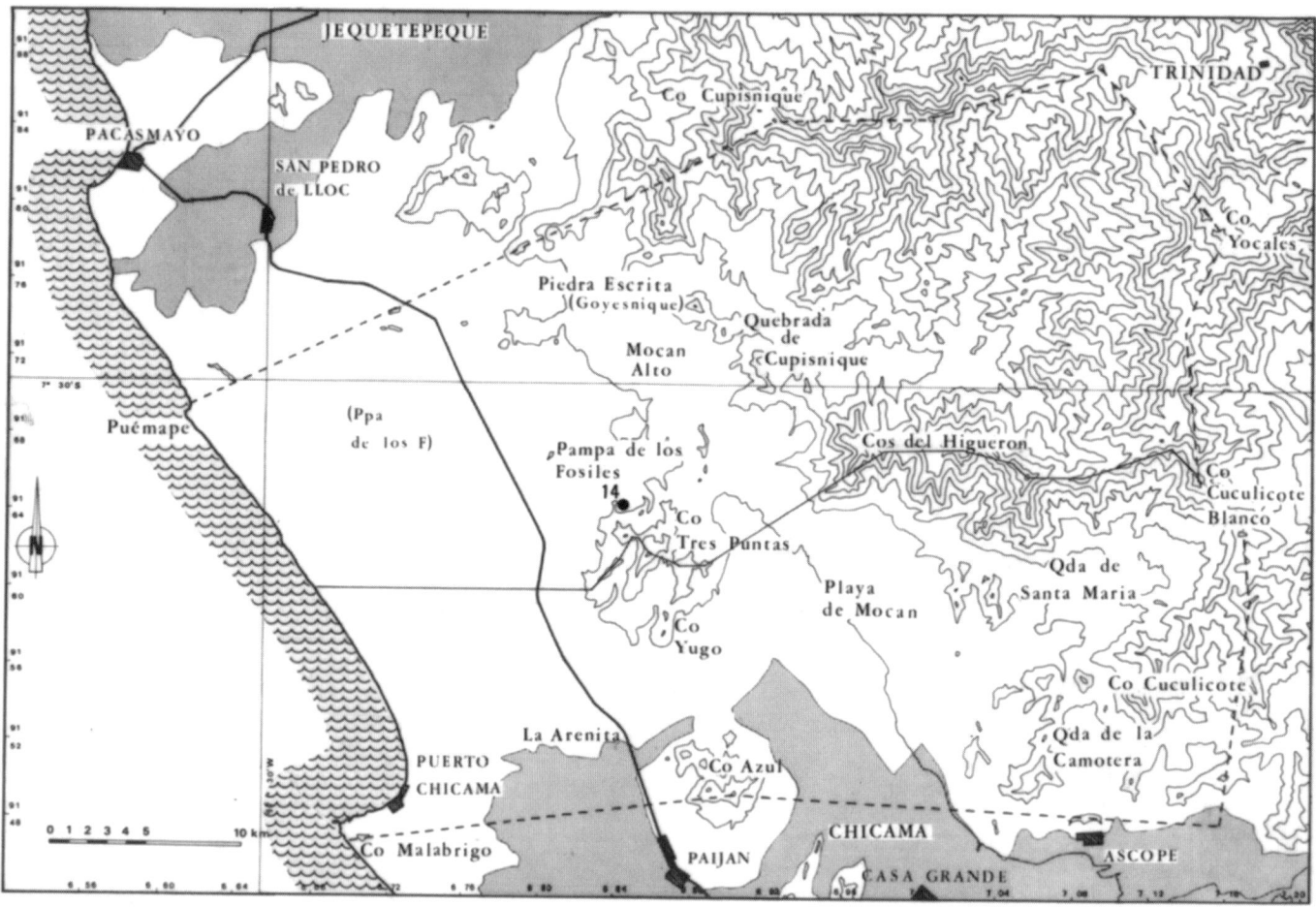

Figure 3. The Cupisnique region: relief (contour interval 200 m); toponymy, location of Pampa de los Fósiles 14.

neously to adopting a completely different design. This design would have been chosen according to explicit technical and functional criteria, rather than as the result of a slow process of derivation from a model point. Two other fishtail points had already been found on the northern coast of Peru, one in the Piura region (extreme north of Peru) without any reliable context (Chauchat and Zevallos Quiñones 1980), the other as part of a group of Paiján point workshops at La Cumbre in the Moche valley, barely 50 km south of the Cupisnique desert zone (Ossa 1976).

It is necessary to question this important, apparently instantaneous change in projectile point forms. We have established its relationship to subsistence remains found in the coastal campsites, since they are associated with knapping workshops where fragments of Paiján points and preforms in all stages of manufacture have been found in association with abundant knapping waste flakes. Because the sediments are loose, the food remains in the living sites were buried by prehistoric trampling. These bones are never those of large Pleistocene fauna of South America, whose fossilized remains are found in abundance on the coastal plain—clearly in this case, however, under the eroded surface and without indication of human presence. On the other hand,

saltwater fish, often very large, are abundant in the campsites (Wing in Chauchat et al. 1992).

The conditions of prey acquisition in terrestrial and marine environments are completely different. A terrestrial animal wounded and weakened by the loss of blood may be overtaken by the hunter and captured at a vulnerable moment. On the other hand, when a prey animal in the ocean escapes it is lost. It is thus necessary to design a weapon that penetrates the animal deeply, assuring its fixation, and that preferably is attached to the hunter. In addition, it is advantageous that the weapon assemblage floats. The morphology of the point is necessarily adapted: a narrow stem ensures its fixation into a reed haft, a narrow and elongated pointed tip ensures maximum penetration of the prey, which the barbs of the point then hold. Abraded edges found on a few points assumed to be finished and even utilized are undoubtedly evidence that the hunters sought a point that would penetrate deeply without unduly cutting and tearing the fish, thus lessening the risk of loss. Perhaps it also served to minimize the size of the hole made in the skin, since the wound stretched the skin instead of tearing it. This aversion to damaging the skin of the fish could be associated with utilizing the skin, such as for making clothing. This utilization is indeed known among other peoples; for example, certain Paleo-Siberian peoples (notably Goldes and Ainus) treat and sew salmon skins.

The change from the fishtail point, which is short and wide,

The Paiján Complex, or Paijánense

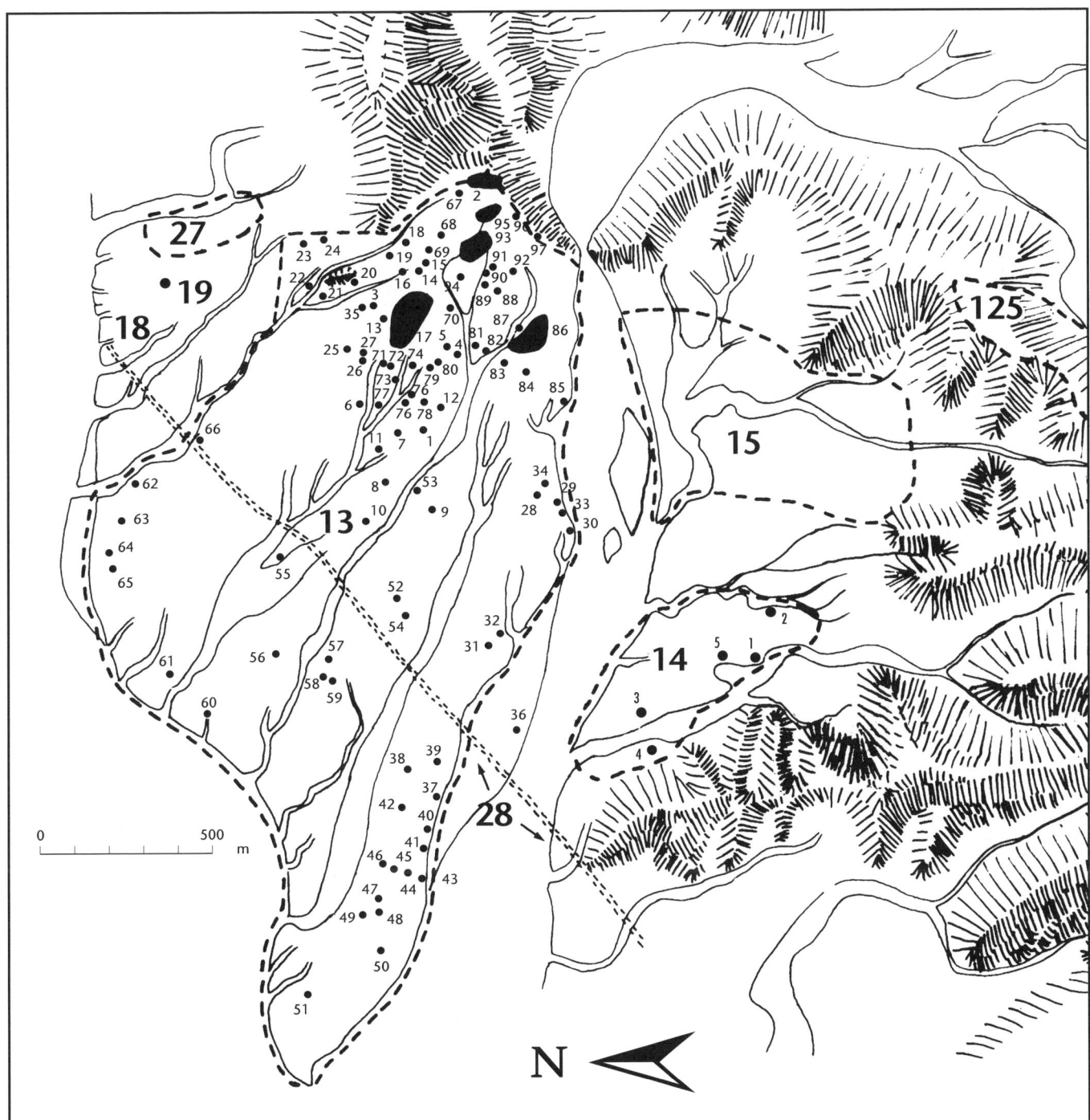

Figure 4. The northern flank of the Cerro Tres Puntas hills and the Paiján sites of Pampa de los Fósiles 13, 14, 15, and 27, as well as the rhyolite quarries of site 125. Sites 18 and 28 date from a ceramic period. Site 18, an enclosure with a loose stone wall, has a road made visible by two parallel lines of cobbles that leads to the enclosure. Site 19 is a final-Pleistocene paleontological site where skeletal pieces of a giant sloth *Scelidodon* sp. have been excavated.

to the Paiján point, which is long and narrow, thus corresponds to a change in game from terrestrial to marine animals. Even if we do not yet know of living sites with fishtail points, we can suppose that this change also corresponds to geographic and ecological changes and could indicate the arrival of the first human groups coming from the mountains to the coastal zone.

More recent research has shown that the Paiján complex, identified by its characteristic points, is found very far in the interior of the territory and fairly high on the western flank of the Andean range at around 2000 m altitude. Because the points known from this zone are few and fragmentary, we cannot reconstruct their complete shape. Nonetheless, they are found at rich sites with large surface areas that leave no doubt as to the density of human occupation in this zone (Chauchat et al. 1998:84). This evidence suggests that Paiján points were utilized in the interior ranges of the territories. However, since these points are always made from local raw materials, we cannot dismiss the possibility that the points and bifacial foliate pieces found at high altitudes are the work of the same Paiján people who made fishing expeditions to the coast. These points would have been made in the mountains, thus taking advantage of good-quality raw materials in anticipation of future fishing expeditions.

We already know that at piedmont sites around or in Pampa de los Fósiles there exist flint fragments that cannot have originated from local outcrops, which are all volcanic or alluvial (Chauchat et al. 1992). Therefore they must come from the extensive limestone outcrops in the mountains. These flint fragments, numbering fewer than ten in each case, are often small knapping remains that we can imagine were forgotten in the bottom of a pouch or basket; thus they more likely suggest expeditions to the sources than exchange with groups based in the mountains. As we have already remarked (Chauchat et al. 1992), this observation leads us to attribute to the Paiján people a high degree of mobility as well as a vast exploitation territory (around 100 km from west to east) across several ecological zones tiered on the western flank of the cordillera.

At around the same time, in several regions of northern South America we observe a tendency toward longer bifacial points. The first known case is at the El Inga site in Ecuador, where elongated points with narrow stems are associated with fishtail points; however, they probably constitute a slightly later component of the site (Bell 1965). At the cave of Chobshi (Lynch 1989; Lynch and Pollock 1980, 1981) these stemmed points are the only ones present. These points have often been identified with Paiján points, but except for a general similarity in form (being rather elongated and stemmed) they are rather different, as the reader will note when comparing our drawings of Paiján points in this volume and in our earlier publications with illustrations of stemmed points from El Inga and Chobshi. In Colombia, large points that are also different from Paiján points, although elongated and with narrow stems, have been found at open-air sites (Ardila 1991; López Castaño 1990, 1995). At the rockshelter site of Pedra Furada in the Piauí region of northeast Brazil, a site famous for its controversial Pleistocene tool industries, the level attributed to the Serra Talhada period yielded a long, massive quartz point. This point is unique in this region, but in spite of lacking its extremities, it is surprisingly similar to Paiján points (Parenti 1993). A final example could be the point, or points, found at Caverna de Pedra Pintada on the Amazon near Santarem, Brazil (Roosevelt et al. 1996). Therefore, in at least part of South America soon after the arrival of the first Paleoindians a tendency toward elongated points appeared, associated with wide, sometimes fluted stems replaced by narrow ones. This tendency could have been manifested in slightly different forms, either adapted to different game in different regions or representing cultural idiosyncrasies.

At Pampa de los Fósiles, the numerous sites of the coastal plain are all surface sites. The same is true for the quarry sites situated a short distance from them on outcrops of volcanic stones, which are mainly rhyolites of good knapping quality. We often examined the material in situ, then replaced it in its original location without collecting it. Other artifacts from several workshop sites were systematically collected. The bifacial pieces were individually mapped and the knapping flakes collected in meter-square units. The results of the study of four of these workshops, several campsites, and a test pit in a quarry site in the same region were presented in Chauchat et al. 1992. The stages of the production process are as follows:

1. On a rocky outcrop, a large, elongated crude biface was knapped with a hard stone hammer. This type of biface is called *Chivateros* after the aforementioned quarry site in the suburbs of Lima (Patterson 1966).

2. After being carried a short distance, these bifaces were first reduced with a soft hammer into elongated foliate pieces, then retouched by pressure into Paiján points.

Considering only the surface knapping remains of the region, we can therefore separate the localities into two types, quarries and workshops, with three phases of knapping processes: stone hammer percussion, soft hammer percussion, and pressure retouch. By convention we have called the piece resulting from soft hammer percussion (starting from the moment of the first blow) a **bifacial foliate piece**; the piece resulting from the pressure technique (from the moment of first removal) we have called a **projectile point**. Of course, this convention does not eliminate the possible diagnostic uncertainty of these two techniques on real objects.

From the beginning of our research on the Paiján complex in this region in 1974, after examining numerous desert surface workshops C. Chauchat envisioned the point knapping process as a flow along the time dimension, resulting in the appearance in the archaeological record of the various by-products of this activity. First there would be flakes, then broken or abandoned objects. It became evident that the objects now present on the surface represented only the rejected pieces, the functional ones having been transported elsewhere for utilization. We can consider this flow the manifestation of the knapper's mental template. This mental template defines not only the shape of the finished object, but also the technical processes that create it. It thus follows that an object in the process of manufacture becomes part of the archaeological record only at the moment when it deviates from the ideal flow and when this deviation cannot be rectified. Obviously this is the case with a broken piece; it also applies to a flaw that the knapper is unable to correct with his level of expertise; for example, a section too thick in proportion to its width, a bump formed by repeated hinge terminations, or a significant asymmetry or curvature of the piece. A different case occurs with objects that any person with a minimum of stone-knapping experience recognizes could not under any conditions be products of the normal process of knapping a Paiján point or even a thin, elongated bifacial foliate point. These pieces thus need a different interpretation. We often observed that they had been intensely reduced until there remained no more than a small blank that was sometimes difficult to hold in the hand. They were thus very likely the result of knapping exercises by children or young adolescents at the beginning of their apprenticeship. For these pieces, what was sought is the simple action of knapping, i.e., the repetition of motor patterns in order to master them, rather than the finished product. The result is a randomly shaped object. Chauchat (1991) has proposed the term "deviant pieces" to describe such objects.

The points finished and ready for utilization were exported from the workshop for this "hunting of fish," undoubtedly toward the shore. The great majority of them were lost, since the shoreline campsites were submerged and destroyed by the rising sea level during the first half of the Holocene (Chauchat 1987). There thus remain only a few broken or whole objects as examples for archaeologists of the Paiján point form that was sought by knappers in the workshops.

However, by studying the whole pieces and broken fragments rejected in the quarries and workshops we can discern the normal morphological evolution from original blank to finished point, on the condition that we distinguish several categories of unequal value. We can expect that abandoned whole preforms were rejected because of morphological flaws or obvious accidents that terminated the knapping process. Naturally some broken preforms exhibit similar kinds of flaws; but others, with no flaws other than fractures, can be considered directly representative of normal knapping processes, all the while maintaining an uncertainty concerning the original length of the preform.

Paiján Projectile Point Technology

In conjunction with our first experiments, we examined hundreds of flakes in the field (at the quarries of Pampa de los Fósiles 12, unit 104, Pampa de los Fósiles 125, and various workshops) and reexamined those from assemblages already collected.

At the quarries, the flakes clearly show distinctive features associated with hard-hammer percussion. These features, identified during experiments conducted with relatively hard quartzite cobbles of local origin, are a relatively thick butt that is plain or rarely faceted; a marked point of impact; and a relatively high frequency of *Siret* (accidental) fractures (Bordes 1961:32; Inizan et al. 1999:156). However, there also exist a few flakes that were clearly detached with a soft hammer (Chauchat et al. 1992:117–118). In addition, it was clearly evident that *Chivateros* bifaces were made from three types of original raw blanks: a) large flakes that were removed from thick blocks, then partially shaped while conserving a good proportion of the ventral face; b) thin plaques with large zones of residual "cortex" (cortex is defined here as a patinated cleavage surface); and c) blocks, or fragments of blocks, that were undoubtedly thicker than the plaques, since they were totally shaped by covering flakes. The knappers' proficiency with these three types of blanks enabled them to exploit different outcrops where the stone fractured and was detached from its bedrock in different ways: in more or less narrow planes, thus providing the plaques; in thicker, prismatic fragments; or in large blocks that could be worked into flake blanks of variable dimensions.

In the workshops the flakes show features identical to those of flakes detached in experiments with direct percussion by a hammer made from the wood of the *algarrobo* tree (*Prosopis pallida*). This tree, common in the north Peruvian desert, is similar to the North American mesquite. These features are a relatively acute exterior platform angle, a faceted butt with a more or less blunted edge, and a strong and clear lip. This latter characteristic reflects the particular fracture mechanism of soft-hammer percussion on a relatively coarse grained and compact stone. Under these conditions the initial fracture tends to tear away the edge rather than drive down the point of contact. These particular features are thus unmistakable diagnostics of direct soft-hammer percussion in the first steps of shaping in the workshops. This is true for large flakes up to 10 cm long and for small, thin flakes less than 2 cm long.

The use of pressure retouch for the finishing stages of Paiján point manufacture is observed or deduced from observations of the points themselves. No form of percussion could possibly have produced the point, stem, and barbs or such a finely regular body of the piece.

These three knapping techniques make it possible to distinguish three main sequences in the *chaîne opératoire* of manufacture, a change in location occurring after the first sequence. These sequences are: 1) on the quarry site, roughing out the blank by hard-hammer percussion; 2) in the workshop, shaping the preform by soft-hammer percussion; and 3) finishing the point by pressure retouch. In addition, our tests have led us to distinguish four distinct phases. We subdivided the second of the three original sequences into two phases, based on observing both a change in objective (transition from thinning to narrowing) and a change in technique (from a heavy hammer to a lighter soft hammer).

More precise estimates of the length of Paiján points sought by the knappers can be deduced by systematically measuring all objects after collecting and excavating. Given that flakes are almost always detached from the longest sides of the piece, the length of the bifacial preform varies only a little during the reduction process. The greatest variation occurs in its width and thickness.

Chivateros Bifaces and Foliate Pieces

A test pit 1 m square excavated at the quarry unit 104 of Pampa de los Fósiles 12 (Chauchat et al. 1992:109–125) yielded numerous whole and fragmentary bifaces. The pieces worked at the workshops of site 12 originate from this quarry. There, as well as in the workshops, the whole objects appeared to be defective and thus provide only distorted or indirect information concerning the knapper's mental template (Pelegrin 1995a). Moreover, it was evident that a number of longer, thicker, sometimes trihedral pieces may have been utilized as picks to excavate blocks for knapping (Chauchat et al. 1992:123, 124). On the other hand, the broken bifaces are very probably the remains of good pieces that were accidentally broken. It was impossible to search for refits among these fragments owing to the presence of an enormous quantity of knapping waste, its intense disturbance by Paijanenses looking for the surface of the stone outcrop, and the small size of our test pit.

Our approach to this situation was to divide the small sample of fragments for which the maximal width was still observable (Table 1) into a subsample composed of what we interpreted as basal (or inferior) fragments and another much smaller subsample interpreted as apical (or superior) fragments.

We thus estimated the missing fragments by using two different calculations and drawing upon two working hypotheses concerning the supposed forms of bifaces (Table 1):

Hypothesis 1: The form of the biface is symmetrical, and the maximum width is at equal distance from the two extremities, the inferior and superior fragments thus being indistinguishable.

Hypothesis 2: The biface is not symmetrical, and the inferior and superior fragments can be distinguished. This distinction arises from the hypothesis that the shape of a biface prefigures that of a foliate piece in the same way that the form of a foliate pieces prefigures that of a finished point. In this case the maximum width of the biface is located closer to the inferior extremity, thus creating two unequal parts.

The first hypothesis (columns 7 and 8) is simple to calculate. It is sufficient to double the distance measured for the existing extremity in order to obtain a first estimation of the distribution of biface lengths: the extreme values range from 82 to 148 mm, and the average is 114 mm. In this case the average of the ratio "estimated length/width" is 1.77, with a standard deviation of 0.32. There was one particular case, biface no. 20, whose length is 96 mm, with the maximum width situated very low at 34 mm from the basal extremity; simply doubling the distance from the basal extremity to the height of maximum width would give an unrealistic estimation of the total length—much smaller than the length of the actual fragment. In this case the value was not noted in the table. This particular object constitutes an additional argument in support of the second hypothesis.

According to the second hypothesis (columns 9–12), the apical portion of *Chivateros* bifaces is differentiated from the inferior portion. The additional hypothesis by which the two fragment types derived from bifaces are assumed to have generally the same form allows us to calculate the average ratio "width/distance from the existing extremity" (columns 9 and 10), which can be used to calculate the missing or incomplete distance for the other bifaces.

Note that the average estimated lengths of the objects in both subsamples (basal and apical fragments) are essentially equal, 65.7 mm and 64.5 mm. This result shows that regardless of the fragment type considered, they are indeed objects with the same characteristics. The ratio of the inferior distance to width is 0.81; that of the superior distance to width is 1.05. Therefore the value of the missing distance is equal to length x 1.05 if it is the superior distance that is missing (column 9), and length x .81 if the inferior distance is missing (column 10). We next add to each value obtained the distance to the existing width measured on each fragment (column 3 or 4) in order to

Table 1. Dimensions of fragmentary bifaces, with maximum width, from the quarry of Pampa de los Fósiles 12, unit 104.

1 No.	2 Length	3 D_{inf}	4 D_{sup}	5 Width	6 Thickness	7 L est$_1$	8 L est$_1$/W	9 D_{sup} est$_2$	10 D_{inf} est$_2$	11 L est$_2$	12 L est$_2$/W
14	98	41		63	41	82	1.3	66		107	1.7
19	90	62		73	43	124	1.7	76		138	1.89
20	96	34		81	36			85		119	1.47
38	84	53		85	37	106	1.25	89		142	1.67
44	66	43		57	22	86	1.51	60		103	1.8
130	109	72		69	32	144	2.09	73		145	2.1
134	83	58		65	32	116	1.83	68		126	1.93
141	92	58		62	38	116	1.87	65		123	1.98
168	106	52		73	31	104	1.42	77		132	1.81
172	114	57		70	36	114	1.62	74		137	1.96
185	81	59		71	72	118	1.66	75		134	1.89
232	90	58		49	27	116	2.37	52		110	2.24
277	81	47		71	45	94	1.32	75		122	1.71
307	72	45		51	28	90	1.76	54		99	1.94
320	99	55		63	35	110	1.75	66		121	1.92
176	74	54		49	35	108	2.2	52		106	
176			54	49	35	108			40	89	1.82
6	97		64	57	41	128	2.24		46	110	1.92
29	109		74	63	37	148	2		51	125	1.98
135	116		68	64	49	136	2.13		52	120	1.88
166	96		66	74	38	132	1.78		60	126	1.7

1 piece number
2 length of the fragment
3 distance from the maximum width to the lower extremity
4 distance from the maximum width to the upper extremity
5 maximum width
6 thickness
7 first hypothesis, estimated total length
8 first hypothesis, ratio of estimated length to width
9 second hypothesis, estimated distance from the maximum width to the upper extremity
10 second hypothesis, estimated distance from the maximum width to the lower extremity
11 second hypothesis, estimated total length
12 second hypothesis, ratio of estimated length to width.

obtain the total estimated length of each biface (column 11). It is then possible to calculate the ratio "estimated length/width" for each piece. A curious case is piece no. 176, for which the calculation revealed a superior distance smaller than the inferior distance. On the other hand, if we suppose that the distance measured is the superior one, we obtain a piece of normal proportions. We noted both hypotheses in the table one after the other, even though we still believe this to be a superior fragment. The distribution of total lengths estimated by this method has extreme values of 80 mm and 145 mm, and an average of 121 mm. The ratio "length/width" of this distribution is 1.87, and the standard deviation of the distribution of the length/width ratios is 0.75. Since the metric values (inferior and superior length limits, average of lengths) differ by less than 1 cm in every case, we note that the two hypotheses do not yield significantly different results.

Table 2 lists for each of the three studied workshops (Pampa de los fósiles 13, unit 3, unit 4–5, unit 11) the counts of pieces, the inferior and superior length limits, and the average of this distribution for typical whole foliate pieces. Since these pieces were reconstructed from several fragments, this sample does not include the whole pieces found on the surface of these workshops.

In the case of unit 11, it should be noted that the most extreme values of length are contributed by one small piece and one large piece. If we remove these two exceptional pieces (leav-

Table 2. Counts, minimum and maximum limits, and average values of the length distributions of complete foliate pieces, reconstructed from fragments, for three of the workshops studied at Pampa de los Fósiles 13.

Site	Count	Min. length	Average length	Max. length
Unit 3	9	114	122	150
Unit 4–5	19	85	122.5	141
Unit 11	16	57	115.4	156

ing n = 14), we observe a much more limited interval: inferior limit, 96 mm; average, 116.7; superior limit, 131. The average lengths of the foliate pieces from the workshops are thus very similar in spite of a relatively high degree of individual variability in each workshop. Therefore, according to our current state of knowledge, pieces longer than 140 mm are exceptional even if they are highly visible in the workshops because of their spectacular nature. These were either produced by exceptionally talented knappers or were the products of some kind of game or contest. Another possibility is that they belong to a particular phase of the Paiján period that we have not been able to isolate owing to the superficial nature of all the workshops.

Finally, the results yielded by the *Chivateros* bifaces from the test pit at the Pampa de los Fósiles 12, unit 104, quarry site, although drawn from fragmentary pieces, do not contradict the workshop data.

Projectile Points

We have already mentioned the rarity of Paiján points in the workshops and the reason for this rarity once the clearly defective pieces are excluded. Unfortunately, this situation hinders statistical analyses of their dimensions and morphological characteristics. We find projectile points in two situations:

- points broken when very nearly finished after much work by pressure retouch. The stem or apex is broken off; we sometimes also find these fragments;
- a few rare examples found in campsites are broken basal fragments that were brought back with the shaft to be replaced by a new point or to be re-pointed if long enough.

We might expect to find exceptional examples of whole isolated points, perhaps lost during travel, but this is not the case. This gives an idea of the care taken with good pieces in anticipation of utilization.

In spite of these limitations, we can nonetheless define Paiján points. The definition stated below, however, does not preclude great variability in detail in stemmed points (Figure 5).

The Paiján point is a bifacial point that is most often elongated. Its base is formed by a stem that is also narrow and elongated. This stem is delimited by barbs whose bases are never rounded, but are pointed and generally oriented toward the base or, more rarely, slightly to the side. The apical part of the point, or tip, is characterized by its long needle shape. On points with convex sides this elongation is manifested as an inflection of the superior edges, which become concave, then rectilinear toward the tip. The supposed finished points are also characterized by clearly detectable abrading along the entire length of the two edges, thus eliminating their sharpness.

Starting from this general morphology, minor variations exist in the shape of the sides (rectilinear or convex), the location of the maximum width (situated at the barb level or higher), the shape of the stem (rectangular or oval or with a medial constriction), and in the length and width of the piece. Serrated edges are exceptional, as is the presence of true wings, which have been observed only on short pieces. The known examples are often of relatively large dimensions, with an average length of 11–16 cm and width of 2–3 cm. In the workshops, however, exist a small number of sturdier pieces, which may have had a different function. We created a subcategory for some very diminutive examples; these were made by marginally retouching flakes and could have been the work of children (Chauchat et al. 1992:199). At present, we have no means of quantifying these differences, for example, by determining types and citing relative frequencies, or by ascribing an evolutionary process and citing early and late forms or dimensions. For example, we could postulate an evolution toward increasingly elongated and sharp points, but at the moment we have no clear proof of this. As discussed in earlier publications (e.g., Chauchat et al. 1992:278, 341–343), the radiocarbon dates obtained from the excavated sites do not offer a solution.

However, on the basis of the collected documents and numerous observations made at the workshops, it is possible empirically to define an ideal point form that appears to have been most frequently desired. This is an elongated point, usually more

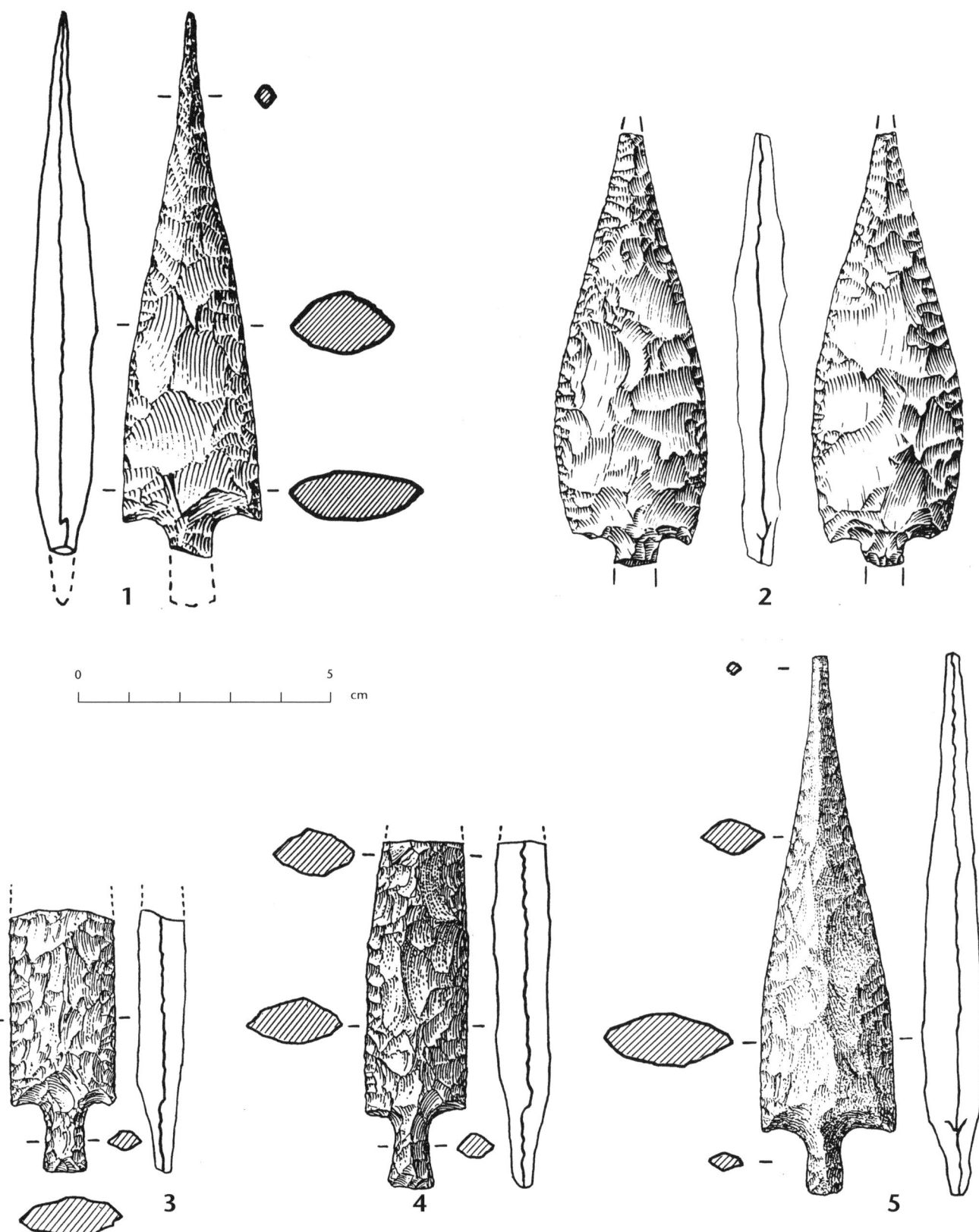

Figure 5. Examples of Paiján points found in workshop contexts in the Cupisnique region. **1**, Quebrada Santa Maria south, site 352; **2**, Quebrada Santa Maria, site 140; **3–4**, Pampa de los Fósiles 13; **5**, Pampa de los Fósiles 25 (drawings: **1**, C. Chauchat; **2**, J.-F. Deridet; **3–5**, P. Laurent).

than 10 cm long; in the majority of cases the length is 10–13 cm, and a few pieces are 14 or even 15 cm long (Table 2). In the excavated workshops, it seems that a broken point was resharpened if the longest fragment was more than 10 cm long. This value is not very far from the inferior limit of the ensemble of foliate pieces found in the workshops (Table 2). The maximum width of this ideal point is 25–35 mm. The sides are convex around the maximum width, then become concave, then straight near the tip, forming what we call the "perforating part" above the two points of inflection of the edges. The stem, almost rectangular or with a medial constriction in the form of an uvula, is 15–20 mm long and 10 mm wide; it is delimited by two symmetrical notches that are joined with the body by two acute angles oriented toward the base of the piece (Figure 5).

Some points adhere to the general morphology except that the sides of the limb are rectilinear or even parallel and that the "perforating part" is less distinct or even completely within the prolongation of the base of the body when the edges are perfectly straight. Known examples seem to be narrower and perhaps longer on average than the former type. A few very long examples were observed, such as one that was reconstituted at 22 cm long and 2.8 cm wide (Chauchat 1979; Chauchat et al. 1992:198–199).

We have thus concentrated our attention on these two elongated forms of Paiján points, which are the focus of our knapping experiments. But we cannot deny the existence of the shorter and sometimes much wider forms found in a few of the workshops. These seem to be generally rarer and are not present in all the workshops. We will see that there is no evidence for the manufacture of these shorter forms at Pampa de los Fósiles 14, unit 1.

Chapter 2
Research Strategy and Experimentation

The Research Strategy

All evidence indicates that manufacturing Paiján points was a significant aspect of Paiján life and was practiced for compelling economic and cultural reasons. Abundant knapping debris visible on the surface of the region is evidence of a significant investment in work to produce these pieces. Moreover, the great number of pieces abandoned on the surfaces of workshops means that an even greater quantity of points were attempted. Finished points were exported, and then most were definitively lost. Finally, it is apparent to an archaeologist experienced with knapping techniques that manufacturing these points required a high degree of expertise, necessitating a long and difficult period of apprenticeship. Beginning in the early 1980s, the desire to address numerous questions like these, raised by the data collected in the field, gradually inspired us to develop the present program of lithic technological research. This project was launched in 1986 by the first series of experiments conducted in the field by Jacques Pelegrin near the rhyolite outcrops of Pampa de los Fósiles, with the collaboration of J. Collina-Girard (then assistant professor at the Université Bordeaux I, France) for recording the knapping tests.

Since the bifaces and points alone could give us only a partial picture of the knapping workshop activities, our main interest was the knapping flakes, which could provide evidence of the manufacture process. The study of the waste products of knapping indeed appeared to be an indispensable complement to the study of the bifaces and points. This was particularly important in revealing certain qualitative and quantitative aspects of the successfully knapped points, which are represented in workshops only by waste flakes, the by-products of their production. This approach had already been applied in earlier research, but there focused on spatial analysis of the structure of the workshops and on determining the placement of individual knappers at unit 11 of site 13 (Uceda and Deza 1979; Uceda and Deza in Chauchat et al. 1992). Moreover, in spite of some interesting results, it appeared during these first studies that meter-square collections lacked the precision needed to define these individual placements.

In developing this program of lithic technology, we thus hoped to be able to identify behaviors and processes (immaterial and dynamic entities) based on archaeological data that are by nature material and static (Binford 1977:5–6). We proposed experimentation as a method to make this transition from the material to the immaterial, i.e., from the archaeological data to the behavior that produced them. We thus study modern, actual behavior associated with reproducing objects that are similar to the archaeological ones. In contrast to ethnoarchaeological observation, the experimental procedure allows us to control and vary the behavior associated with reproducing archaeological objects and thus detect the various factors and mechanisms involved. The goal is to supplement archaeological interpretation with the causal pair of processes and the materials that result from them.

With the objective of studying the knapping processes as completely as possible, particularly the relationship between the bifaces and knapping flakes, we constructed a research program with two main phases.

The first phase consists of creating an experimental reference base through well-documented tests, while respecting as much as possible the observations made in the archaeological workshops. This operation has two purposes:

- to refine the classification of different kinds of knapping flakes according to pertinent phases of the knapping process, blank types, and dimensions;
- to estimate the quantity of flakes of different categories that result from producing a Paiján point according to its dimensions and the nature of the original blank, and to estimate the time required to execute various sequences.

We knew from the start that it would be impossible to reproduce all the point forms recognized in the archaeological workshops, particularly the shorter ones, which have a greater morphological variability. Moreover, we do not know whether these latter were meant to be utilized or whether they represent knapping exercises with no practical application. So we chose to focus on the most frequently occurring form, the elongated point defined above, specifically on the form with convex edges and a well-defined "perforating part" (tip). The elongated and narrow form with straight edges also identified in the workshops can be obtained from the same foliate pieces during the pressure-flaking phase. One experimental piece having this particular shape was manufactured during the knapping tests (Figure 6, left). For a foliate piece of the same length, the working time does not seem to be very different for the production of one or the other forms.

The main results of this phase of experimentation have been presented elsewhere in a recent article (Pelegrin and Chauchat 1993) and will be only summarized here. However, we emphasize the qualitative and behavioral conclusions drawn from this experimentation concerning the principles, constraints, and strategies of knapping perceived by the knapper. These apply to the physical properties of the material (a hard stone), the final objective (a Paiján point), and the *chaîne opératoire* applied (from a bifacial rough-out knapped with a stone hammer to a foliate piece knapped with a soft hammer).

In **the second phase** we conducted a new study of an archaeological workshop with exacting attention to spatial precision and data collection in the field. We analyzed the collected material according to criteria defined in the experimental tests in order to estimate the amount of labor expended, the number of points produced, and the number of functional points exported from the workshop (Pelegrin 1995a). We present here a detailed description of this second phase and the results of a study of the group of workshops from Pampa de los Fósiles 14, unit 1.

Of course, once the data obtained during experimentation are summarized, they will be applied not only to the projectile point manufacture activities of site 14, but all the data collected from this site will be considered, whether or not they are related to the projectile points.

Experimentation

Based on the first conclusions drawn from the field data, we can

Figure 6. Experimental Paiján points (Jacques Pelegrin). From left to right, tests no. 5–9 and 11.

summarize what we still do not know or do not know in sufficient detail about the knapping processes. We can then develop a research strategy to address these questions.

From a qualitative perspective Once the knapping techniques are determined, can we then identify the nature of the tools utilized, the different phases of production, the nature of the waste flakes produced in each phase, and the degree of expertise necessary to manufacture these points?

From a quantitative perspective Based on the study of an archaeological workshop, can we estimate the number of pieces produced and the time necessary to produce them? In other words, can we estimate the quantity of waste flakes and the labor expended in the various stages of point manufacture according to the dimensions of the point obtained and the original shape of the blank?

Our experiments must thus satisfy two main conditions. The first is to ensure correlation between the local conditions and the archaeological data. This implies utilizing the same raw materials as the prehistoric knappers or at least materials available locally, either the knapped stone or the hammers. We must also succeed in creating finished products that are sufficiently similar to the prehistoric ones while adhering to the different stages discerned in the archaeological materials (Pelegrin 1991).

The second condition is equally important. The modern knapper must have a level of expertise sufficient to choose from several techniques and methodological variants those that lead to the desired result. The knapper must also precisely understand what he is doing and why, in order to apply the strategy and choices involved in the knapping process.

In November 1986, during his first work session in Peru, the experimenter (J. Pelegrin) thus spent several days reexamining the lithic collections as well as lithic materials in the field at various quarry and workshop sites.

Next, after some initial experiments with different local stones and a preliminary attempt (test no. 1), the first series of ten knapping tests (tests no. 2–11) was conducted in place at Pampa de los Fósiles in order to ensure sufficient access to local raw materials. Two additional tests were performed in 1988, and a final one in 1992 in the city of Trujillo, utilizing the same local raw material but recorded in a simplified manner (tests no. 12–14). For all these tests, we varied both the nature of the original blank (block, plaque or flattened prism, or large flake) and the dimensions of the finished piece. Pressure flaking was performed in only eight of these tests (Figures 6 and 7), which seemed sufficient to address the one pertinent parameter of this phase, the duration of work.

The main characteristics of these tests are described below. Rough-outs were produced archaeologically with a stone hammer at the quarries; since we are more interested in the workshops, we give only a summary description of the experimental rough-outs at the stage at which they usually arrived at the archaeological workshops (what we call stage 1). For these tests we sought to vary both the length of the pieces and the nature of the original blanks in accordance with the archaeological material from Pampa de los Fósiles.

Test 2 Performed on a fragment of a block with a large, flat patinated surface; stage 3: foliate piece 100 x 37 x 10 mm (1 cm was accidentally lost during phase 2b).

Test 3 Performed on a block; one face was completely flaked, and the other had a wide central cortical area; stage 3: foliate piece 220 x 48 x 13 mm.

Test 4 Performed on a plaque; one face was completely flaked, and the other had a wide central cortical area; stage 3: foliate piece 149 x 39 x 10 mm.

Test 5 Performed on a flake; the inferior surface was highly reworked, and the other face was 50 percent cortex; stage 4: projectile point 140 x 30 x 9 mm.

Test 6 Performed on a block; both faces were flaked; stage 4: projectile point 121 x 30 x 8 mm.

Test 7 Performed on a block; both faces were flaked; stage 4: projectile point 169 x 32 x 10 mm.

Test 8 Performed on a flake with remaining cortical base and inferior face almost intact; stage 4: projectile point 106 x 37 x 9 mm.

Test 9 Performed on a prism with a flattened triangular section; one remaining flat face had a large central cortical area; a lateral, semi-abrupt face had some cortex; stage 4: projectile point 147 x 31 x 8.5 mm.

Test 10 Performed on a plaque with residual cortex on two faces (40 percent and 80 percent); broken just at stage 3: foliate piece 127 x 33 x 9 mm.

Test 11 Performed on a flake with 15–20 percent cortex on the side of one face; stage 4: projectile point 127 x 31 x 8.5 mm.

Test 12 Performed on a plaque; stage 4: projectile point 128 x 29 x 10 mm.

Test 13 Performed on a flake; stage 4: projectile point 146 x 29 x 11 mm.

Test 14 Performed on a block; stage 4: projectile point 140 x 32 x 9 mm.

Of course, other data from these tests were also recorded. The knapping processes were divided into stages by the knapper. Each phase was timed, and the flakes were collected on a cloth, counted, and weighed, as was the piece resulting at the end of each phase; i.e., at the corresponding stage (Table 3). The flakes from each phase were then briefly described one by one using a simple coding system.

We can calculate the average of the ratios "length/width" and "width/thickness (based on the values given in Table 3). The ratio "length/width" of the experimental bifaces at stage 1 ranges from 1.3 to 1.9, with an average of 1.6 and a standard deviation of 0.17. This means that the broken bifaces from the quarry at Pampa de los Fósiles 12, unit 104 (average 1.87, see above) are slightly narrower than the experimental bifaces. Moreover, as indicated above, the bifaces from the quarry site range in length from 89 to 145 mm, with an average of 121 mm. They thus fall within the inferior range of variation chosen for the dimensions of experimental pieces. This seems to be due to the fact that the quarry bifaces are slightly "deviant" (Chauchat 1991), since the foliate pieces from the workshops are much longer. In fact, the results of the tests agree nicely with the dimensions of the reconstituted foliate pieces from the archaeological workshops already studied (Table 2). The ratio "width/thickness" ranges from 2.4 to 4, with an average of 3.2. We observe, moreover, that the width is generally proportional to the length. Nonetheless, the distribution of the dimensions of the experimental pieces is not random, since these dimensions were chosen such that a small sample would cover the variations observed in the workshops. The correlation observed thus has no statistical value.

Qualitative Results: The Phases of the *Chaîne Opératoire*

From a qualitative perspective, the experimental tests confirmed

Table 3. characteristics of experimental bifacial pieces and the duration of the different work phases (B, block; F, flake; P, plaque). Tests 12–14 and phase 4 of test 9 were conducted during knapping demonstrations or photographic sessions; interruptions prevented calculating their durations.

	Test												
	2 B	3 B	4 P	5 F	6 F	7 B	8 F	9 P	10 P	11 F	12 P	13 F	14 B
Original dimensions													
length	300	320	210	192	220	250	110	195	160	170	-	-	-
width	230	240	150	151	140	180	82	110	90	100	-	-	-
thickness	80	100	40	28	70	80	32	38	24	40	-	-	-
weight	988	6124	1721	833	613	3725	349	1438	509	639	2173	1590	1659
Phase 1 duration	8	15	10	2	7	10	2	10	2	5	-	-	2
Stage 1 dimensions													
length	120	220	160	150	125	185	113	165	134	131	-	-	-
width	65	135	90	102	97	117	72	90	87	85	-	-	-
thickness	25	35	27	27	40	40	28	30	22	27	-	-	-
weight	254	1539	521	546	280	943	275	478	370	354	372	678	716
ratio length/width	1.85	1.62	1.78	1.47	1.29	1.58	1.56	1.83	1.54	1.54			
ratio width/thickness	2.6	3.86	3.33	3.77	2.42	2.92	2.57	3	3.95	3.15			
Phase 2a duration	8	20	25	17	10	15	15	25	10	10			
Stage 2a dimensions													
length	110	220	152	145	122	176	112	150	132	131			
width	60	104	60	75	60	90	60	68	66	67			
thickness	18	27	18	18	12	21	15	15	18	14			
weight	137	821	324	232	113	453	111	127	166	152	214		
ratio width/thickness	3.3	3.9	3.3	4.2	5	4.3	4	4.6	3.7	4.8			
Phase 2b duration	20	70	30	40	20	55	25	45	20	22			
Stage 2b dimensions													
length	100	220	150	144	121	172	108	147	128	130			
width	40	63	47	42	44	57	45	49	43	44			
thickness	10	13	13	10	9	12	10	10	11	10			
weight	57	566	107	77	56	137	50	86	74	71			
ratio width/thickness	4	4.8	3.6	4.2	4.9	4.8	4.5	4.9	3.9	4.4			
Phase 3 duration	15	37	35	25	10	40	10	25	20	22			
Stage 3 dimensions													
length	100	220	149	141	121	169	106	147	127	128			
width	37	48	39	35	35	37	38	36	33	35			
thickness	10	13	11	9	9	9	9	9	9	9			
weight	42	255	68	56	43	74	39	54	51	47	51	72	62
ratio width/thickness	3.7	3.2	3.6	3.9	3.9	4.1	4.2	4	3.7	3.9			
Phase 2+3 duration	43	127	90	82	40	110	50	95	50	54			48
Phase 4 duration				70	90	60	30			46			63
Stage 4 dimensions													
length				140	121	169	106			127	128	146	140
width				30	30	32	37			31	29	29	32
thickness				9	8	11	9			8	10	11	9
weight				33	28	54	30			31	35	46	41
ratio width/thickness				3.3	3.8	2.9	4.1			3.9	2.9	2.6	3.6
Total duration				109	130	170	80			100			113
Length of piece (mm)	100	220	149	140	121	169	106	147	127	127	128	146	140

and clarified what we had already deduced by examining the archaeological material.

The piece produced at the end of each phase was labeled "stage" and accompanied by the number of the phase in which it was produced (Figures 8–10).

Phase 1

General
In the archaeological context, this phase occurs on the quarry site. It is the short phase of reducing a block, plaque, or large flake into a biface by hard-stone percussion. It does not occur at the known workshops. It was sometimes performed at the foot of the quarries, as demonstrated by concentrations of knapping waste flakes, each representing the reduction of a few bifaces.

The rough-outs produced at the quarries by hard-stone percussion, traditionally called *Chivateros* bifaces (stage 1 of the *chaîne opératoire*, Figure 7), can be made from three types of blanks:

a) a block or fragment of a block bifacially reduced by removals with a hard hammer, with concave flake negatives that create pronounced ridges;

b) a large flake, cortical or not, with a slightly convex ventral face, conserved as is;

c) a thin plaque, of which both faces conserve a large area of cortex (this "cortex" is in fact an altered state of ancient diaclastic surfaces).

Research Strategy and Experimentation

Knapping Principles

- Attempting to produce rough-outs too thin with a hard hammer risks breaking them; instead, thin the thicker ones while preserving a comfortable width. This technique does not eliminate the possibility of breakage when "qualifying" a blank that is initially very thick and not correspondingly wide with one powerful blow: if it works, success; if it breaks, there are no regrets because this was the only possibility. This is the significance of certain large axial removals observed at quarries, evidence of a high risk of overshots, or "plunging" flakes. We call these removals "qualifying" because they radically alter the morphology of the piece and qualify it for continuing the shaping process. The best-prepared knappers would have brought a large soft hammer to the quarry site to detach certain qualifying flakes rather than risk failure with a hard hammer.

- Do not pay undue attention to length at the expense of the overall quality of the section. This consideration also explains the reason for certain oblique or longitudinal removals, which are costly in terms of length but very efficient for thinning.

Figure 7. Experimental foliate pieces (Jacques Pelegrin). Above, test no. 10 broken during fabrication; below, from left to right, tests no. 3, 2, and 4.

- Verify the quality of the raw material and ascertain the absence of fissures to avoid carrying to the workshop rough-outs that are likely condemned from the start.

The objective of stage 1 is to leave the quarry site with finishable rough-outs: not too thick, sufficiently wide, at least 11 cm long, of acceptable raw material. At stage 1 the biface is still thick but already elongated.

Phase 2

General

Phase 2 marks the beginning of work by soft-hammer percussion. Given the rarity of Cervidae (*Odocoileus virginianus*) and the small size of their antlers, we infer that hammers were made from the heart of *algarrobo* wood. This tree is common in the north Peruvian desert, and its hard wood is suitable for this function. Phase 2 requires a relatively heavy billet, around 500–700 g. For purely methodological reasons, we separated this phase into two subphases, 2a and 2b. Phase 2 consists essentially of thinning the *Chivateros* biface by removing covering flakes with a soft hammer.

In subphase 2a the first series of covering flakes are removed by soft-hammer percussion, thus reworking the initial surfaces of the *Chivateros* biface and creating a bifacial preform with a rather thick biconvex section. The large characteristic flakes produced are cortical, thick, elongated, or "Kombewa" (see definitions below, "Recognizing Blanks," and Figure 8). The small quantity of soft-hammer flakes collected in the test pit of the quarry at Pampa de los Fósiles 12, unit 104 (Chauchat 1978; Chauchat et al. 1992) belong to this phase. Thus, in some cases initial work by soft hammer was done at the quarry, undoubtedly for the purpose of testing the raw material and to lighten the piece as much as possible before transport.

The first series of covering flakes detached by soft-hammer percussion during phase 2 at the workshop can indicate the type of original blank from which the *Chivateros* biface was shaped (Figure 7):

a) a bifacially reduced block or block fragment produces several thick flakes (>5 mm on the mesial part) with pronounced ridges, and a few elongated flakes, which are sometimes skewed (Figure 8, no. 1–3; and Figure 10, phase 2a: lower row);

b) a rough-out on a flake results in at least one clear Kombewa flake (Figure 8, no. 4);

c) a plaque with large areas of residual cortex produces several large highly cortical flakes (Figure 8, no. 5; and Figure 10, phase 2a: lower row, right).

We call these various flakes (thick, elongated/skewed, Kombewa, and cortical), which necessarily come from the beginning of phase 2 (thus 2a), "type 2a" flakes. Our experimental tests show that their presence is a clear sign that phase 2 was indeed begun at the workshop and that their respective proportions indicate the types of blank used to produce *Chivateros* bifaces. We must keep in mind that a rough-out on a block could have re-

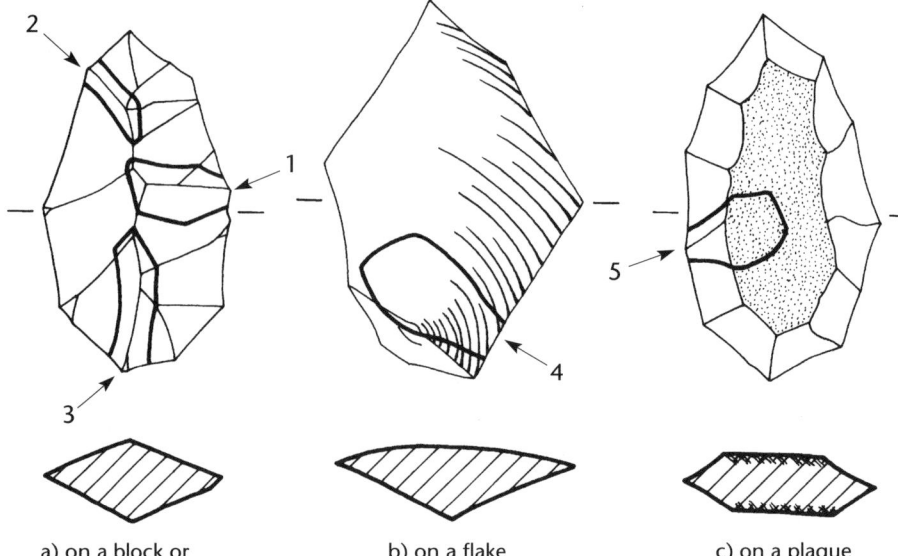

Figure 8. The various types of *Chivateros* bifaces and the first characteristic flakes produced during thinning (type 2a flakes): **1**, thick flake; **2**, skewed flake; **3**, elongated flake; **4**, Kombewa waste flake; **5**, cortical flake. Approximate scale 1/3. (Drawing by M. Reduron.)

tained some cortex, that a thick plaque could present one knapped face and one cortical face, and that a flake can have cortex or pronounced ridges on its upper surface.

Subphase 2b defines the next series of removals almost until the definitive thinning of the piece. The resulting flakes are large and covering, but thinner, and sometimes have a teardrop-shaped outline that often extends beyond the middle line of a still rather wide preform. The butt is sometimes reduced by a particular "blunted spur" preparation (Pelegrin 1981). At stage 2b (Figure 9, stage 2b) the preform is now a thinner foliate piece, almost at its definitive thickness, but still rather wide.

Knapping Principles

First, thin the preform under the most favorable conditions, meaning early, in order to take advantage of the width preserved during stage 1. When the preform is still rather wide, solid zones of impact can be prepared on the edges by convex faceting to ease the task of detaching large covering flakes while preserving a section thick enough to withstand the shock.

Phase 3

General

In phase 3 the piece is thinned by carefully removing thin covering flakes (Figure 10, phase 3). These flakes are small, thin, and so fragile they often break. A lighter soft hammer (approximately 300 g) is now used. In definitive shaping it is advantageous to reduce to a minimum the amount of material removed by pres-

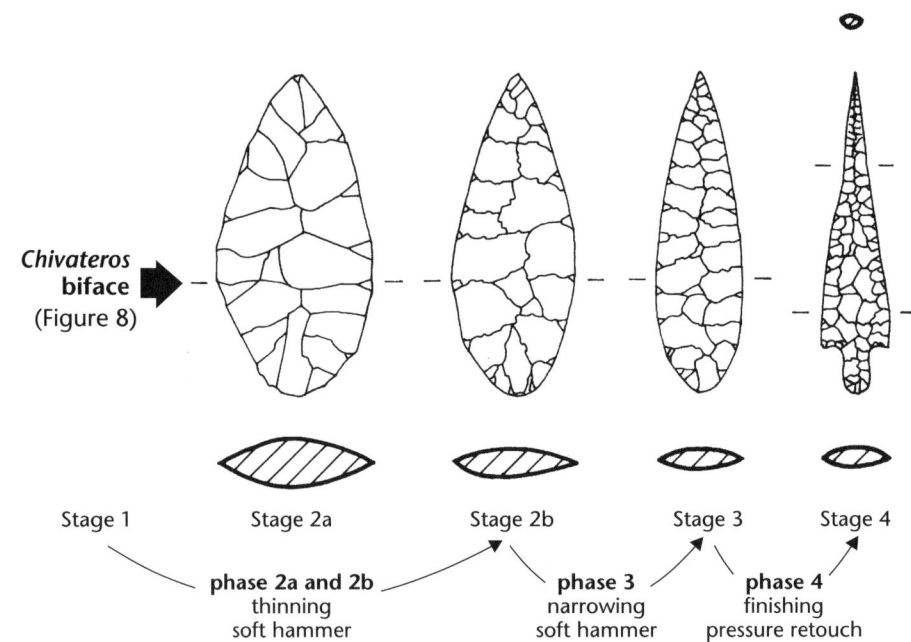

Figure 9. The various phases of shaping a Paiján point; approximate scale 1/3. (Drawing by M. Reduron.)

Research Strategy and Experimentation

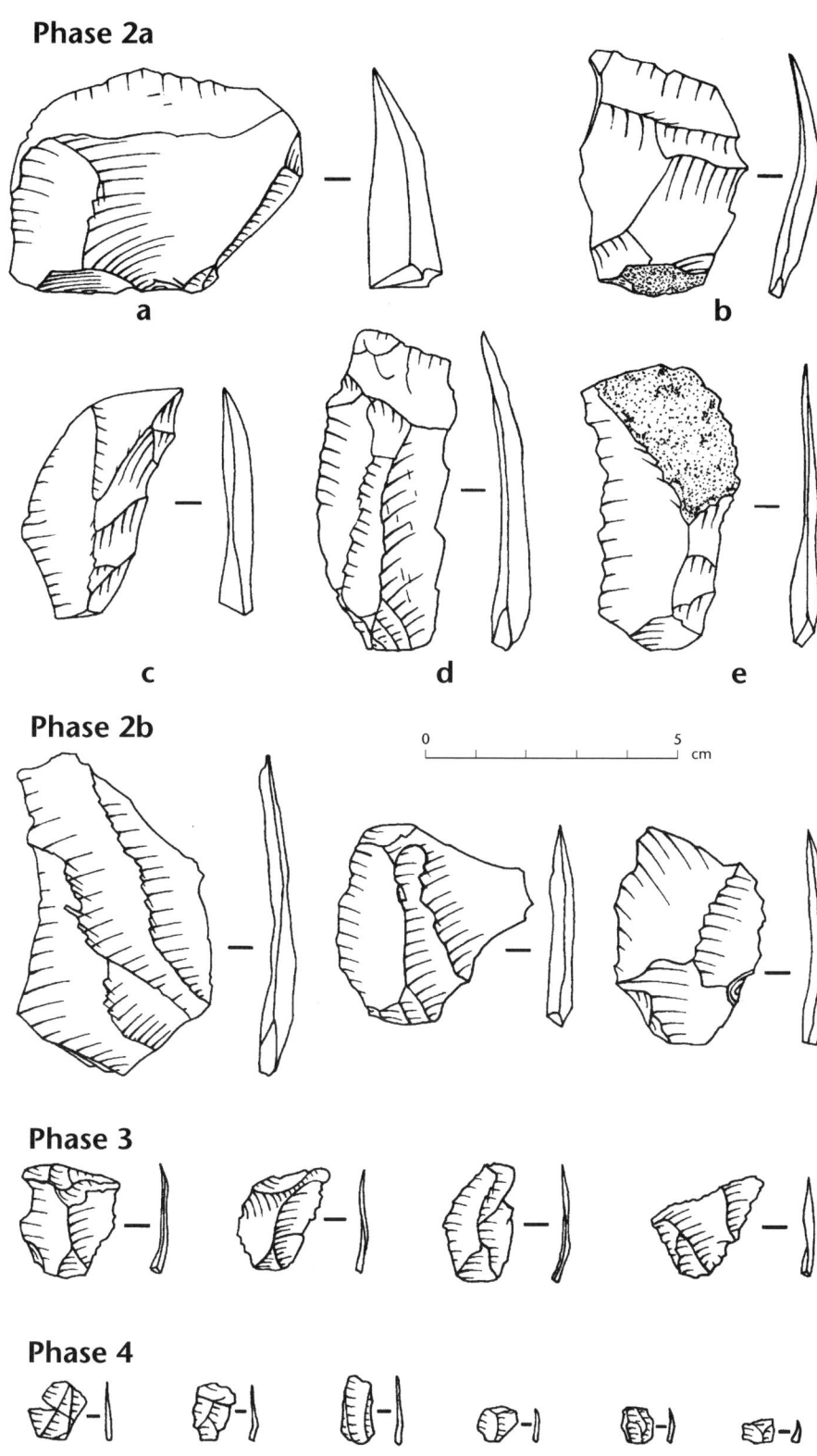

Figure 10. Examples of typical flakes from the different experimental phases of knapping a Paijan point. Phase 2a: **a**, thick flake; **c**, skewed flake; **d**, elongated flake; **b** and **e**, cortical flakes. Phase 2b: wide and thin flakes. Phase 3: short, very thin flakes. Phase 4: minute flakes detached by pressure flaking. (Drawings by G. Montbel.)

sure retouch; if the foliate piece is large this can take a long time and become very painstaking. At stage 3, the preform has a width in the basal third of about 3 cm, which is barely wider than in the finished point. The thickness of the piece is 10–11 mm, 7–8 mm at its basal extremity.

Knapping Principles

- Since the section has become rather thin (stage 2) and more fragile, it is sufficient to thin it a little while simultaneously regularizing it by removing many thin, short flakes (stage 3); carefully avoid hinge terminations or deep negative scars.

- Where work by percussion ends represents a compromise. If the piece is still wide (more than 35 mm in the basal third), finishing it by pressure retouch requires inordinate effort. On the other hand, the more it is thinned by percussion, the greater the risk of breakage, especially in the case of long pieces, which are more susceptible to breaking by vibration, or "end shock."

The objective of stage 3 after first thinning by percussion is to regularize the edges by very short removals using pressure retouch, rather than abrading by percussion. The section should be regularly biconvex in shape or slightly plano-convex. The thickness, already nearly achieved during stage 2, is now definitive since it is practically impossible to thin a preform by pressure retouch, even under optimal conditions. The moment of transition from phase 3 to 4 is thus defined by a compromise of effort and risks, while considering the quality of the raw material and the advantages and limitations of the two techniques.

Phase 4

This is the phase of work using pressure retouch. It is used primarily on the needle-shaped perforating part of the point and on the stem. These are the two most difficult parts to shape and the most fragile, which explains why they are the fragments most often missing from broken archaeological points in the workshops. The stem is shaped by bilateral narrowing, resulting in intermediate forms with large stems that are often found in the archaeological workshops.

Knapping Principles

- Provided the piece was acceptable at stage 3, this phase may take a lot of time but does not present great risk.
- According to some archaeological observations, it seems the base was finished before the point. This would be a more reliable tactic to avoid breaking the extremity of a finished, and thus fragile point while shaping the stem. A few pieces broken when the base was finished or nearly completed bear evidence of this process. Moreover, it seems that in these cases the fracture was caused by using a soft hammer during phase 4, undoubtedly while attempting to overcome unexpected difficulty in reducing part of the body of the piece by pressure retouch.
- The stem and barb angles are best formed progressively, not from the extremity of the base but from the two lateral edges. After definitively calibrating and regularizing the section and the edges at the point where the barb angles will be situated, several small series of adjacent or alternating removals by pressure retouch gradually narrow the basal 20 to 25 mm of the point. As always, it is crucial to avoid all hinge terminations that would compromise the continuation of the operation. The last retouch flakes give the stem and barb angles their symmetry and exact outline.
- The shaping of the upper part is even more delicate, since it becomes more and more susceptible to flexing exerted during pressure retouch. It is also a time-consuming process because, starting from the preform of stage 3, more than 1 cm of width must be reduced by pressure retouch along a length of several centimeters. Repeated adjacent, then alternate removals are thus necessary while perfectly maintaining the axis of the extremity viewed from the face and profile. The removals from the first series can be relatively powerful (possibly employing a shoulder crutch) and covering, especially near the medial part of the point where the section remains relatively massive (Figure 10, phase 4). Note that the width of the point is reduced while its thickness remains nearly constant. Therefore the dihedral angle of the lateral edges rapidly attains 90°, and it becomes impossible to detach anything more than small, short semi-abrupt flakes, which necessarily follow an alternating pattern in a "spiky" progression. To detach the next flake on the opposite face, the extremity of the pressure flaker is placed at the edge of the concave negative scar of the preceding flake, following a more or less oblique direction oriented in the direction of the progression of the series along the edge. Now the care taken during preceding phase 3 is justified, since any excessive thickness or irregularity (bump or hinge termination) risks interrupting the last series of alternating flakes. The risk of breakage is greatest when we attempt to reduce a bump by a forced, deep removal made by pressure or even by a light percussion blow.

The objective of stage 4 (Figure 9) is found in the definition of the Paiján point (body, stem, barb angles, remarkably slender point).

Evaluating Constraints

The manufacture of Paiján points clearly falls in the category of "difficult" lithic productions, along with Solutrean laurel-leaf points, Paleoindian bifacial pieces, and even some blade debitage methods of the European upper Paleolithic. Such an appreciation is only relative, since absolute quantitative criteria for measuring the "difficulty" of ideo-motor activities do not exist. However, this difficulty can be estimated in terms of apprenticeship duration (Roux 1991) based on the experience of modern knappers. We estimate that to manufacture, or attempt to make, several dozen or even hundreds of Paiján points required a considerable level of proficiency. Not only is it necessary to master three very different techniques (hard-hammer percussion, soft-hammer percussion, and pressure), the craftsman must also be intimately familiar with the characteristics of the raw material. At Pampa de los Fósiles, this material was essentially rhyolite, which presents more constraints than both flint and obsidian. This material does not forgive negligence: a poorly prepared or poorly struck removal either crushes the edge in that area or creates a hinge termination, which can immediately or ultimately condemn the piece. We have also demonstrated that knapping principles were precise and that the correct order had to be respected. To shortcut or attempt to alter the thickness or symmetry of the piece too late increases the risk of accident. Therefore, from beginning to end the manufacture of a Paiján point demands sustained attention, consistent motor execution, and a very fine appreciation of the risk of fracture, all of which can be learned only after long individual experience. It is thus rewarding that in our study we have the opportunity to introduce to beginners and apprentices skills whose acquisition must have extended over several years.

The phases of the *chaîne opératoire* do not depend on the knapper. They are **mechanically** conditioned by the characteristics of the desired point and by the initial decision to knap a biface rough-out with a stone hammer. This option is itself conditioned by the original forms of the blocks found at the outcrop. The only way to deviate from this option (as the Paijanenses sometimes did) is to work with a large flake or thin plaque. This is an option that carries a great risk of breakage because violent blows must be applied to these thin blanks.

A Paiján point has a sharp "perforating part" and a narrow stem at its extremities. These traits, as well as the general slenderness of the piece, imply the constraint of thinness. The piece must be between 8 and 12 mm thick. In turn, this necessary thinness requires some work by soft-hammer percussion. To shape the stem and the perforating part also implies utilizing pressure retouch as soon as the piece becomes too narrow to withstand violent blows, especially for the particularly delicate work of forming the lateral notches. We emphasize that the toughness of the rhyolite utilized by the prehistoric knappers and for our experiments clearly limits the effectiveness of pressure retouch. Even with a shoulder crutch (and sufficient training with hard flints), we found it impossible to detach flakes more than 10 mm wide or 15 mm long, a limit that in practice prohibits invasive removals and thus late thinning of the piece by pressure. We also deduce that unfailing motivation was required of the craftsman (inspired by the functional imperatives presented above) to give the Paiján point its particular characteristics, carrying the price of at least 30 to 40 minutes of hard and delicate work.

We thus begin with an oval-shaped biface that is much wider than the definitive piece. Since the desired point is elongated, the reduction process proceeds with removals starting from the two longest opposite edges of the biface. The removed material narrows the biface through successive removals at the butt of the flake and thins it when the flakes extend to the zone of maximum thickness, generally in the middle of the piece. Next, the biface is narrowed and thinned at the same time while its length is barely diminished (Table 3), except in the case of an accident, which almost always occurs in the form of a transverse fracture. The length of the *Chivateros* biface is thus a reliable gauge of the length of the desired point, as we proposed above based on our study of archaeological *Chivateros* bifaces.

Our experimental tests clearly demonstrated that it is crucial to reduce the section of the piece to its definitive thickness early, i.e., while it is still wide enough to withstand covering removals. This implies two successive phases with different objectives. The priority during phase 2 is thinning; during phase 3 the priority is narrowing without more thinning, since the piece becomes increasingly fragile. During phase 2 the width/thickness ratio (Table 3) increases because the piece that remains relatively wide is thinned; during phase 3 the ratio decreases because the piece that retains approximately the same thickness is narrowed. In phase 3 the detached flakes, which are more invasive than covering, are thin and short and become more so as the piece is narrowed. If the piece is not first maximally thinned, it develops a relatively thick section with a narrow and elongated outline. Postponed thinning of such a piece almost inevitably results in breakage, since a piece made fragile by excessive narrowness cannot withstand the impact of blows required to detach additional thinning flakes (covering flakes, therefore relatively thick in such a raw material).

Probably we could refine some of these observations by expanding this experimental reference base through additional tests and additional knappers. However, we believe that the relationships described above would not be invalidated, since they result from unavoidable techno-morphological constraints implied by the materials and techniques. Once the margin of length for finished pieces and *Chivateros* bifaces is specified—as we did above, based on the known archaeological materials—the average section of the preform is precisely fixed.

It is fixed, on one hand, because it is impossible to thin a long, wide piece with a hard hammer without breaking it; on the other hand, it is fixed because a reserve of width must be retained in order to detach numerous covering flakes with a soft hammer. Moreover, we have already mentioned that the characteristics of the raw material preclude thinning the piece during the pressure retouch phase. Thus there clearly exists an optimal operational scheme; by successively employing the three available techniques (hard hammer, soft hammer, and pressure retouch), labor and risks are distributed throughout the entire manufacturing process.

Finally, our technological analysis of the *chaîne opératoire* avoids the argument of whether technical stages exist as concepts, or mental templates, in the minds of prehistoric knappers. The notion of *steps*, and thus *stages*, is implied by the characteristics of the raw material and by the efficiency and risk of fracture associated with different techniques. It is not necessary to call upon an *a priori* cognitive analysis (Young and Bonnichsen 1984; Young et al., 1994), which, on the other hand, we agree is very useful in the analysis of blade and Levallois debitage (Pelegrin 1995). The attentive reader will recognize that we have empirically determined the phases of the reduction process, and thus stages (morphological states), which are nothing more than steps in this process. The approach we have taken in our research program is thus different from that of Shott, who states that "the notion of stages in the reduction process requires that all members of a stage essentially be identical or at best differ only trivially with respect to its diagnostic attributes" (Patterson 1997; Shott 1996, 1997). The author clearly indicates that he is speaking of the knapping flakes resulting from this process, and he next proceeds to enumerate the *attributes* to be measured on these flakes: "Weight (in grams), and by length, width and thickness (in mm). Platform width thickness (also in mm), types of platform, percentage of dorsal cortex, number of dorsal scars, types of fragments." The result of this analysis is a continuum of variation through the reduction process, which seems predictable to any knapper so long as there is no intervening change in technique.

The phases we have defined in the bifacial knapping process are completely different in concept. They are based on a technological and behavioral approach; only secondarily are they cognitive in nature. We thus approach from a direction different from the perspective of Young and Bonnichsen (1984). If we redefined the phases distinguished above from a cognitive perspective, phase 1 would be defined as the manufacture of a large bifacial rough-out by large removals with a hard hammer. Phase 2 would be defined as the **intention** to thin the piece while retaining a sufficient width. Phase 3 would begin when the piece was **judged** to be sufficiently thin and would be redefined as the **intention** to narrow the piece until it possessed dimensions close to that of the definitive point, with the main goal of avoiding a difficult phase of work by pressure retouch. It would end when the risk was **judged** too great to continue percussion. Phase 4 is thus defined by a different technique and the appearance of particular morphological characteristics that are otherwise impossible to obtain.

The characteristics chosen by Shott to measure the variations of knapping flakes are exactly those that are susceptible to continual variation. The flakes of the first series of our phase 2a do not appear in his analysis, and the two phases of thinning and then narrowing are particularly difficult to detect using his criteria. However, it would undoubtedly be possible to distinguish most large flakes removed from the area extending beyond the median zone of the biface in phase 2 and most shorter flakes removed in phase 3. It is true that these phases, including the manufacture of a biface with a stone hammer, are in part culturally determined—and thus do not exist in the reduction process of North American Paleoindians—and also depend on the morphology of the piece being produced. It follows that Shott's conclusions are valid only for the one type of biface that he produced; moreover, they could be biased from the start by observations that focused exclusively on a small number of characteristics of knapping waste flakes.

Quantitative Results and Principles of Application

The flakes (whole or fragmentary) produced during the knapping process were sorted into three categories based on their maximum dimension in any direction: large (L > 35 mm), medium (L 20–35 mm), and small (L < 20 mm). The small flakes were not described, only counted and weighed. During the knapping process, the length and section of the flakes diminishes; they become more fragile and break into ever smaller fragments. Thus phase 3 produces very few distinguishable flakes, and phase 4 only minute fragments and dust.

Although for each experimental test the flake counts for each dimension category are available, we consider only flakes and fragments from the large and medium categories, since, as we will see below, small flakes cannot be used for archaeological comparisons.

Recognizing Blanks

Among these "large" and "medium" flakes, we have already described a particular type of flake produced during phase 2a. We call it a "type 2a" flake because of its specificity to this moment in the *chaîne opératoire*. Since type 2a flakes are the first flakes detached from the preform by soft-hammer percussion, surfaces or ridges on the superior face identify the nature of the original blank as it arrived in the workshop. Since these flakes are relatively few in number, they can be easily counted. The following is a detailed description of their characteristics (Figures 8 and 10).

An **elongated flake** removes part of the central zone (often in the form of a pronounced ridge) of a surface initially roughed-out with a hard hammer and significantly contributes to thinning the piece. It is called a **skewed flake** when it develops obliquely in relation to the direction of the blow.

A **thick flake**, more than 5 mm (away from the bulb), is evidence of pronounced ridges. Its thickness indicates that the flake removed a surface roughed-out with a hard hammer.

A **cortical flake**, total or partial, indicates a block, plaque, or large flake blank with a more or less cortical superior face. A flake both cortical and thick—which is rare because cortical faces are always flat—was classified as cortical. Only test 3 produced several flakes that were both cortical in their distal portion and thick in the mesial portion.

A **Kombewa flake** or **partial Kombewa flake** is actually a Kombewa waste flake (Figure 8b). The Kombewa technique, named after an early-Paleolithic site in Kenya, utilizes a large flake as a core for removing a smaller flake from its lower (ventral) face (Owen 1938). The resulting flake thus possesses its own bulb of percussion, and on its superior surface part of the bulb of the flake from which it was removed (Inizan et al. 1999:68–71). Kombewa flakes, which have an oval or circular outline, were sought for their regularity, particularly for the manufacture of Acheulian cleavers. By extension, in the case of the *chaîne opératoire* of bifacial reduction we include with Kombewa flakes the knapping waste flakes that are produced during the first series of removals from the inferior face of large flakes. These flakes are easily recognized because they remove and bear on their dorsal surface a portion of the convex ventral surface, often with a portion of the bulb, of the flake blank from which they were detached. This portion appears convex in section, not concave as would be a normal scar from a previous shaping flake, thus indicating a large flake blank. It is partial when other removals have obliterated part of the characteristic convex or smooth surface. Note that this is a knapping waste flake, as are all the flakes defined here, and that the term Kombewa does not here refer to the debitage method of the same name. Of course, we must not confuse these flakes with bulb scars, which are spontaneously produced during debitage and can be very large when associated with large flakes, as we learned from the quarry test pit mentioned above.

Table 4 lists the counts of these different flakes resulting from the experimental tests.

We have observed the weak specificity of these flakes for identifying the blank type. Only Kombewa flakes are certain indicators that the shaped blank was a flake since, by definition, they remove part of the bulging bulbar zone of the inferior surface of the flake-blank. However, note that plaques generally produce many more cortical flakes than thick flakes, as would be expected.

In our study of archaeological assemblages, the first step is to detect whether flake blanks were knapped. Next, if thick flakes greatly outnumber cortical flakes, we deduce that the blanks were predominantly blocks and not plaques, which are largely roughed-out with a hard hammer. This procedure is less reliable when flake assemblages comprise waste flakes from only a few pieces.

Principles of Quantitative Evaluation

Next, we determine the number of points actually produced and exported by analyzing the characteristics of associated waste flakes obtained from our experimental tests. We first calculate the range of variation in number and weight of flakes produced during the manufacture of experimental points of different lengths. Based on what we previously deduced about the length of Paiján points from Pampa de los Fósiles, we divide the test results into three categories:

1) small points (actually small and medium), 6 pieces 100–128 mm long;
2) large points, 5 pieces 140–149 mm long;
3) very large points, 2 pieces, one 170 mm long, the other 220 mm long.

Table 5 shows the characteristics (number and weight) of the different kinds of flakes produced for each of these three categories of points. However, it is first necessary to verify that the beginning of phase 2, evidenced by type 2a flakes, is represented in the assemblage. To do this, we first consider the ratio "type 2a flakes/all large and medium flakes" in terms of number and weight.

For all categories of points, the weight of flakes is more reliable than their number for analyzing the ratio "type 2a flakes/all large and medium flakes." (Because of uneven fragmentation that occurs during flake production, the number of flakes produced varies more than their total mass.) Indeed, the number of "type 2a" flakes varies grossly in proportion to the global count of flakes according to length; the longer the preform, the greater is the area of the initial surface of the *Chivateros* biface, and thus the more type 2a flakes will be removed from its surface.

But the weight ratio is more reliable, although it varies from simple to double, without permitting a distinction between small and large points (Table 5). Indeed, we have:

- 28.6–56.3 percent for the small points;
- 34.5–55.6 percent for the large points;
- 37.3–51.1 percent for the two very large points.

Therefore, when this ratio for an archaeological assemblage approaches 30 percent, we safely assume that phase 2 is well represented in the workshop, including its beginning (subphase 2a). On the other hand, a ratio that approaches or exceeds 60 percent should alert us to the possibility that a piece was abandoned during phase 2, even if the piece itself is absent; it may have been rejected elsewhere, collected, or later displaced from the excavated zone of the site. Furthermore, if the type 2a flakes are mostly cortical, it is likely that a very thin plaque was knapped, producing few ordinary flakes before phase 3. This was the case in test 10 of our knapping experiments.

Once it has been verified that phase 2 is represented, we can use the tables to infer the kinds of point corresponding to the flake assemblage:

- small point: 60–100 L + M flakes weighing 100–200 g
- large point: 130–180 L + M flakes weighing 280–500 g
- very large point: 200–300 L + M flakes weighing 600–1100 g

For each of these groups, the margin of uncertainty goes from 1 to 2, and slightly less for the number of flakes than for the weight (e.g., for a certain quantity of flakes, we could estimate the existence of 3 to 6 points, but absolutely no more or no less). However, we cannot absolutely deduce the length of the corresponding points simply by counting and weighing an archaeological flake assemblage; for instance, a total of 180 large and medium flakes can result from knapping 3 pieces about 12 cm long, or 1 piece about 15 cm long. The margin of uncertainty is thus 1 to 3 points. To infer the length of corresponding points

Table 4. Detailed counts. global count, and global weight of the large and medium type 2a flakes resulting from the experimental tests. according to support type and length of the piece produced.

Test no.	Blank type	Length (mm)	Large and Medium Type 2a flakes					
			Elongated	Thick	Cortical	Kombewa	Total 2a flakes	Total weight (g)
8	flake	106	2	6	5	4	17	61
11	flake	127		8	8	3	19	94.6
5	flake	140		3	11	3	17	121
13	flake	146	3	10		1	14	156
10	plaque	127	1	3	32		36	112.6
12	plaque	128		5	9		14	74
9	plaque	147		8	39		47	192.4
4	plaque	149		6	10		16	100.8
2	block	100		4	9		13	40.2
6	block	120		6			6	42
14	block	140		11	24		35	268.4
7	block	169	1	15	7		23	234.8
3	block	220	2	20	30		52	529.6

Table 5. Quantitative data of the large and medium experimental flakes grouped into small points, large points, and very large points. The large number of 2a flakes in test 3 is due to the fact that many large flat flakes from phase 2b are still more than 5 mm thick.

Test no.	Blank type	Length	All flakes L + M		Type 2a L + M flakes		Ratio of type 2a/all flakes (%)	
			Count	Weight (g)	Count	Weight (g)	By count	By weight (g)
2	block	100	64	106	13	40.2	20.3	38
8	flake	106	76	145	17	61	22.4	42
6	block	121	69	147	6	42	8.7	28.6
11	flake	127	109	200	36	112.6	33	56.3
10	plaque	127	86	180	19	94.6	22.1	52.5
12	plaque	128	102	216	14	74	13.7	34.3
	average		84.3	165.7	17	70.1		
5	flake	140	135	323	17	121	12.6	37.5
14	block	140	164	487	35	268.4	21.3	55.1
13	flake	146	177	414	14	156	7.9	37.7
9	plaque	147	159	346	47	192.4	29.6	55.6
4	plaque	150	140	292	16	100.8	11.4	34.5
	average		155	372.4	25.8	167.3		
7	block	169	226	629.2	23	234.8	10.2	37.3
3	block	220	280	1037.2	52	529.6	18.6	51.1
	average		253	833.2	37.5	382.2		

with confidence, we must consider the maximum dimension of the large flakes, as shown in Table 6.

Our tests clearly demonstrate that the maximum dimension of the flakes in each test increases with the length of the piece produced. The reason is purely technological. A large rough-out made with a hard hammer must be wide enough to avoid breaking during the knapping process. Therefore, since a large proportion of the thinning flakes of phase 2 must exceed half the width of the preform, a long, thus wide, preform will produce longer flakes than a shorter and correspondingly narrower one.

Another general rule is that the number of flakes increases with an increase in the length of the point. There are, however, exceptions to this rule; test 4 is a notable example. This was a thin plaque that was carefully knapped, but because of the poor quality of the material, many thin flakes broke into small fragments often less than 35 mm long. More precisely, we observe that among the 6 tests of the small point group, only one flake (test 12) exceeded 65 mm in maximum dimension. On the other hand, for each of the 5 tests of the large point group, we find one or several flakes that exceed 65 mm. The number of very large flakes, as well as their maximum dimension, increases significantly in tests 7 and 3, with respective foliate piece lengths of 169 and 220 mm (Table 7).

The last two columns of Table 7 show that flakes longer than 65 mm distinguish medium pieces from small ones except in the case of plaque blanks (tests 4 and 9). We also observe that the ratio type 2a flakes/all flakes for large flakes alone varies slightly more than the same ratio for large and medium flakes together. We thus prefer the latter for determining whether phase 2a is represented in the workshop (Table 5).

Moreover, in order to visualize better the relationship between the length of a knapped piece and the length of its waste flakes, we have constructed histograms that correlate the counts of the "large" flakes characteristic of phase 2a (hatched lines)

Table 6. Distribution of flakes and large fragments resulting from experimental tests according to their maximum dimension by 5 mm increments, for each experimental test arranged according to the length of the piece produced (same order as Table 5).

Test no.	Blank type	35–39	40–44	45–49	50–54	55–59	60–64	65–69	70–74	75–79	80–84	85–89	>90	Total
2	block	5	3		1									9
8	flake	9	6		1	2								18
6	block	4	3	2	1	1	1							12
10	plaque	11	4	2	3									20
11	flake	5	4	5	1	1	1							17
12	plaque	14	6	1	1	1	1	1						25
5	flake	10	3	5	2	2	2				1	1		26
14	block	21	7	9	1	1	2	1	2		1			45
13	flake	13	13	3	1	1	2	3			1			37
9	plaque	10	12	5	4	2	1							34
4	plaque	6	6	3	2				1					18
7	block	17	9	7	7	2	3	1	1	1	1	1	2	52
3	block	26	14	8	8	5	7	3	3	4	2	1	3	84

Research Strategy and Experimentation

Table 7. For each experimental test (arranged in the same order as in previous tables): global count of large flakes, number of type 2a flakes and other large flakes, ratio of 2a flakes to the total flakes, maximum dimension of the largest flakes, number of flakes longer than 65 mm, and percentage of the latter in relation to the global count of large flakes.

Test no.	Blank type	Length of piece	Total flakes	Type 2a flakes	Other flakes	Ratio (%)	Max. dimension (mm)	>65mm	Ratio (%)
2	block	100	9	5	4	55.6	55	0	0
8	flake	106	18	10	8	55.6	60	0	0
6	block	121	12	3	9	25	65	0	0
11	flake	127	17	9	8	52.9	65	0	0
10	plaque	127	20	13	7	65	55	0	0
12	plaque	128	25	9	16	36	70	1	4
5	flake	140	26	9	17	34.6	90	2	7.7
14	block	140	45	21	24	46.7	85	4	8.9
13	flake	146	37	11	26	29.7	90	4	10.8
9	plaque	147	34	23	11	67.6	65	0	0
4	plaque	150	18	8	10	44.4	75	1	6.7
7	block	169	52	14	38	26.9	115	7	13.5
3	block	220	84	34	50	40.5	105	16	19

and simple flakes (in white) along the y-axis with their maximum dimension in increments of 5 mm along the x-axis, beginning at 35 mm (the inferior limit chosen for "large" flakes). For each test the appropriate histogram shows the proportion of large type 2a flakes (also confirming that this phase was performed when applied to archaeological materials) and indicates the approximate length of the preform from which they originated according to the number and dimensions of the flakes represented. The histograms for the experimental tests shown in Figure 11 are organized by the length of the point obtained and the kind of original blank (block, plaque, or large flake). For convenience, we will call this kind of small histogram a "spectrum," since it shows at a glance the number and dimensions of large type 2a flakes and other flakes for a given test or archaeological assemblage. Keeping in mind that a margin of uncertainty is implied, these spectra nicely summarize tests that were conducted. The longer the foliate piece desired, the greater the total number of large flakes and the greater the dimensions of these flakes.

Naturally these spectra alone cannot specify the nature of the original raw blank (roughed-out block or fragment, more or less cortical flake, or plaque); once stage 1 of the *Chivateros* biface is completed, the nature of the initial blank has almost no effect on the following phases of the *chaîne opératoire*. As we saw above, we can infer this information by examining the characteristics of type 2a flakes. These results are summarized in Table 7, where the data are arranged by ascending order of the lengths of the finished foliate pieces or points.

Conclusions

The large (> 35 mm) and medium (20–35 mm) flakes or fragments, and the flakes or fragments characteristic of phase 2a, are relatively easy to separate from the ensemble of flakes at a workshop and can be rapidly counted and weighed. By comparing these results with the knapping tests, we can thus:

1) deduce with reasonable confidence the nature of the original blank;

2) determine from the length of the longest flakes the length of the corresponding piece (small-medium, long, or very long point);

3) after choosing from several hypotheses, estimate, with a margin of error of 1 or 2 pieces, the number of pieces produced at a workshop by considering the number and weight of combined large and medium flakes.

To estimate the number of finished pieces exported by the knapper, it is necessary to subtract pieces remaining at the workshop and to determine the stage of the *chaîne opératoire* during which they were abandoned and their dimensions.

It is important to remember that, except in the case of an accident, the length of piece is barely reduced during the entire knapping process. The finished point itself is barely 1 cm shorter than the *Chivateros* biface from which it was made.

We attempted to develop other criteria that would improve estimates of the average length and number of pieces produced, based on an assemblage of archaeological flakes: number and weight of medium flakes alone; number and weight of large flakes alone; ratio, in number and weight, of large to medium flakes. These data in all respects were no more useful than the criteria discussed above. Only the ratio of large/medium flakes can indicate the production of large points when they exceed 35 percent in number and 50 percent in weight (Table 8).

Using our adopted criteria, we developed the model shown in Table 9, which will be systematically used in analyzing the bifacial knapping process at Pampa de los Fósiles 14, unit 1. In this table we assembled the data that are useful, for an assemblage of knapping flakes of a given material or variety of materials, in determining the number of worked bifacial pieces, their dimensions, and the nature of the original blanks. These data concern large and medium type 2a flakes, as well as other large and medium flakes and their relative proportions of principal interest.

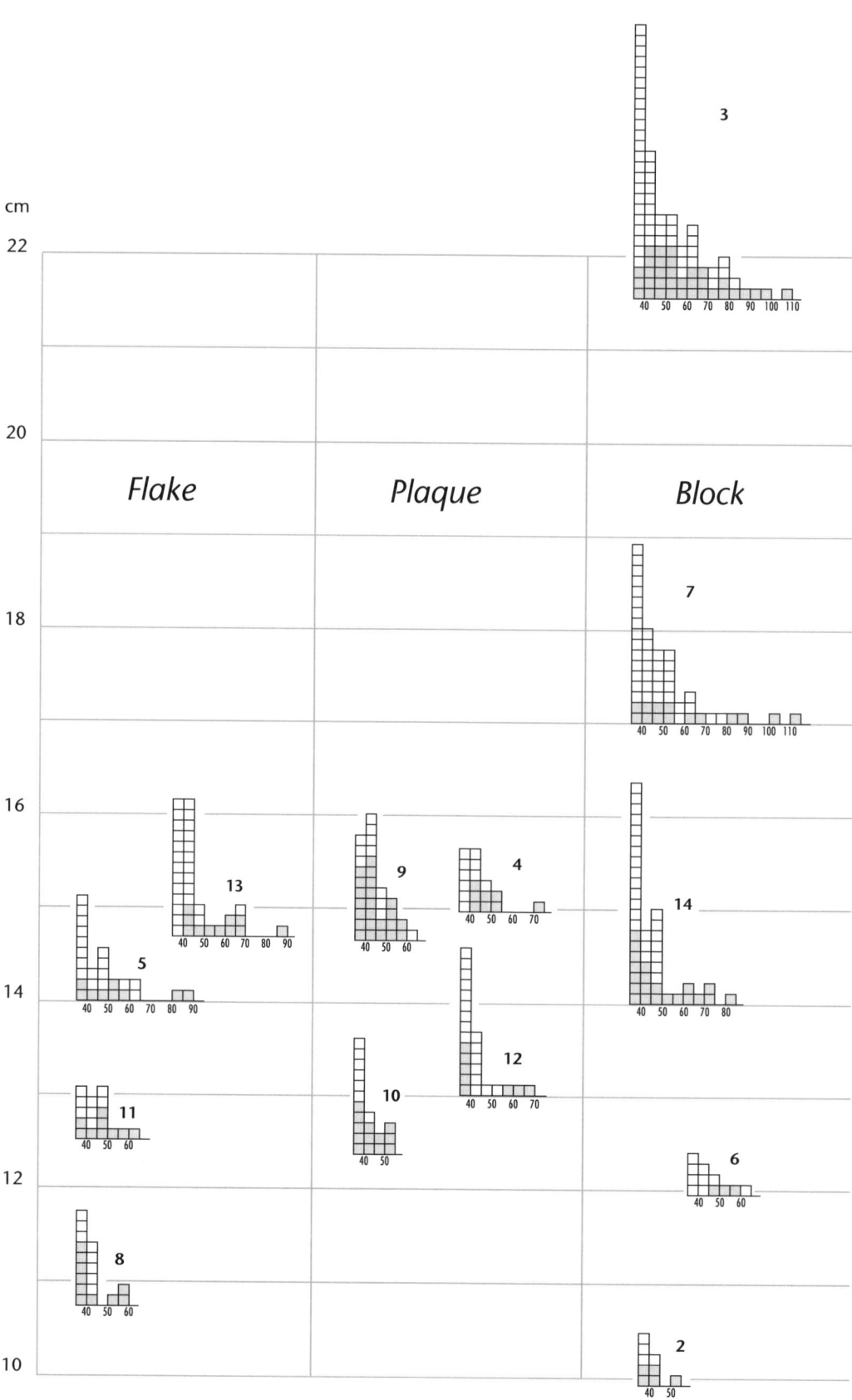

Figure 11. Histograms (spectra) of the counts of large flakes (length >35mm), including type 2a flakes (gray cells) from experimental tests 2–14, in increments of 5 mm in length, arranged according to the original blank and the length of the piece obtained (along the vertical scale).

Table 8. For the three groups of tests arranged in the same order as in previous tables, according to the length of the knapped piece, number and weight of large and medium flakes, and ratio of large to medium flakes by number and weight.

Test no.	Blank type	Length	M flakes		L flakes		Ratio L/M flakes (%)	
			Count	Weight (g)	Count	Weight (g)	By count	By weight (g)
2	block	100	55	66	9	40	16.4	60.6
8	flake	106	58	74.6	18	70.2	31	94.1
6	block	121	57	76	12	71	21	93.4
10	plaque	127	89	113.8	20	86.6	22.5	76.1
11	flake	127	69	77.4	17	102.2	24.6	132
12	plaque	128	77	88	25	128	32.5	145
	average		118					
5	flake	140	109	115	26	208	23.8	181
14	block	140	119	147	45	340.4	37.8	232
13	flake	146	140	164	37	250	26.4	152
9	plaque	147	125	151	34	195	27.2	129
4	plaque	149	121	167.2	18	125	14.9	74.7
	average		144.4					
7	block	169	174	202.4	52	426.8	29.9	211
3	block	221	196	238.2	84	799	42.8	335
	average		195					

Table 9. Model of the table of counts and weights of type 2a flakes, as well as large and medium flakes from phases 2 and 3, and the main ratios between these values for the subject assemblage or concentration and raw material variety. Gray cells denote data that do not apply in this case.

Concentration X:	Variety					
	Large		Medium		Total	
Type 2a flakes	n	W (g)	n	W (g)	n	W (g)
elongated and skewed						
thick						
cortical						
Kombewa						
total						
all flakes						
ratio 2a flakes/all flakes			%	%		
Number and dimensions of the largest flakes: n = x; class x mm						

Chapter 3
Return to the Archaeological Record

Pampa de los Fósiles 14, Unit 1

The primary objective of this chapter is to describe the second phase of this research program, which is the study of a workshop excavated in 1988, and to compare these archaeological data with the modern, experimentally produced reference base.

Because of the abundant interesting material visible on the surface, as well as the ease of access to this zone, the Paiján sites of Pampa de los Fósiles have been the most studied in the region. A projectile point knapping workshop in site 12 (unit 42) was first summarily described (Chauchat 1979, 1991). Other workshops that have been previously published are units 3–5 and 11 of site 13 in the same zone (Chauchat et al. 1992:179–227) (Figure 4). Although these three workshops can yield the same kind of information as we obtain here, there are several reasons why they are not good sites for this purpose:

- The zone in which they are situated is highly affected by violent winds that blow over the plain. These winds create trails of flakes spatially sorted in decreasing dimensions by saltation. Material is also highly worn by eolian processes.
- Because flakes were collected by meter-square units, it is difficult to delimit knapping localities precisely and to distinguish clearly the material belonging to each one.
- Relatively few varieties of raw material are observable in these workshops, but flakes resulting from knapping operations are very abundant. This circumstance, further complicated by deterioration of the flakes by eolian processes, renders attempts at refitting very difficult.

Pampa de los Fósiles 14 is located on an alluvial fan, or several coalescing alluvial fans, that descend directly from the northern flank of the Cerro Tres Puntas. The basal extremity of this fan is transversally cut by a *rio seco* (dry wash) that comes from the same massif but is oriented towards the west as soon as it

Figure 12. Site 14, unit 1, looking toward the southeast after the excavations of 1988. About halfway up the hill behind the person standing on the site is the large vein of pale rhyolite that constitutes the northern slope of the outcrop where the quarries of site 125 are found. (Photo by C. Chauchat.)

exits from the canyon onto the alluvial plain (Figures 4 and 12). A secondary, rather deep wash cuts through the alluvial fan and across the archaeological site.

This site as a whole contains five units (Figure 4). Unit 1 is located on the right bank of the wash in an area where the bluff is now very steep. Unit 2, located 150 m to the east, is a well-defined and concentrated living site. It has been studied by C. Chauchat, P.-Y. Demars, and E. Wing and is presented in the publication already cited (Chauchat et al. 1992:247–278). This unit yielded a large tool assemblage, hearths, and pits, as well as several thousand identifiable animal bones. Spatial analysis of these various objects suggests several successive, undoubtedly seasonal occupations. Five radiocarbon dates were obtained, which extend over the entire Paiján period. The oldest are GIF 9405: 10,640 ± 260 RCYBP (unpublished) and GIF 5161: 10,380 ± 170 RCYBP (Chauchat et al. 1992:278). Even though this living site is the closest to unit 1, there is no proof that both units were occupied by the same people. Units 3 and 4 contain the same kind of knapped tool assemblages as the other living sites but in weaker densities. They are located farther away, downstream from unit 1. Unit 5 comprises at least two small pale rhyolite workshops; the nearest is about 100 m to the north of unit 1. In fact, it is possible that a few of the objects collected from the northern extremity of unit 1, about 20 m from concentration D, belong to unit 5. The whole of site 14 is protected from southern trade winds by the Cerro Tres Puntas massif and a lower rocky hill that develops in a north-south direction a few hundred meters west of the site.

The group of workshops that constitute unit 1 of site 14 have distinctive characteristics that make them attractive for study, according to criteria chosen for our program of technological analysis:

- sheltered area reduces displacement by wind and deterioration of surface material;
- several small-sized workshops are clearly separated;
- relatively small quantity of knapped material consists of many varieties of raw material.

Moreover, this workshop enjoys a particular feature that does not exist as clearly in the other workshops of Pampa de los Fósiles: abundant "unifaces," knapped from different types of stone but all by soft hammer. This feature introduces one more element into our study.

Since this workshop clearly constitutes a unique case, it is not certain that the behavior suggested from a study of its material will be found in the other workshops in this zone. It will thus be interesting in the future to study a workshop of more classic form.

Unit 1 includes five concentrations of rejected knapping wasteflakes of unequal dimensions and densities. They are organized in a partial elliptical shape whose larger axis, approximately 25 m, is oriented in a south-north direction. The smaller axis is around 15 meters long (Figure 14). The five concentrations were named A through D. Concentration B is actually formed of two coalescing concentrations that are difficult to separate. The northeast quarter of the ellipse is unoccupied; it is interesting to note that this zone lies in the path of the wind, as shown by small trails of waste flakes transported from the concentrations. The Paiján workshops found in proximity all have an eolian trail of flakes oriented toward the north, conforming to the modern direction of the trade winds. We obviously do not know whether the trade winds of the less arid climate that dominated this region during the Pleistocene-Holocene transition followed a different direction. Some landforms observed along the great Cupisnique dune ridge indicate a probable variation of a few degrees, but the chronology of this variation is not known. The deviation of about 45° from the direction of these trade winds indicated by the surface of our workshop is thus due to the nearby hills, which protected the site to the south and southwest.

Methodology

Field methods

The unit was studied in three phases. In the first, we systematically collected all tools visible on the surface in and around the concentrations. Given their weak densities, we proceeded by triangulation following two parallel axes oriented north-south, which later served to establish a metric grid. The 75 objects collected were recorded on a plan and consecutively numbered for the whole workshop. In addition, the approximate outlines of the concentrations were drawn on the plan so that we could associate the spatial distribution of tools (Figure 13). This collection phase was done in 1974, long before we developed the program of lithic technology presented above. Drawings of some tools had also been completed, but no publication followed this field work.

In the second phase, undertaken in June 1988, a few months after the first knapping experiments, we collected knapping flakes within the metric grid described above. This grid was divided in increments of 25 cm on each side, resulting in 16 subdivisions per square meter. Each subdivision was assigned a number so that we could record the location of objects found within its boundary. Because knapping flakes were so numerous, they were not numbered individually, but labeled according to the square meter and subdivision in which they were found and with the letter "S" for surface. This phase was centered on a zone of 586 m^2, although some tools had been collected from beyond the limits of this area, mainly to the north and northeast (Figure 14). During this operation we verified that this zone completely encompassed all visible lithic scatters, thus leaving no material on the surface after collection.

In the third phase, which immediately followed the second, we rapidly excavated 20 cm in depth the richest areas of the workshops (in the interior of the dashed line in Figure 14). All sediments from this excavation were systematically screened on the spot. The flakes collected were marked in the same manner as those described above, but with the letter "E" for excavation. A few tools also found during this excavation were precisely located on the plan. The surface excavation covered 87 m^2, primarily in the richest zones of each surface workshop.

A detail proved to have unexpected consequences for the com-

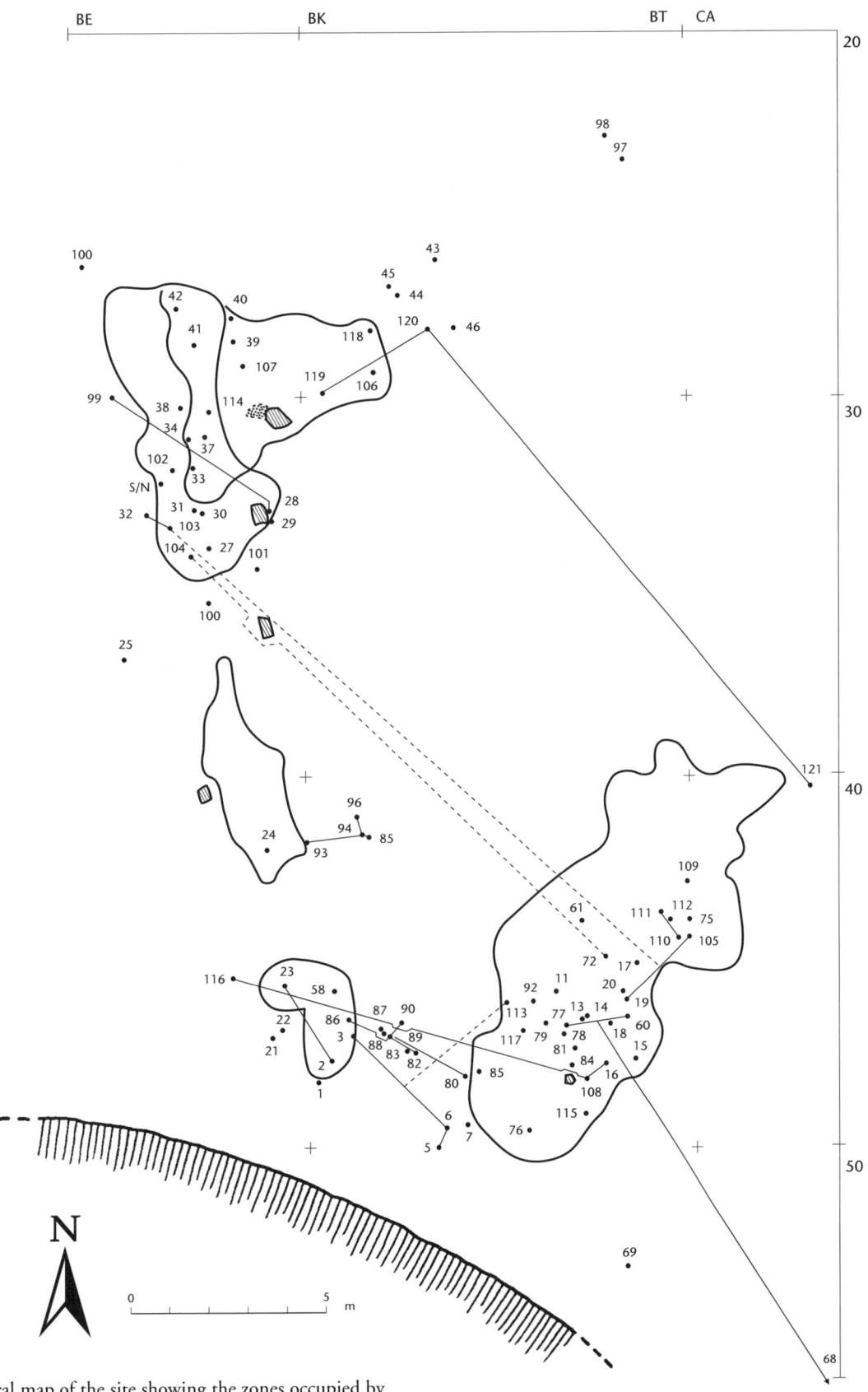

Figure 13. General map of the site showing the zones occupied by the concentrations, the bluff of the terrace to the south, the distribution of collected tools, and the connections between tool fragments.

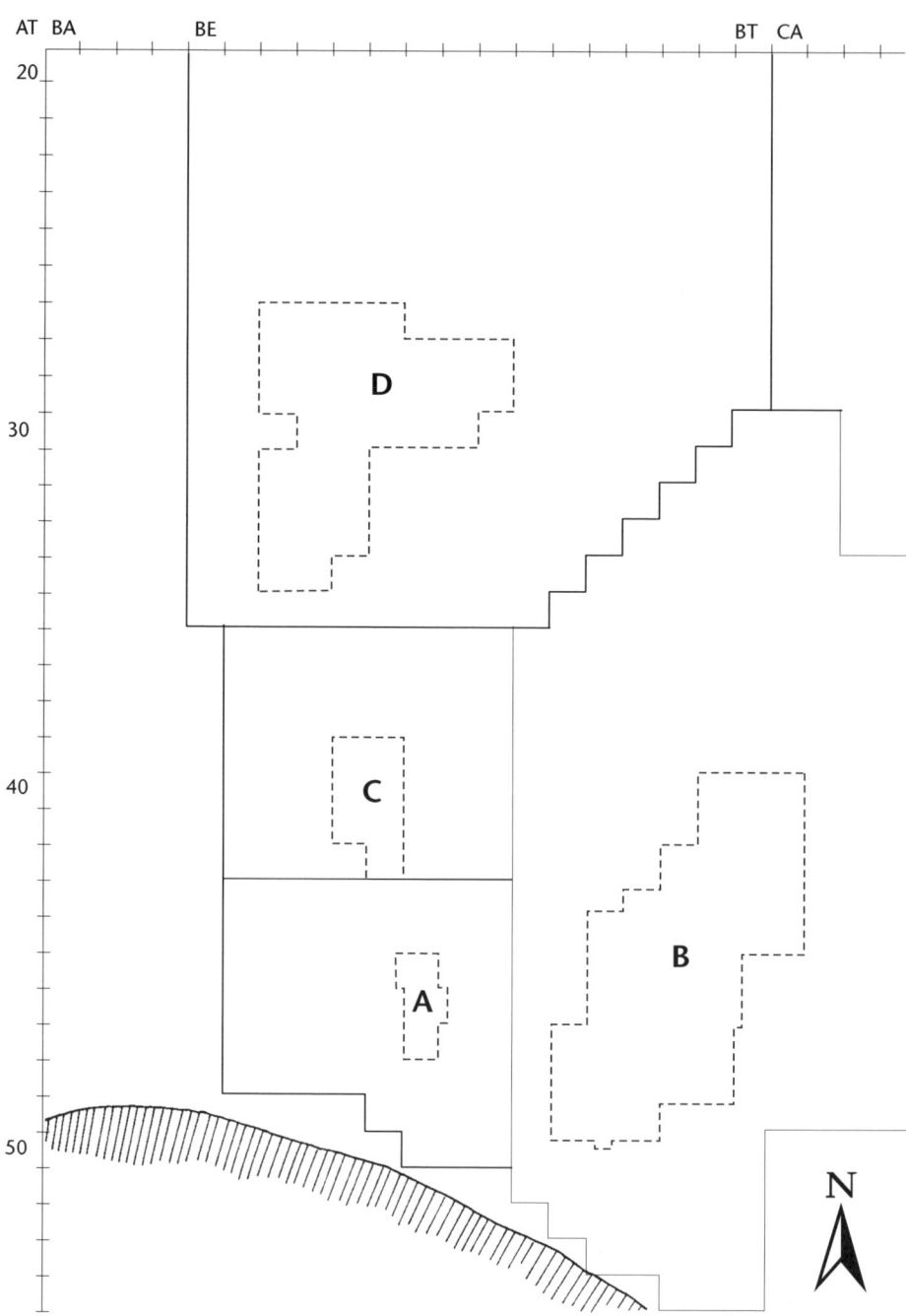

Figure 14. General map showing the grid and the zones subject to surface collection (solid line) and excavation (dashed line). The scale of both axes is in meters.

pleteness of this collection. The excavation, which in principle should have covered all the zones occupied by the workshops, was done immediately after completing the surface collection. Therefore precise records locating flakes by 25-cm subdivisions were not yet available; we had only the distribution of tools on the surface and the approximate outlines of workshops that were mapped during the first phase. We subsequently realized that these outlines, drawn by eye, did not exactly correspond to those that would have been drawn according to the plans of the distribution of flakes. As a result, a few zones of limited dimensions were not excavated even though they should have been, considering the number of flakes found on the surface. It is thus possible that we missed some flakes, and even tool fragments, in these zones. It must be stressed, however, that we stopped digging in a zone only when several sub-squares failed to yield knapped material, even after we sieved the sediment.

At this time we were also unaware of the possibility of a central hearth, which later appeared during spatial analysis, especially when we drew the outlines of the knapping localities shown in Figure 31. Consequently the area in the center of the ellipse was not explored. This is one of the greatest shortcomings of field work in this site.

The various areas that were not completely explored could thus explain why certain fragments are missing. The presence of a steep bluff and a wash below close to concentrations A and B is another possible reason for the disappearance of various pieces. However, we have observed in the other workshops previously studied that numerous fragments are also inexplicably absent, even though collections were made over the entire area of the workshops and sometimes over vast surfaces around them.

During the different stages of field work a total of 121 pieces were collected, precisely localized, and numbered. However, these objects do not all have the same status. The list of tools in Table 12, according to our typological records, does not include the hard-hammer flakes and small debris that were initially individually collected (Chauchat et al. 1992:54–65). Moreover, we collected some tools at a distance from the workshops on the theory that they could have been thrown away there, without considering that other workshops towards the north could equally have been the source of these objects; we later removed these artifacts from the definitive inventory. These last two phases of field work required 10 days of work by a team of five persons, including the authors of the present publication.

Lithic Analysis
Data analysis in the laboratory was begun immediately after the field work session (June 1988) and continued during the following month. Analysis was subsequently pursued intermittently from 1989 to 1991, in the absence of J. Pelegrin and C. Chauchat, by the other three authors. In March–April 1992, Pelegrin and Chauchat returned for four weeks to Trujillo, where the material was stored, with the goal of completing the study. We intended first to interpret the inventories and plans by category and by concentration, work already begun by C. Galvez, R. Esquerre, and R. Becerra. Checking these inventories, J. Pelegrin observed some difficulties in classifying a small percentage of the lithic material (identifying the raw material and technological value of some pieces). We then decided to reclassify the whole lithic collection with the help of our Peruvian colleagues. The experimental collection was also reclassified in order to maintain consistency for comparison with the archaeological material, as defined by J. Pelegrin at the start of the project.

With the whole of the material displayed on large tables, J. P. observed that different varieties might be distinguishable within the pale rhyolite. This discovery encouraged him to regroup the flakes assigned to particular varieties. In several cases it was found that a group containing no more than a few dozen flakes could have resulted from knapping a single piece. Moreover, while grouping the flakes a few refits were quickly found, some of them from two different scatters, thus supporting the validity of such subdivisions. Suddenly the search for breakage and debitage refits (Tixier 1980) became pertinent. The task was a reasonable investment of time and would be an effective method for validating the distinctions we made and for detecting natural and anthropogenic displacements.

This fine distinction, to the level of individual blanks or a very small number of blanks, opened new perspectives for estimating the number of finished pieces exported by the knappers, since all that remained was the by-products of their activity. Unfortunately, this discovery occurred rather late, when it was no longer possible to extend the analysis session or to return later. Despite the determined work of J. Pelegrin, this study thus suffers from the incompleteness of certain analyses and records that were judged of low priority at the time but which we now know would have clarified certain details. For example, except in rare cases we do not have a complete record of the spatial location of flakes attributed to each variety of raw material, only of those that are components of refits.

Classification: The Data Sheet
The set of collected lithic material was recorded on a data sheet according to raw material and a first-level technological distinction. Four technological categories were distinguished:

1) Flakes from the bifacial *chaîne opératoire*, detached by soft-hammer percussion. While this technique is relatively easy to recognize on the butt-bulb area of whole flakes and proximal fragments, it is obviously more difficult to detect on flake fragments without butts. It is, however, often revealed by the thinness of the flake, by a profile that is usually slightly curved, or by the presence of opposed negatives on the dorsal surface. Numerous observations at other similar sites confirmed that the two main stones utilized for the manufacture of Paiján points, pale rhyolite and green tuff, were in fact worked exclusively by this technique. Not one flake made from these materials was assignable to a different technique or *chaîne opératoire*. At Pampa de los Fósiles 14, unit 1, the only difficulty in classifying occurred with a small series of flakes of gray tuff, some of which are definitely the by-products of bifacial knapping, others of unifacial retouch, and a small number of dubious attribution.

2) Flakes detached by hard-hammer percussion. These are very few in number and are made from particular materials such as black quartzite. They correspond to the rare products and by-products of flake debitage and to the reworking of a few unifaces.

3) Flakes of an undetermined technique. These are rare, following our descriptions above.

4) Retouch flakes from unifacial pieces, each recognizable by its plain butt and the curvature of its distal extremity.

For each of these classes, flakes were subdivided according to their maximal dimension and in accordance with the experimental tests: large flakes and fragments (> 35 mm); medium (20–35 mm), and small (< 20 mm). The nature of the butt of rare flakes detached by a hard hammer was also recorded: cortical, plain, dihedral, or faceted. As with the experimental tests, particular types of large and medium flakes (type 2a flakes) were distinguished: elongated or skewed, thicker than 5 mm in the mesial area, cortical, and Kombewa. The maximum length of all large flakes was also recorded. Finally, the number and weight of the flakes in each of these categories were recorded.

The Problem of Small Flakes

All the material produced during the experimental tests was collected on a cloth and saved. However, during the analysis of archaeological materials it became apparent that we could not compare the smallest experimental flakes, approaching the dimensions of dust particles, and the smallest flakes (minute chips) recovered from the surface collections and screening of excavated sediments. These flakes were sometimes displaced by wind or rare rainfall events, and the smallest had practically disappeared. It was thus necessary to establish an arbitrary limit that would be valid for the two categories of data. We set this limit at 20 mm for the greatest dimension of each flake. This means that we did not include the counts of small pale rhyolite or green tuff flakes assignable to bifacial knapping in our quantitative estimations of the number of worked bifacial pieces. On the other hand, because they have technological value, we examined and classified as precisely as possible the smallest flakes of other kinds of raw material, particularly those produced in the manufacture or resharpening of unifaces.

The Two Approaches Applied to the Study of the Bifacial Knapping Concentrations

Each concentration was considered a "unit of study." First, we estimated the number and certain characteristics of the bifacial pieces produced (present and absent) based on the qualitative and quantitative spectra of the knapping products.

Next, we subdivided the knapping products of each concentration into raw material types. We thus achieved finer qualitative and quantitative results when documenting refits of flakes on flakes and of flakes on broken or abandoned bifacial pieces. All flakes and fragments at least 2 cm long and assignable to bifacial knapping were reexamined and their technological classifications checked.

Spatial analysis

If we strive to fulfill all the objectives of archaeological research, simply to determine the *chaîne opératoire(s)* and technical processes employed is insufficient. Whenever possible, spatial analysis should also be done, since it is an indispensable constituent of technological analysis if we hope to understand human behavior in all its complexity. It complements the detailed distinction of raw material varieties, for by studying the spatial distribution of objects, especially knapping flakes, we can identify where knapping operations were performed. In the case presented here, we see that the multiplicity of these locations reveals a complex history during occupation of the site.

The archaeological lithic objects are found on the surface where they were deposited following various actions:

- involuntary actions, resulting from mechanical operations associated with knapping activity and its context;
- voluntary actions that modify the nature, composition, and localization of concentrations of knapping waste products;
- actions occurring during the long period between the prehistoric occupation and intervention by the archaeologist, including various natural post-occupational processes.

Supposing the knapper sits or stands still, waste flakes resulting from knapping are distributed in an involuntary manner in accordance with gravity, the influence of wind, the nature of the forces that the knapper applies to the block of material, and any obstacles between the block and the ground, such as the legs of the knapper or a protective apron. In all these cases except the last (flakes collected in an apron could be carried elsewhere), they would fall in the immediate vicinity of the block of raw material being worked, thus forming a concentration of flakes. Such a concentration marks the location where the knapper worked, in other words, a "knapping locality." In practice, knapping localities are identified by a density of flakes higher than elsewhere. After identifying a knapping locality, we made plans of refitted flakes belonging to the varieties of pale rhyolite previously distinguished. In many cases we were able to determine which knapping locality contributed to the knapping of this variety. Ultimately the superposition of several varieties at the same knapping locality leads us to theorize a single knapper. By augmenting this deduction with other particulars, such as estimating (and differentiating) the levels of technical expertise attained by individual knappers, we can add a little flesh to the shadows of these prehistoric craftsmen.

Experimentation has shown that these knapping localities rarely exceed an area of 1 m^2 (Kvamme 1997; Newcomer and Sieveking 1980). In particular, the first author emphasized the theoretical distribution of flakes, whereby the number of flakes decreases with distance from a center representing their origin (e.g., the vertical line from the point where the block is knapped). In our case the knapping localities are spread out and have been blurred by the various post-depositional processes outlined above, but they are still visible.

In theory, all the flakes belonging to a knapping locality should refit onto one another, resulting in one or several blocks from which only the finished piece would be missing if it was exported. This type of reconstitution requires an enormous amount of work, and other factors can make it impossible—for example, the knapper may have relocated while the operation was in progress, a frustrated knapper may have thrown away flakes, flakes may have been swept away to create a more comfortable workspace, children may have introduced objects during play or educational activities, flakes with sharp cutting edges may have been removed for non-knapping activities elsewhere, etc.

It is obvious that if a knapper interrupts his work to move elsewhere and then returns to work in exactly the same location and position, it is impossible to distinguish these two separate phases unless he continued to shape one or several pieces in the second location. This displacement would thus be registered in the archaeological record by a series of successive flakes from the two locations that could be refitted. It is, however, necessary to avoid confusing such a temporary displacement with the situation when a heap of flakes that got in the way was simply thrown out; in this case the dispersion would undoubtedly be larger. We are of course describing ideal conditions; in practice these diverse behaviors are not easy to detect.

Instances of these types of behavior can be very numerous,

and the spatial evidence often allows no more than a supposition as to their exact nature. These are the voluntary actions that occur during or slightly after the knapping operation.

After the site is abandoned, natural processes are prevalent but human actions can also take place. The site may be disturbed by people of the same culture returning to visit a camp or workshop occupied during a previous season, perhaps to procure flakes with a good cutting edge. But we cannot exclude occasional disturbance by travelers long after the site is abandoned if the concentrations stand out in the landscape by their color, as is sometimes the case. For example, a foliate piece and a projectile point were collected somewhere and abandoned near a stone windbreak at site no. 56, which contains ceramics of the Cupisnique style (ca. 1000 B.C.) (Chauchat et al. 1998:44). Of course, we cannot exclude visits by modern collectors; although the desert has been less frequented in the modern period, we know that stone "arrowheads" found on the desert floor aroused interest in curious travelers well before their discovery by archaeologists. It is not surprising to find moderate dispersal of surface concentrations and a few objects absent on a surface that has been exposed for 10,000 years. We could even expect the effects to be much more pronounced.

In the workshop under study, we conducted the spatial analysis in the same manner as the technological analysis, by successive approximations, i.e., by mapping increasingly precise categories on site plans, essentially guided by the raw material varieties distinguished during the technological analysis. This analysis did not include calculations to distinguish possible spatial groupings; only groups whose outlines were visible to the naked eye were distinguished. Indeed, at least for the moment all the calculations to discern spatial groupings are far less effective than the human brain, although they are certainly cumbersome.

Unless otherwise noted, the grids on the maps and plans of the sites and particular concentrations are metric.

Post-Occupational Formation Processes

Since the occupation by Paiján knappers, the flakes and debris concentrations have been subjected to various phenomena that contributed to their present aspect. Some of these phenomena are common to all the region; others are specific to this location and its unique properties. It is necessary to isolate every one of them in order to understand why this particular workshop is what it is and to determine whether the distribution of archaeological material is the result of natural processes or a human agent.

We noted above that the site is located on an alluvial fan or a series of coalescing alluvial fans coming down from the Cerro Tres Puntas massif. Actually, the slope of the surface is not very pronounced, probably on the order of 4°, and it is regular from north to south, more like a regular alluvial terrace than an alluvial fan. A possible effect of this direction of slope is that most flakes from the knapping localities moved northward. The slope, practically devoid of vegetation but littered with small angular stones, is not steep enough for gravity to move objects across its surface. However, sheet-flooding or the formation of gullies during rainy episodes such as El Niño events can move objects along this preferential direction. In fact, a shallow gully about 1 or 2 m wide exists in the northern part of the site where it crosses the concentration D (Figure 25). Migration of flakes toward the north was observed along this gully (Figures 36, 38, 40–42). Some south-to-north movement that seems to have occurred sporadically is visible in some, but not all, of the plans of distribution of varieties of materials (Figures 34–36). Since this phenomenon is supposed to have occurred after occupation by the Paijanenses, all the varieties of material were already in place and should have been affected. However, this is not the case, which means that some agent disturbed some varieties of materials, but left other varieties undisturbed or affected them in a different way. The only agent that could operate differently on different varieties of material on the same spot is the agent responsible for their original deposit, the human agent. Since blanks were worked one at a time at each knapping locality, different behaviors could result in different spatial distributions of the waste products. This does not mean that downslope movement by surface water did not exist; it means that it was weak and had little effect on the concentration of flakes except in the case of the above-mentioned gully across concentration D.

During the analysis we occasionally mention absent fragments that normally should exist in the archaeological record. We found the same problem when studying other biface knapping workshops: numerous small fragments of bifaces without any apparent functional interest were missing, even though we explored around the workshops well beyond throwing range and recorded every piece (Chauchat et al. 1992:179–227). However, in Pampa de los Fósiles 14, unit 1, we cannot forget the presence of a steep bluff near the southern end of the site, where pieces or fragments thrown away would have been irretrievably lost.

Another crucial problem when interpreting surface sites in arid land is wind deflation. Given trade winds continuously blowing across a supposedly soft terrain consisting mainly of sand and silt, one would expect quite a depth of superficial sediment to have been blown away, leaving on the surface eroded stones without their sedimentary context. Strangely enough, that does not seem to be the case, since buried features such as firepits, refuse pits, and human burials found in a majority of Paiján campsites have not always been truncated by wind erosion. In cases like Pampa de los Fósiles 12, unit 7, and Pampa de los Fósiles 13, unit 1 (Chauchat et al. 1992:85–92, 140–146), there is even a buried archaeological deposit that, in our opinion, was formed by prehistoric people trampling and disturbing the upper soil layer, thus driving quite a few faunal remains and artifacts under the surface. In the first instance where this phenomenon was discovered a sedimentological analysis was conducted at the Institut du Quaternaire, University of Bordeaux, France, by C. Thibault, who found that the sediment containing the faunal remains and artifacts was not eolian but was the same silt as the upper layer of the alluvial substratum. This layer of buried faunal remains and artifacts is also found in the Paiján campsite closest to the one studied here, Pampa de los Fosiles 14, unit 2,

150 m from unit 1 and in the same sedimentological context (Chauchat et al. 1992:247–278). Even on a very soft sediment this superficial disturbance by trampling cannot affect more than 15–20 cm. This does not mean that wind erosion has been nonexistent, only that it has been weaker than one would expect and quite variable, depending on the presence or absence of intervening hills and distance from the sea. A factor that could account for this situation is that the superficial sediment always contains a coarser component, generally in the fraction 0.5–1 cm, which forms a micro-pavement within the first few centimeters of erosion that very soon stabilizes the surface and prevents further deflation. Another factor is hypothetical: it could be that present arid conditions are too recent to have taken their full effect and that deflation is still going on. In any case, we are tempted to ascribe to deflation in the Pampa de los Fósiles zone a *maximum* depth of 20–30 cm, and this only in the more exposed areas of site 12.

In the workshop we are studying here, as in other instances, we found that spatial analysis isolated some concentrations of buried material. They were interpreted as the result of intensive trampling in a small area and thus indicated some activity of relatively long duration at the same spot. In the present site, concentrations of buried flakes disclosed a knapping locality of some importance (Figures 28 and 29). These finds underscore the fact that almost nowhere in the region did we find evidence of sediment deposit following the Paiján occupation. Of course, occasional sand dunes may have passed upon a lithic site or accumulated around a bush as frequently happens now; and if some sediment buried a site that was later uncovered again by wind deflation, there is no way to know it. There is just one instance of a partially buried midden in the nearby campsite of Pampa de los Fosiles 13, unit 1, set against a low alluvial ridge, whose fine material covered part of the fauna- and artifact-bearing layer (Chauchat et al. 1992:140–146). Other instances of buried middens can be found at the upper end of the Quebrada de Cupisnique, especially at sites 101 and 102 of this zone, where middens rich in land snails are visible only on their eroded margins, most of their area being covered by a thin (5–10 cm thick) layer of silt (Chauchat et al. 1998:56–57).

But wind has another effect: like sheet-flooding and gullies, it can displace small, thin flakes along a preferential direction. Trade winds continuously blowing in the same direction have a tendency to sort objects by decreasing size in this direction, starting from the actual knapping locality. Most Paiján bifacial workshops in the Pampa de los Fósiles area have a trail of such flakes, sometimes visible over distances exceeding 10 m and oriented toward the north. In Pampa de los Fósiles 14, unit 1, since all flakes were collected by individual 25-cm squares we were able to map rather precisely these eolian trails and separate them from the actual knapping locality where they originated. It seems that the effects of wind were weaker and also deflected from their original direction, since small but recognizable eolian trails extend toward the northeast. We also observed that only flakes in our small-flakes category, i.e., whose maximum dimension is less than 20 mm (see "Lithic Analysis" below), were visibly affected by movements along the eolian trail. We assume that larger flakes probably also moved, either within the knapping concentration or slightly outside, but over smaller distances. For instance, it is quite possible that some of the directions of preferential refits visible on Figures 34–36, which are from north to northeast, were caused by wind as well as by sheet-flooding.

We have also observed a "windshield wiper" effect, half-circle sweeping of objects by dead plants, still fixed to the ground by their roots, that swing across the ground when wind gusts rapidly change direction.

A concentration of waste flakes on the surface can be subject to other post-depositional processes that are still observable in the Peruvian desert. Accidental movement of objects, whatever the objects, the frequency of displacement, or the distance and direction of displacement, in the long term separate objects from each other. Short but repeated random movements disperse a concentration of waste flakes and can even obliterate it if there are other objects nearby with which pieces can become intermixed. Disturbing by desert animals such as lizards, snakes, and small mammals and by the growth of plants, a process called bioturbation, can have an appreciable effect of this kind over thousands of years. This phenomenon alone can account for the fact that archaeological knapping concentrations, especially in Pampa de los Fósiles 14, unit 1, are significantly larger than experimental concentrations.

During the whole research program on the Paiján complex, the existence of lithic sites on the surface obliged us to pay particularly close attention to possible causes of mixing of flakes from different periods on the same spot as well as to possible causes for the various visible concentrations. Two main conclusions arise from this experience gathered over 30 years.

1) The Paijanense is a complex of various kind of sites with varied lithic equipment. Some of these are characterized by flake tools and few, if any, projectile points; the others are specialized sites for the manufacture of these projectile points.

2) The site under study here, Pampa de los Fósiles 14, unit 1, is one of these specialized sites where several concentrations visible on the surface are primarily of waste flakes from projectile point manufacture and therefore of human origin. So far, the only natural post-occupational processes isolated are: a) some spreading out of the material after lying on the surface for many years; b) eolian trails of minute flakes originating at the original concentrations and trending toward the northeast; and c) a gully crossing concentration D that displaced flakes along its course. Probable downslope movement by sheet-flooding on the whole site can be deduced from the existence of this gully, but the effects are nearly nonexistent. Wind erosion is minimal, its effects visible only as a slight polishing on the surfaces of the flakes. Displacement by wind action is visible mostly as trails of small flakes toward the northeast and may even be responsible for moving larger

flakes over short distances; however, wind is unable to disperse or even to blur perceptibly the knapping concentrations.

The Collected Material

The material collected in unit 1 consists primarily of lithic objects, the majority of which are flakes removed by soft-hammer percussion (Tables 10 and 11). It also includes a small number of stone tools, a few unknapped objects, one bone tool, and a small faunal assemblage. These faunal remains will be treated

Table 10. Numbers, weight, and ratio to all flakes of each raw material category in all of unit 1.

Raw material	Number of flakes	Ratio to whole by number (%)	Weight (g)	Ratio to whole by weight (%)
pale rhyolite	6743	77.6	6742	75.6
green tuff	1454	16.7	1443	16.2
black quartzite	150	1.7	335	3.8
gray tuff	150	1.7	142	1.6
brown rhyolite	47	0.5	125	1.4
quartz	37	0.4	34	0.4
quartzite	12	0.1	9	0.1
miscellaneous	92	1.1	92	1
total	8685		8913	

Table 11. Number, weight, and ratio to all flakes of pale rhyolite and green tuff flakes for each dimension category in all of unit 1.

	Count	Ratio to whole by count (%)	Weight (g)	Ratio to whole by weight (%)
Pale rhyolite				
large	453	6.7	2539	37.6
medium	2029	30.1	3008	44.6
small	4261	63.2	1195	17.7
total	6743		6742	
Green tuff				
large	108	8.1	489	37.4
medium	465	34.9	585	44.8
small	759	57	232	17.8
total	1332		1306	

separately. It must be stressed that our study affected the whole surface of the site with the limitations outlined above, mainly that some areas were searched more intensively than others because of the presence of archaeological material on the surface. However, we made every effort to collect all existing material, including making the kind of shallow excavation previously described. We consider our lists and inventories of collected material a comprehensive record of the real set of lithic material existing on this site.

Raw Materials

The lithic object that was knapped can be sorted by its constituent materials. The majority is pale rhyolite, a volcanic rock whose color varies from cream to violet and orange. It is dotted with various inclusions such as feldspar, pyrite, and iron oxide. Our surveys discovered a large outcrop and several secondary points

Table 12. Inventory of the tool assemblage of unit 1.

Common tools		deviant piece	1
naturally backed knife	7	small fragment	5
utilized flake	5	projectile point	6
tranchet	3	total	28
scraper	2	**Unifaces**	
notch	2	typical pointed uniface	4
massive denticulate	1	typical rounded uniface	2
micro-denticulate	2	atypical uniface	1
splintered piece	1	total	7
pebble tool	2	**Non-worked tools and miscellaneous pieces**	
total	25		
core	1	cobble or hammerstone	3
Bifacial tools		small pebble or gravel	1
Chivateros biface	2	utilized bone splinter	1
bifacial foliate piece	14		

of this material about 1 km from the site; they show evidence of intensive quarrying activities during prehistoric times. We have called this quarry site Pampa de los Fósiles 125. The blanks utilized in our experimental tests come from this same quarry site. It is possible that other outcrops of pale rhyolite were exploited to obtain raw material for the site (in particular, units 104 and 135 of site 12), but as we will see below, this would have been on a very minor basis.

The second most often used lithic raw material was a volcanic tuff called green tuff, which is in fact greenish gray under an olive-green patina. We originally considered this material a dacite (Chauchat et al. 1992) because of its apparent similarity to *"la dacite du Ténéré"* described by Africanist archaeologists (Tixier 1978:33 and Figure 4). The origin of this material has not been precisely established. This material was found in concentrations of large soft-hammer flakes, which are probably the remains of the beginning stages of bifacial shaping, at the foot of rocky hills formed of volcanic-sedimentary stone (cinerites or volcanic tuffs), about 7–8 km north of site 14. However, the exact stratum from which the material originates has not been determined. In any case, this material comes from a zone located northward and farther from the site than the source of pale rhyolite.

The other raw materials found in the unit are much less abundant than those described above (Table 10). The fine-textured black quartzite was not utilized in the bifacial *chaîne opératoire*; it is associated only with the unifaces and a few ordinary tools. It has been observed in other sites of Pampa de los Fósiles, primarily camp sites, in the form of knapped cobbles or flakes, and in other workshops in the form of unifaces and their rejuvenation flakes. This material, which at Pampa de los Fósiles is always in cobble form, was clearly imported, since the local alluvial material is never rolled to the same degree. On the other hand, cobbles of the same black quartzite, which are more or less suitable for knapping, are frequently found in the wash of the Quebrada de Cupisnique. We thus infer that the cobbles found at Pampa de los Fósiles originate either from this wash or from alluvium along its course to the ocean. In either case, they originate directly or indirectly from at least 8–10 km north.

Another variety of tuff of a variable gray color and sometimes finely stratified is regularly found in sites of the region. Its nearest source is the rocky foothills to the north of Pampa de los Fósiles previously mentioned in association with the green tuff. This is indeed the only other raw material that we observe in the green-tuff workshops on these foothills. It was often employed for the manufacture of unifaces and ordinary tools. Only a few rare points were made from this material.

Brown rhyolite, despite its name, has not been petrographically defined; it was deemed similar to pale rhyolite. This is a fine-grained dark brown stone with scattered white inclusions that seem to be feldspar. Its geological provenience is unknown.

In some sites, despite difficulties of extraction and knapping, the Paijanenses extensively employed quartz, which exists in this region as large inclusions in granite. It is found in the form of rock crystal and quartz veins and all intermediate forms between them. In our site only traces of this material were present.

Other varieties of quartzite also exist in the region. These have a slightly coarser grain and are found in various colors. Extensive outcrops of large orange and purple slabs can be found on the current coastline of Puerto Chicama in the southern part of the region. However, a few tests conducted in 1988 indicate that many blocks are not suitable for knapping. Another outcrop of a gray veined or violet color at the upper end of the Quebrada de Cupisnique was extensively knapped. A third outcrop was recently identified in the northernmost section of the Mócan valley in the foothills separating the Mócan area from the Quebrada de Cupisnique.

The category "miscellaneous" in Table 10 lists the raw materials that are difficult to define or too rare to be counted separately.

Tools

Tools associated with the knapping debris observed on the surface (Table 12) are mainly bifaces and points in various stages of manufacture. These are made from the same raw materials as are most flakes, pale rhyolite and green tuff. However, our records do not include a small number of objects collected at the very beginning from locations 15–30 m from the workshops themselves. These include three poorly made bifaces and a fragment of an excellent foliate piece found to the north, as well as a few rare tools and isolated knapping products.

Compared with the workshops of site 13 already studied, which often included several hundred bifacial pieces, the site presented here is not very rich. Considering the detailed nature of the study we have undertaken, this paucity of objects can be seen as a benefit. The present workshop includes 20 bifaces (*Chivateros* and foliate pieces), of which 3 consist of several fragments, and 10 projectile points (pieces on which pressure retouch can be observed), of which 2 consist of several fragments.

As mentioned above, a peculiarity of unit 1 noted at the time of its discovery in 1970 is the abundance of unifaces relative to bifaces. Unifaces, also knapped by soft-hammer percussion, are commonly found in workshops, sometimes more frequently than in campsites. However, in the workshops we have studied, generally only two or three unifaces are found for every hundred or more bifacial pieces. The proportion of 7 unifaces for 30 bifaces found here is thus quite uncommon. However, the workshops near Ascope, on the northern margin of the Chicama valley, are an exception, since there the proportion is inverted, undoubtedly owing to the abundance of high-quality gray volcanic tuff, which was preferentially employed for the manufacture of this tool category (Chauchat et al. 1992:299–324). We believe that these objects were originally much larger and were intensively "curated," meaning they were gradually reduced by repeated rejuvenations over a long life cycle. They do not become archaeologically visible until they are abandoned after they become too small or are broken during reworking, or because the retouched edges become too steep. These unifaces are most often made of gray tuff or dark quartzite, not of rhyolite or green tuff as are most of the bifacial pieces.

The two tool categories produced by workshop activities, the bifaces and points, and the unifaces, will be described in detail below with consideration of each raw material type and each workshop. For descriptive purposes, especially in the context of spatial analyses, the identification number of a piece will sometimes be given in the text. A tilde (~) between two numbers indicates two fragments of the same piece that have been refitted. Suspension points between two numbers (...) indicate two fragments that do not fit exactly together but which nevertheless probably come from the same piece and are thus "associated." We will also sometimes use the label of a square-meter, composed of two letters and a number (e.g., BK30), to locate a precise zone on the plan, as seen in Figure 13 and 14.

Since bifaces and points of light-colored material found on the surface tend to monopolize our attention, it was unexpected that common tools characteristic of the Paiján campsites would also be present. Their presence, although difficult to quantify, indicates a certain emphasis on daily activities related to food processing, the manufacture of organic tools, etc. Moreover, excavations conducted during field work revealed a small refuse pit containing the remains of animals consumed by the knappers during their stay. This occurrence is exceptional for the Paiján workshops known by us.

As far as we can judge, given the small number of common tools, the quantitative composition of this category is not different from that of other campsites in this zone (for definitions of these tool types see Chauchat et al. 1992:54–65). Tools of the *"a posteriori"* types (Bordes 1967, 1970) are particularly numerous, especially naturally backed knives (Figure 15, no. 1 and 2) and utilized flakes (no. 4 and 5). These latter pieces are large green tuff flakes with a smooth superior face. They were detached by soft-hammer percussion and thus probably came from a bifacial *chaîne opératoire* beginning on a flake or the surface of a plaque. Despite considerable effort to find refits, none of the flakes that would normally have followed this detachment were found. It thus seems they were brought to the site as is to be utilized for their unaltered sharp edge, which could explain the presence of a few chips and notches.

After a detailed analysis of the pale rhyolite varieties employed for the manufacture of projectile points in this workshop (presented below), two relatively large knapping flakes stood out be-

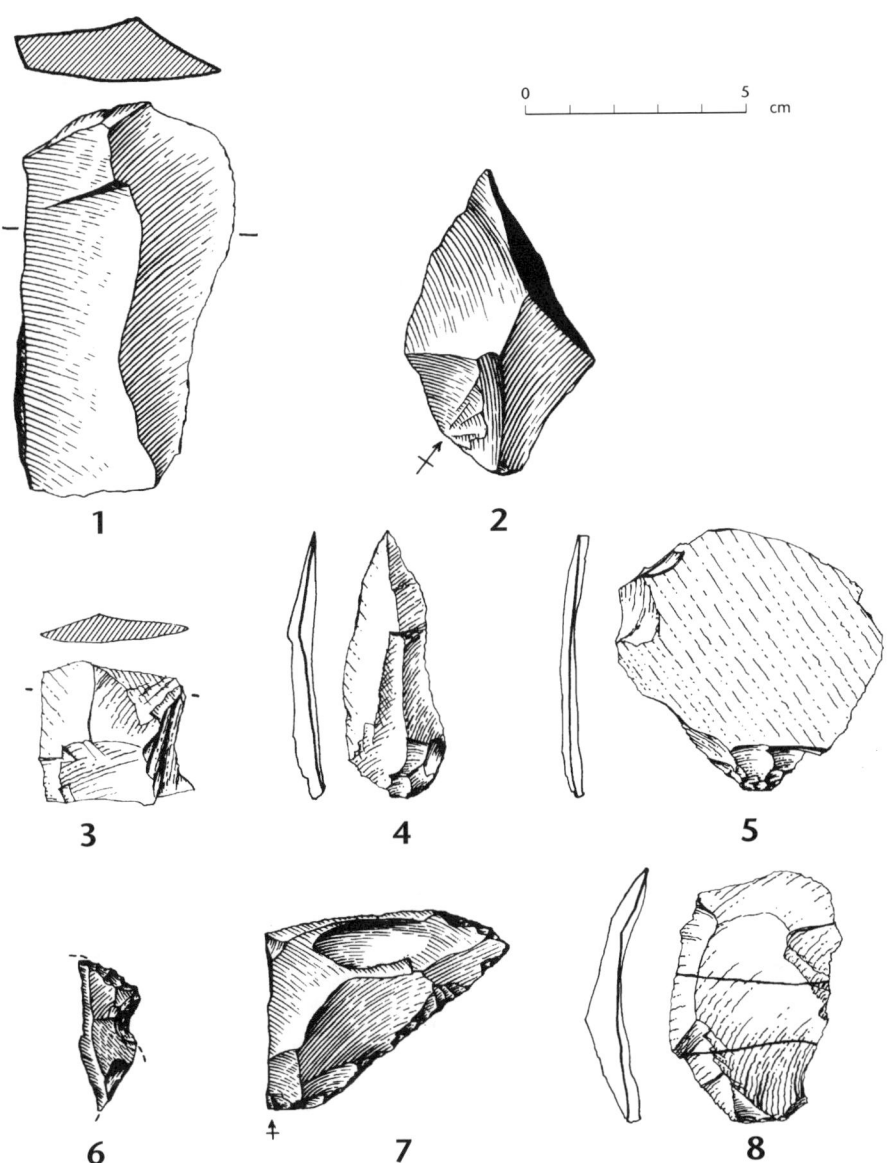

Figure 15. Common tools: **1** and **2**, naturally backed knives; **3**, *tranchet*; **4** and **5**, utilized flakes; **6**, micro-denticulate; **7**, sidescraper; **8**, flake fragmented in three pieces—the distal fragment is a naturally backed knife, the mesial fragment is a *tranchet*. (Drawings 1, 2, 6, and 7 by C. Chauchat; 3, 4, 5, and 8 by M. Reduron.)

cause they do not belong to any known raw material, and also because knapping flakes are usually found in lots of tens, even hundreds. We conclude that they were brought to the site already knapped to serve as knives, as was the case for the large green tuff flakes described above. They were thus included in the category "utilized flake." The first is a large flake of gray-greenish rhyolite; its exact provenience was not noted, but it comes from concentration A. The second, from square BG32 of concentration D, is made of a yellow-gold rhyolite (Figure 13 and 19).

We found three almost certain *tranchets*. Figure 15, no. 3 shows somewhat dubious evidence of a voluntary fracture at its distal end. One shaping flake of green tuff broken into three fragments shows no signs of voluntary fracture (no. 8). However, the distal fragment was found quite far from the others, which could indicate that it was utilized. We have chosen to interpret this object as being constituted of a naturally backed knife (the distal fragment found in workshop B) and a *tranchet* (the mesial fragment) that could have easily been obtained by flexion (given the curvature of the flake). This latter was utilized in concentration D, close to the refuse pit. The non-utilized proximal fragment would have fallen to the ground at the location where the flake was fractured (Figure 19). Only one microdenticulate and one sidescraper were found (Figure 15, no. 6 and 7).

The pebble-tool category includes two tools, one of which is a pebble-scraper (Ossa 1973:124). Although rare, this tool is characteristic of the Paiján lithic assemblage. It consists of a chopper made from a flat cobble that was carefully regularized on its largest side by rather long retouch flakes in order to form a sharp, convex, regular edge like that of a sidescraper. This tool was found beyond the limits of the workshops. The second pebble tool is a globular black quartzite cobble with an irregular edge. It also served as a hammerstone on the side opposite the sharp edge. None of the numerous flakes of this same material found in concentration B refits onto this object.

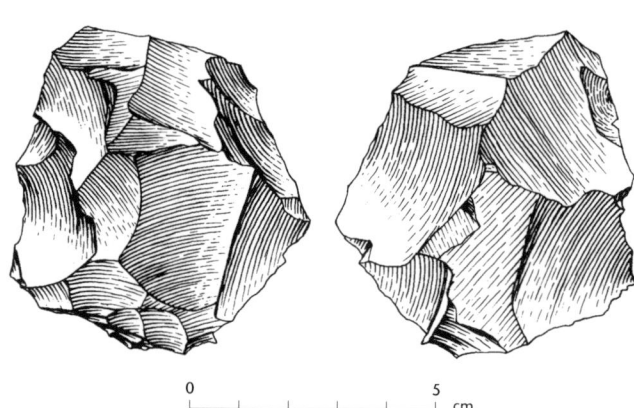

Figure 16. Discoid core. (Drawing by C. Chauchat.)

In comparison, the debitage, in the strict sense, barely deserves mention since only one discoid core was found (Figure 16), along with a few hard-hammer flakes. The lack of any refits among them shows that these objects must have been brought to the site as is. It is possible that these flakes represent *a posteriori* tools, even though they show no macro-traces of use. Other objects described as tools, such as the massive denticulates, could have served completely or partially as cores.

We should not forget to mention the presence of a few unknapped tools, sometimes clearly in association with knapping activities, sometimes enigmatic. Several cobbles that undoubtedly served as hammerstones were then reused in a hearth, where they exploded. Similarly, the very rounded "small pebbles" or "gravel" (1–2 cm maximum dimension) were clearly imported to the site. Because of their small size, their function is unknown.

One poorly preserved bone splinter that was found during excavation has one blunted, better conserved end, suggesting it was used as a pressure flaker (Figure 17). Moreover, it comes from the zone richest in point knapping remains (concentration B) and close to a block that could have been used as a seat (Figure 19). During its time buried in the sediment, this object was reduced to several heavily eroded fragments. These fragments refit only partially onto each other; thus we do not know if it was abandoned whole. Nonetheless, this bone splinter was sufficiently massive to be held in the hand and to withstand the significant physical forces of a tool used as pressure flaker. The appreciable blunting seen on the microphotograph is evidence of such utilization, even if bone is usually considered inferior to antler for this purpose.

A few large stones are visible on the surface of the unit, some of which could have been used as seats. The refuse pit is located alongside one of them. No traces of hearths were found, despite the presence of thermally broken cobbles. Most of the blocks located in the northern part of the workshop, particularly in concentration D, are deeply embedded in the sediment (Figure 13,

Figure 17. Possible retoucher on a bone fragment. Top, approximately 4/5 actual size; bottom, microphoto (X5) of the two faces of the active extremity (arrow). (Photos by C. Chauchat.)

shaded objects). They certainly existed before the workshop, and it is possible they were used as seats during the human occupation. On the other hand, two smaller blocks in C and to the south of B were deliberately placed on the surface, suggesting they were manuports (natural objects brought to the site).

Spatial Distribution of Tools

The dispersion of different categories of tools reflects in large part the primary activity carried out at this site. In other words, the distribution of tools corresponds to the distribution of the knapping products. This is evidently the case for the bifaces and points that were produced in the workshop, as well as for the unifaces that were at least reworked there for the last time (Figure 18). The bifacial tools are indeed distributed in two main zones: in the southern part of the ellipse of the workshops, thus in B and A; and at the other extremity, in D. Only one object was found in C. Bifaces contribute very little to the evacuation trail northeast of D, which consists mainly of ordinary tools (Figure 18 and 19). It is interesting to refit fragments taken from both extreme concentrations. In the case of the bifaces, these matches are not absolutely certain, since they are only based on the identity of raw materials and not on true refits (and thus indicated by dashed lines on the plan). *However, a parallel connection exists in the category of common tools (Figure 19)*. The utilized bone splinter was found barely 1 m from the block-seat of concentration B. The unifaces (Figure 18) are mainly concentrated in the south of B and in A, except for one found in D. One uniface collected in 1970 without precise provenience also came from the south of B or from A. The distribution of these tool categories will be further examined below in relation to that of the flakes resulting from their production.

The spatial distribution of common tools is similar to that of the bifacial tools (Figure 19). The only refits between fragments of common tools are found in concentration C, a flake of green tuff fractured by percussion with a notch and wear traces on one edge. Common tools are much more numerous in D than in the southern zone and are also very dispersed. We could imagine that the refuse pit in D constitutes the common terminus of three different trails of common tools: toward the northeast, the northwest, and the south. The northeast trail is the clearest. On it we found five tools and a core distributed over a distance of more than 10 m. Since common tools are clearly associated with subsistence activities in the campsites, this association with food remains is not surprising.

The unknapped tool assemblage is restricted to a trail of fragments originating from two burnt cobbles, a sort of ball of undetermined stone to the southeast of B and one small pebble in D. Another small pebble was collected, but from well outside the unit. It is interesting to note that these small rounded and polished pebbles (generally 1–2 cm in diameter), perhaps originating from the beaches, have been observed several times, even if only one or two specimens at a time, in the projectile point workshops, while they seem to be absent from the campsites.

Table 10, a quantitative comparison of raw material types in the entire workshop, reveals that pale rhyolite is the most abundant material (except in concentration D). The next part of this study will thus concentrate on pale rhyolite in two main phases: first, we investigate the significance of this material in each concentration; then we study subvarieties of pale rhyolite to refine our perception of tool production with this material. Green tuff, the predominant material in concentration D, will be analyzed in the next chapter, along with the much less abundant green tuff from concentration B. With the exception of gray tuff, the rarer materials such as quartzite, quartz, and brown rhyolite were not used for bifacial knapping but only in the production of unifaces; or they are only found in hard-hammer debitage, very likely corresponding to *a posteriori* tools that were not recognized as such at the beginning of the study. Gray volcanic tuff will be discussed after green tuff, and the other raw materials following these.

Bifacial Knapping Activity

We consider each concentration a unit of study, as stated above, and first inventory the counts and characteristics of large and medium flakes, large type 2a flakes, and other kinds of flakes in order to estimate the number of pieces worked. In the first part of this chapter we will study the four concentrations in order to distinguish knapping locations, dense concentrations of flakes that indicate a location occupied by a knapper.

In analyzing knapping waste products, we will present three kinds of tables for each concentration. The first lists the counts of flakes and their weight (in grams) for each kind of raw material present. The second details the counts and weights of large, medium, and small flakes (according to our definition given above) for the two most abundant raw materials, pale rhyolite and green tuff. The third kind of table, mentioned in the preceding chapter, is more complex; it contains detailed information that is essential for interpreting the technological processes for each raw material. These tables list data first for pale rhyolite, then for each variety of pale rhyolite, then for green tuff. In addition, the count of large flakes and type 2a flakes will be presented following the models that were constructed for the experimental tests.

> NOTE: In the discussions and tables that follow, the count and weight of flakes do not correspond exactly to the area for which the outline was drawn, but to the total of flakes drawn on the plans of each concentration, which are slightly larger. However, this small difference has no effect on interpreting the data.

Concentration A

The surface area of concentration A is estimated at 5m^2, of which nearly 4m^2 was excavated (Figures 20 and 21). Concentration A has the lowest count (256) and weight (560 g) of pale rhyolite flakes. Green tuff is present in insignificant quantities (9 flakes, 16 g). The composition of concentration A in terms of raw materials and flake dimensions is shown in Tables 13 and 14. Those flakes dispersed outside the limits of concentration A and those close to concentration C (as defined on the plan) are fairly numerous in the eastern zone and nearly absent toward the west. This distribution defines a rather clear western limit for the workshop along concentrations A and C.

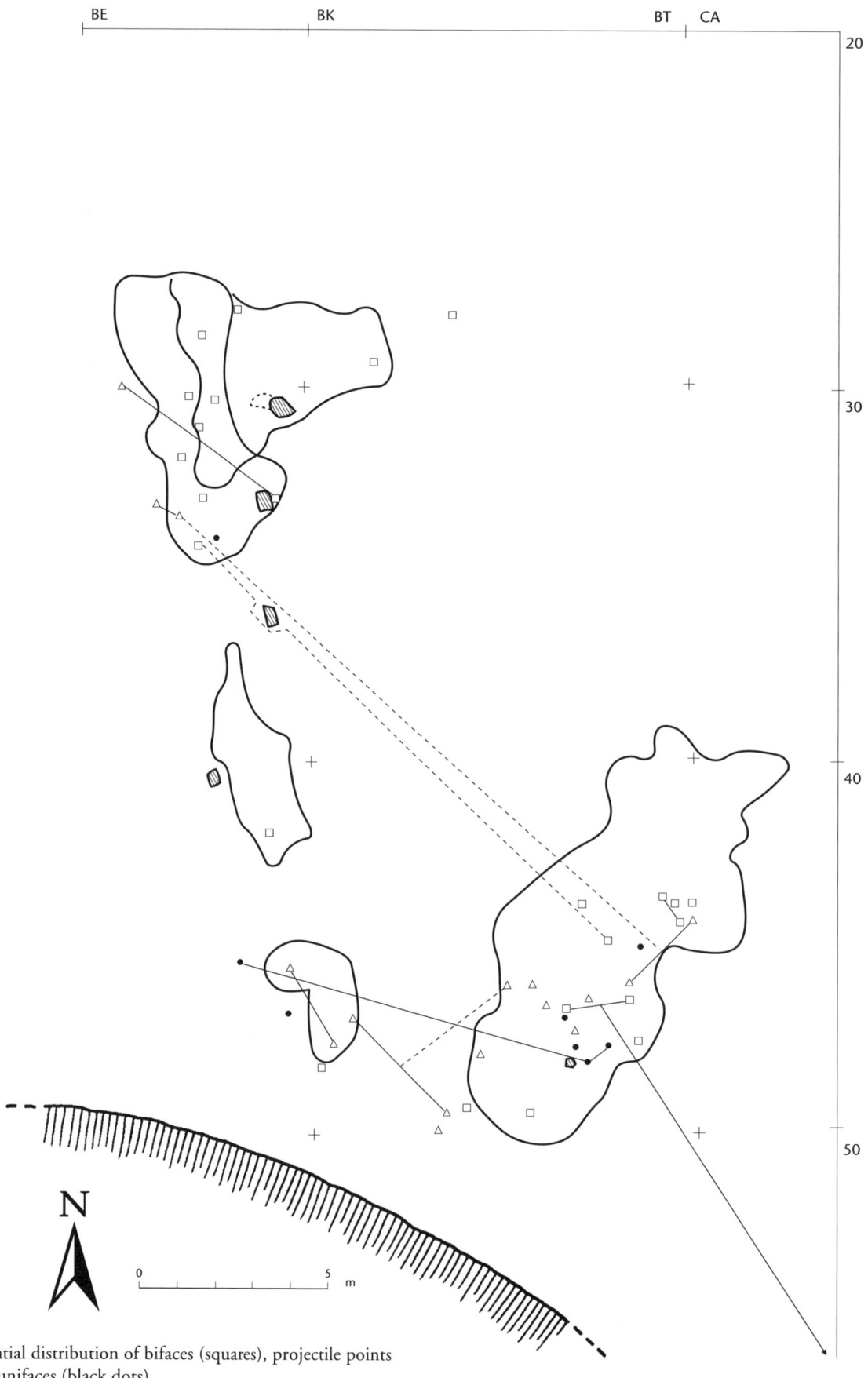

Figure 18. Spatial distribution of bifaces (squares), projectile points (triangles), and unifaces (black dots).

Return to the Archaeological Record

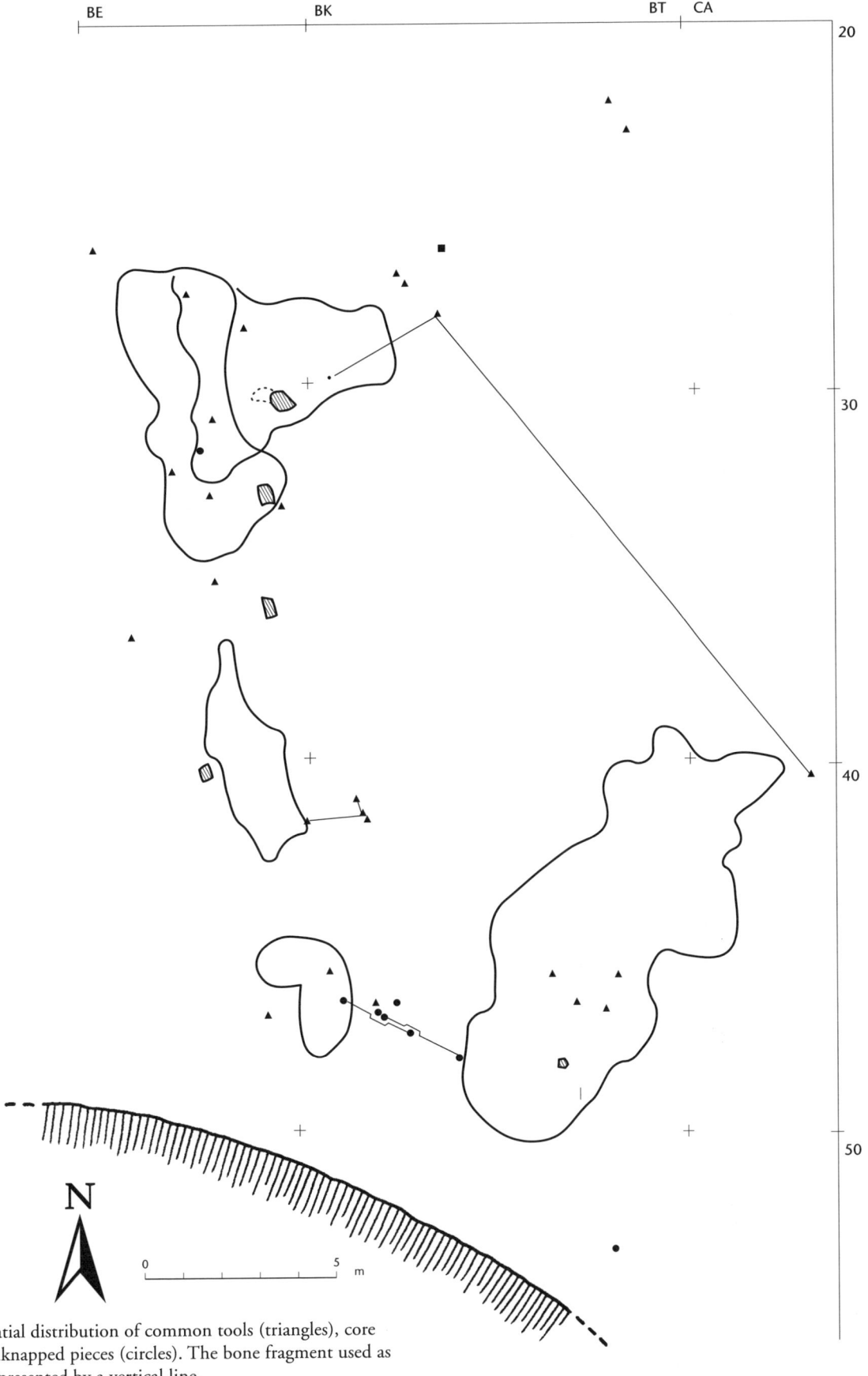

Figure 19. Spatial distribution of common tools (triangles), core (square), and unknapped pieces (circles). The bone fragment used as a retoucher is represented by a vertical line.

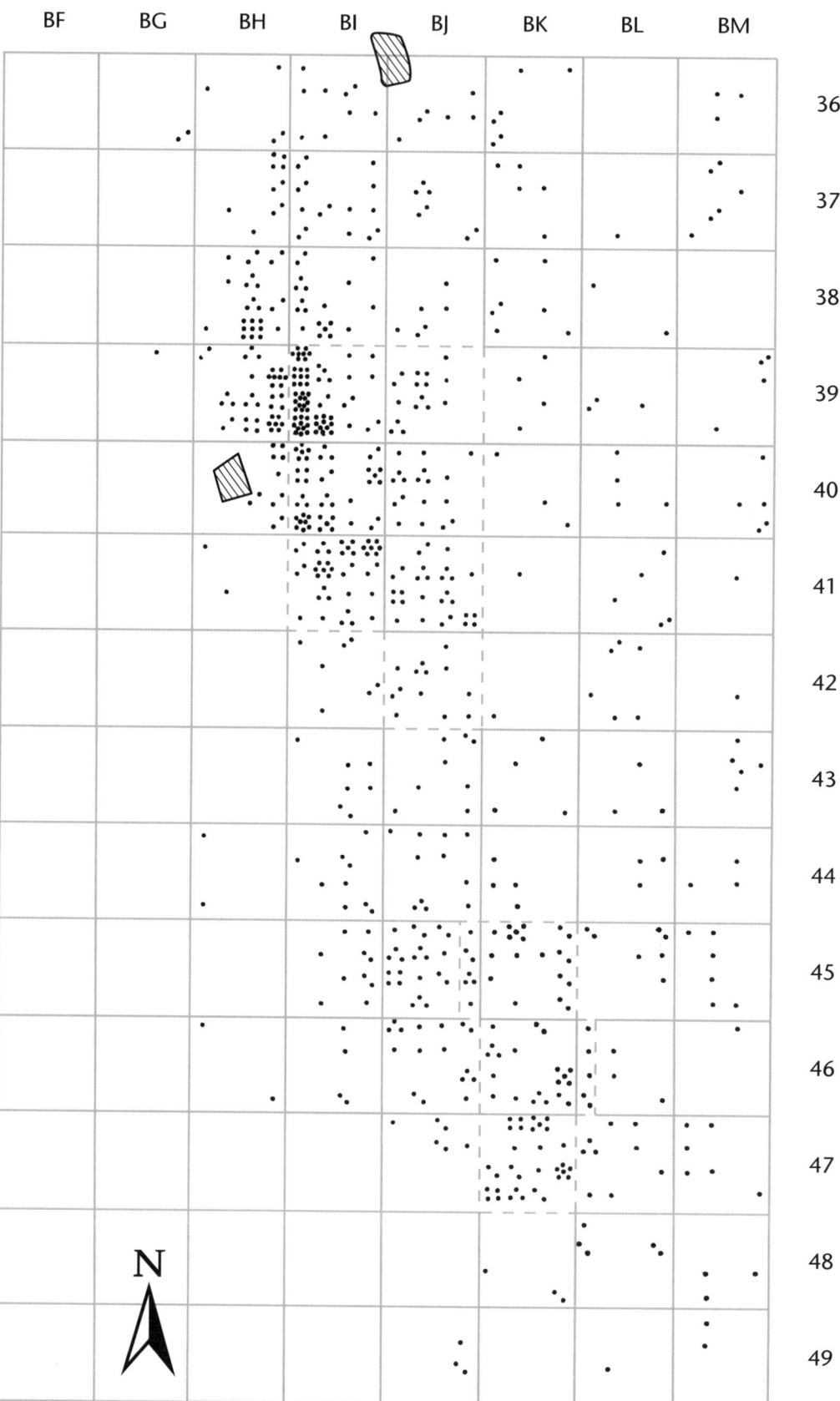

Figure 20. Concentrations A and C; spatial distribution of pale rhyolite flakes by 25-cm squares.

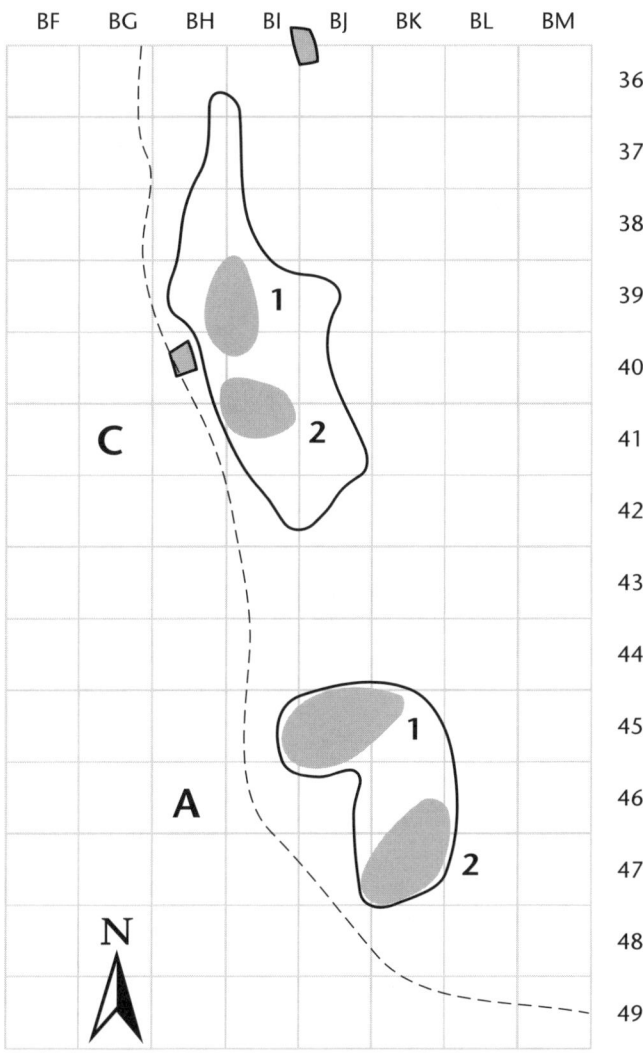

Figure 21. Structure of space and knapping localities in concentrations A and C; the shaded areas indicate the knapping localities interpreted according to the distribution of flakes (Figure 20).

Because of the low density of knapping localities in concentration A, it is difficult to detect them by the distribution of flakes; but it appears there were essentially two. One is centered on square BJ45, the other on BK47. In both cases they are rather diffuse and extend slightly beyond these squares (Figures 20 and 21). These knapping localities are called A1 (for BJ45) and A2 (for BK47). Tools are more numerous toward the east and include a group of six objects found outside the limits indicated in the zone separating concentration A from concentration B (Figure 13).

The majority of these bifacial knapping flakes are pale rhyolite. The composition of characteristic flakes is given in Table 15. From this table we were immediately able to conclude that the original blanks were large flakes and blocks (the small quantity of cortical flakes made it improbable that plaque blanks had been knapped). There are 39 type 2a flakes weighing 249 g (29 percent of the total by number, 47 percent by weight). Type 2a flakes are thus rather strongly represented, undoubtedly indicating in situ knapping from the beginning of phase 2a.

These data, taken together with the spectrum of large flakes (Figure 32, no. 1), indicate two or three small or medium pieces were knapped (note that all flakes are less than 60 mm in maximum dimension). The rather high number of non-cortical type 2a flakes suggests we might be missing one or two phase 3 sessions, which could have been conducted elsewhere, or not at all if all the pieces were broken at the end of phase 2. The qualitative composition of type 2a flakes indicates the blanks knapped were thick-sectioned *Chivateros* bifaces: at least one large, thick flake blank and one or two fragments of thick blocks with a bit of residual cortex. In concentration A we find three fragments of bifacial pieces, but only one seems to be of the same variety of

Table 13. Numbers, weight, and ratio to all flakes of each raw material variety in concentration A.

Raw material	Number of flakes	Ratio to whole by number (%)	Weight (g)	Ratio to whole by weight (%)
pale rhyolite	256	83.9	560	81.6
green tuff	9	2.9	16	2.3
black quartzite	18	5.9	27	3.9
gray tuff	6	1.9	16	2.3
brown rhyolite	8	2.6	60	8.7
quartz	8	2.6	7	1
quartzite				
miscellaneous	3	0.9	11	1.6
total	305		686	

Table 14. Number, weight, and ratio to all flakes of pale rhyolite and green tuff flakes for each dimension category in concentration A.

	Count	Ratio to whole by count (%)	Weight (g)	Ratio to whole by weight (%)
Pale rhyolite				
large	49	19.1	289	51.6
medium	122	47.6	247	44.1
small	85	33.2	24	4.3
total	256		560	
Green tuff				
large	1	11	8	50
medium	3	33	4	25
small	5	55	4	25
total	9		16	

Table 15. Number and weight of large, medium, and type 2a flakes of pale rhyolite in concentration A.

Concentration A:	**Pale rhyolite (total)**					
	Large		Medium		Total	
Type 2a flakes	n	W (g)	n	W (g)	n	W (g)
elongated and skewed	6	30			6	30
thick	17	152.4	11	40.4	28	193
cortical	4	23.2			4	23
Kombewa			1	3.2	1	3
total					39	249
all flakes	49	289	122	247	171	536
ratio 2a flakes/all flakes					29%	47%
Number and dimensions of the largest flakes: n = 2; class 55–59 mm						

rhyolite as the flakes in this concentration; this is piece no. 3, half of a point broken during phase 4, with which pieces no. 5 and no. 6 (between A and B) of the same raw material can be associated, although true refits are lacking (Figure 22, no. 1).

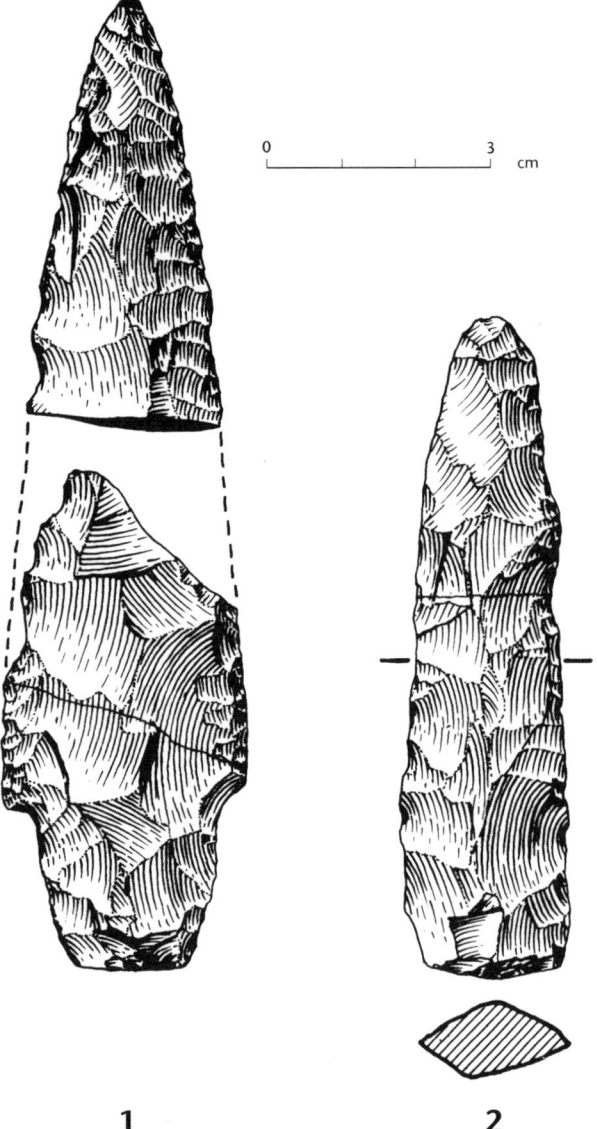

Figure 22. Pale rhyolite points in concentration A: **1**, superior fragment no. 3 and inferior fragments no. 5-6; **2**, superior fragments no. 23-2. (Drawings by C. Chauchat.)

The other two fragments (Figure 22, no. 2) are of raw material types that are absent or nearly absent among the flakes in concentration A, if not in the whole site.

For our global quantitative evaluation, we maintain that the flakes from concentration A correspond to the production of two or three points, of which one was broken. The evidence suggests complicated knapping behavior at concentration A: two of the associated fragments of pieces were knapped very little at this location, and one or two other pieces may have been finished elsewhere.

Concentration C

Concentration C runs north-south and covers an area of 8–9 m^2 (Figure 20), of which 7 m^2 was excavated. The flake density is relatively low, although a little more significant than concentration A in terms of quantity (483) and weight (795 g) of pale rhyolite flakes (Tables 16 and 17). As in concentration A, there are only a few green tuff flakes (n = 6, 13 g); these flakes, all found dispersed on the surface, are probably intrusions either from concentration B or more likely from concentration D, where green tuff is better represented. As with concentration A, the limit of concentration C is sharply defined towards the west and much more diffuse in the northeast. This is precisely the location of the empty zone in the ellipse of the knapping concentrations, where a long trail of flakes probably displaced by wind extends into concentration D at the limit of separation between D and B (Figures 23 and 25). Unfortunately, in the tables these flakes were counted in concentration D. Thus the total count of pale rhyolite flakes in concentration C is slightly reduced.

Based on the spatial distribution of flakes, two knapping localities can be distinguished. The first (C1) is located in BH-BI39; the second (C2), which is somewhat less clear, is located in BI41 (Figures 20 and 21). These localities are associated on their west side with a stone block that may have served as a seat. However, the rare tools (five objects) associated with this concentration lie to the southeast in an eastward-oriented band that extends beyond the limits of the workshop. This configuration,

Table 16. Numbers, weight, and ratio to all flakes of each raw material variety in concentration C.

Raw material	Number of flakes	Ratio to whole by number (%)	Weight (g)	Ratio to whole by weight (%)
pale rhyolite	483	94	795	95.2
green tuff	6	1.2	13	1.6
black quartzite	6	1.2	9	1.1
gray tuff	4	0.8	4	0.5
brown rhyolite	9	1.8	8	1
quartz quartzite	2	0.4	2	0.2
miscellaneous	4	0.8	4	0.5
total	514		835	

Table 17. Number, weight, and ratio to all flakes of pale rhyolite and green tuff flakes for each dimension category in concentration C.

	Count	Ratio to whole by count (%)	Weight (g)	Ratio to whole by weight (%)
Pale rhyolite				
large	62	12.8	364	45.8
medium	209	43.3	366	46.1
small	212	43.9	65	8.1
total	483		795	
Green tuff				
large	1	16.6	4	30.7
medium	2	33.6	6	46.1
small	3	50	3	23
total	6		13	

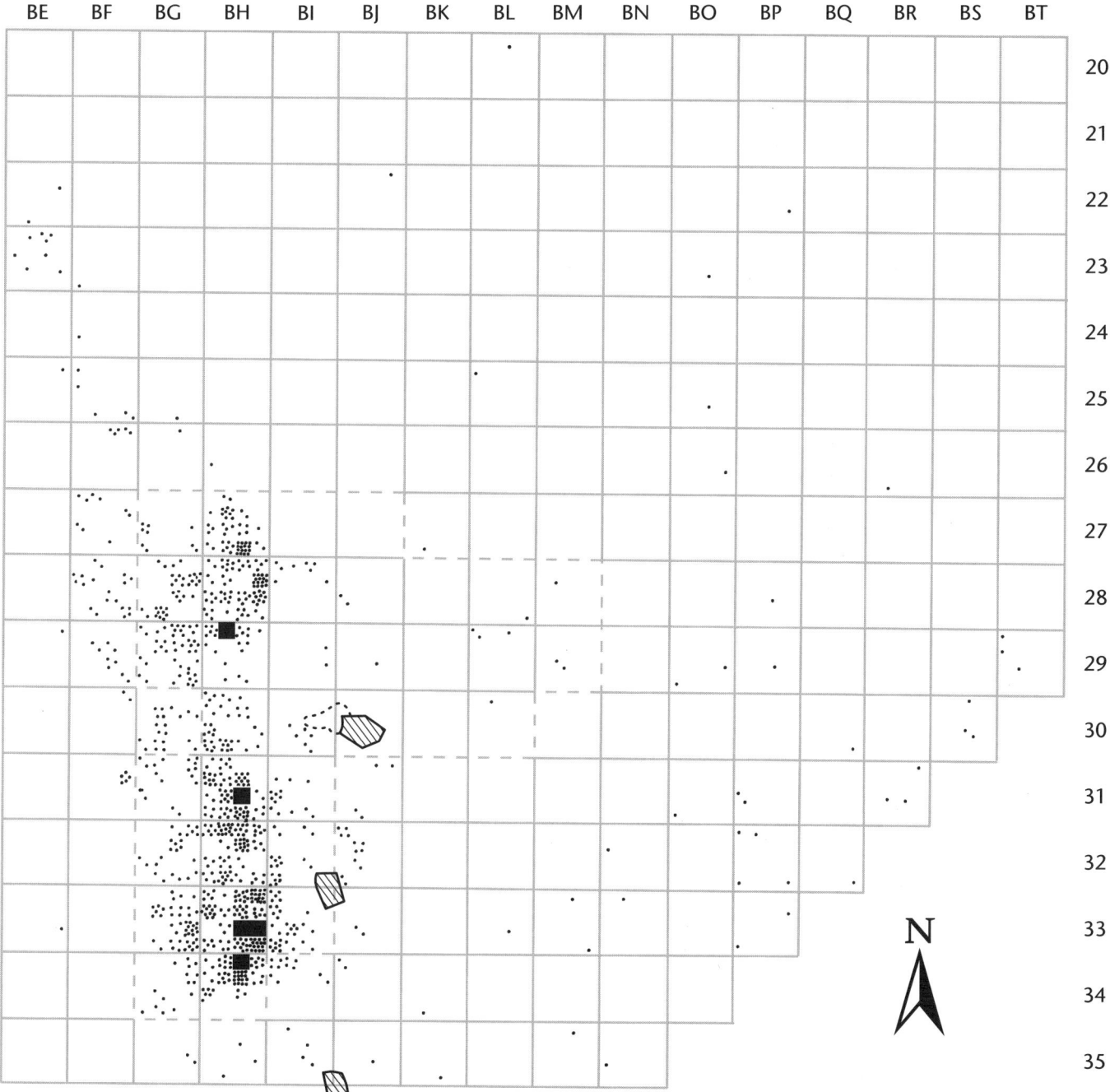

Figure 23. Concentration D; spatial distribution of pale rhyolite flakes by 25-cm squares.

similar to the one found in concentration A, is even clearer. A second stone block, situated between concentration C and concentration D, appears to be isolated and is probably of natural origin. As with concentration A, the knapping activity of concentration C appears to have been relatively limited, especially compared with concentrations B and D.

Large and medium flakes of pale rhyolite number 271 (weight 730.4 g). Examination of the spectrum of the dimensions of these flakes (Figure 32, no. 2) immediately indicates that the number of knapped pieces seems to be low. The maximum dimensions of the large flakes indicate that small to medium preforms were knapped (flakes with a maximum dimension greater than 65 mm are absent). The large count of type 2a flakes indicates that the incidence of this phase exceeds the average of our tests.

The ensemble of data persuades us that two to four objects were knapped by percussion in concentration C. The absence of Kombewa flakes and presence of cortical flakes indicate that block and plaque blanks were knapped.

In addition, a fragment of a stage 2b piece was found (no. 24, square BI41). A fracture on a diaclastic fissure, oblique to the long axis, shortened the potential point by about 4.5 cm. The other fragment, which probably was not long enough to be worked, was not found at the site or nearby. In several cases, unworkable preform fragments like this one were found several meters from the knapping locality or were secondarily displaced. Therefore, of the two to four pieces estimated to have been knapped, only one to three were exported.

Concentration D

This concentration covers a surface of around 37 m², of which 34 m² was excavated. It has the second greatest number (815) and weight (1004 g) of pale rhyolite flakes, and the greatest number (1290) and weight (1227 g) of green tuff flakes (Tables 19 and 20). This concentration is also significant because it contains two areas of partially mixed pale rhyolite and green tuff (Figures 23 and 24). We observe a larger concentration of green

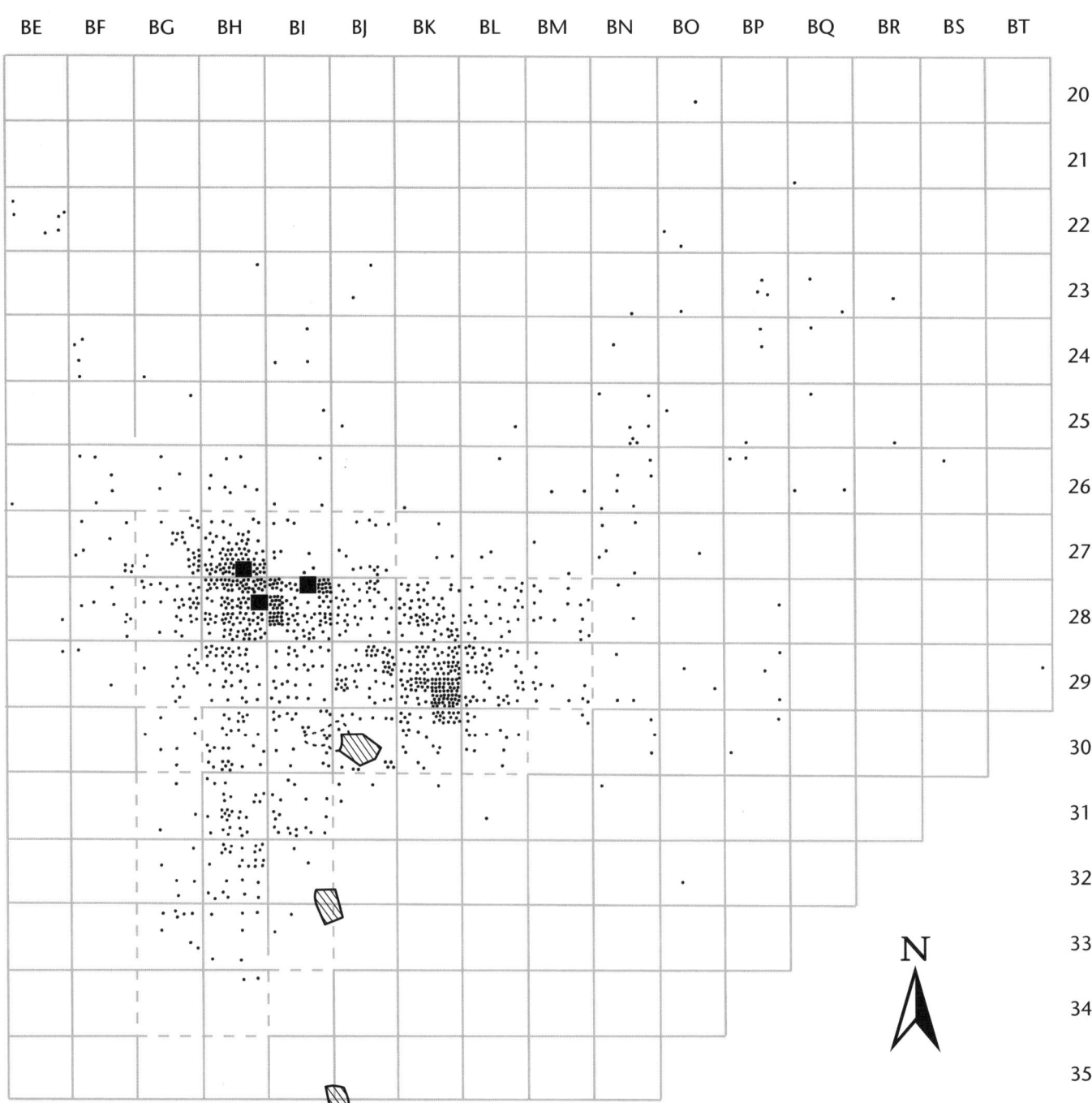

Figure 24. Concentration D; spatial distribution of green volcanic tuff flakes by 25-cm squares.

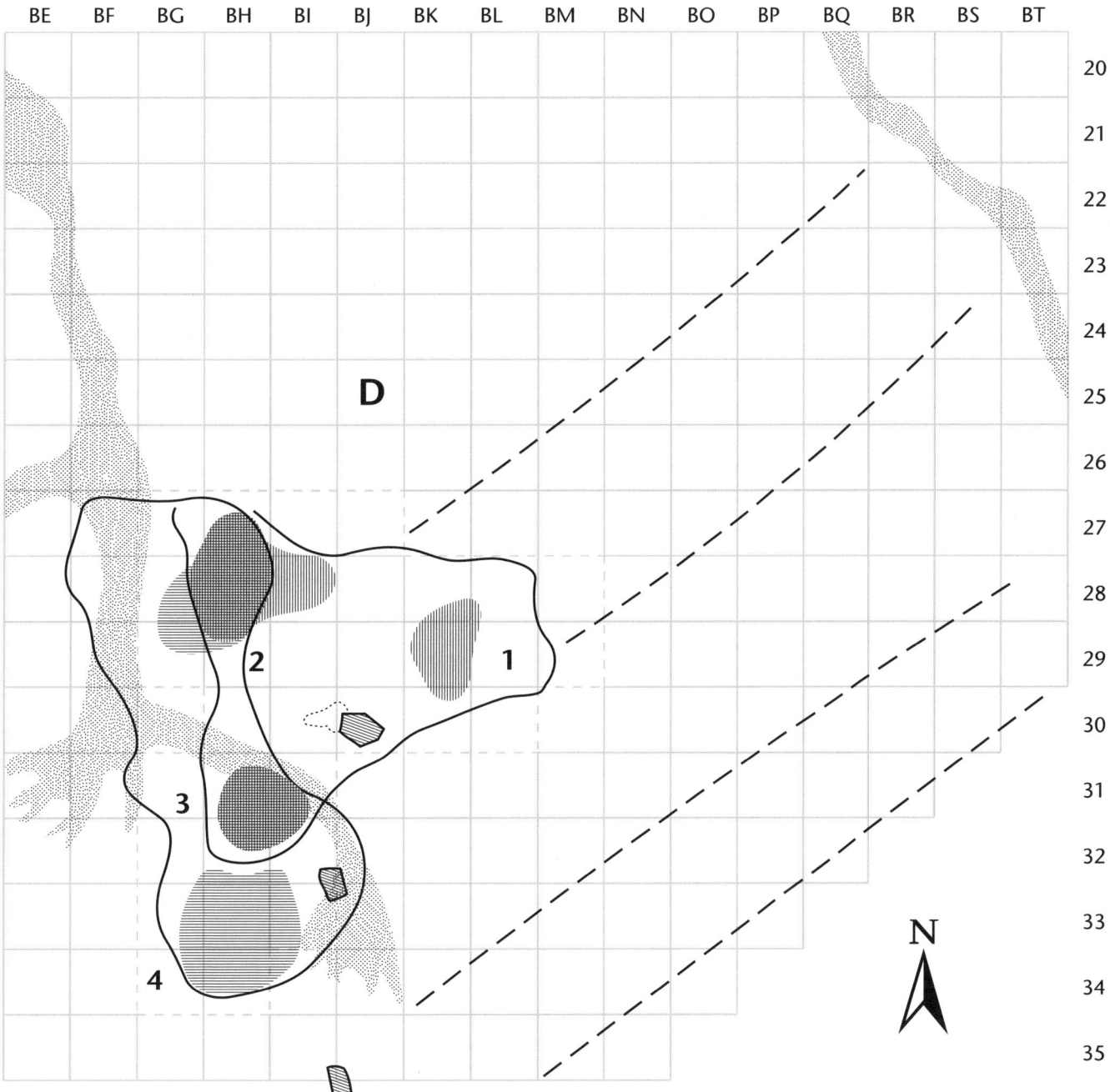

Figure 25. Concentration D; structure of space and knapping localities no. 1 to 4 according to the distribution of flakes (Figures 23 and 24); the horizontal lines represent the pale rhyolite, the vertical lines represent the green volcanic tuff; the dashed lines delimit the trail of evacuation of tools and flakes toward the northwest, and below, the trail of flakes originating from concentration C. Gullies flowing from south to north are illustrated by random dots.

tuff in its northern and eastern parts, where two knapping localities are centered in BH28 and BK29, and a barely visible concentration is situated around BH31 (Figure 24). The BH28 knapping locality was also used for knapping pale rhyolite; in BH31 this material is largely predominant and only a little green tuff was knapped. Only pale rhyolite is found in the last locality, situated at the southern extremity around BH33 (Figure 23). The plan in Figure 25 summarizes the spatial structure of concentration D: D1 is the green tuff knapping locality in BK29, D2 is the mixed knapping locality of BG-BI28, D3 is the mixed locality of BH31, and D4 is the pale rhyolite knapping locality of BH33. In summary, pale rhyolite and green tuff were concurrently knapped at both knapping localities D2 and D3; green tuff was clearly less predominant in D3. Only one material was knapped at each of the two peripheral localities, green tuff to the east at D1, and pale rhyolite to the south at D4.

A small gully originating in concentration D and flowing toward the north carried a few flakes in this direction. A small number of fine pale rhyolite flakes, along with a larger number of green tuff flakes, were dispersed by wind in a northeast direction. A portion of this trail of objects may be the result of intentional evacuation, since it includes a narrow zone in which were found some heavier tools and even a core (Figures 18 and 19). The plan in Figure 25 also shows a trail of flakes originating at concentration C, which consists exclusively of pale rhyolite (Figure 23) and is undoubtedly of eolian origin.

Three large stone blocks found on the margins of concentration D were apparently too far from the knapping localities to have served as seats, except for the block in BI32-33, which may be associated with D3 and D4. The stone farthest to the north is associated with a pit on its west side (BI-BJ30) that contains food remains, whose contents are detailed in the appendix. The shape of this pit resembles that of a ventilated fireplace; it may have served this function, however for only a short time, since it contains very little charcoal and no rubefaction of its bottom was observed. This pit occupies a central position between the northern and southern groups of knapping localities.

With 369 large and medium pale rhyolite flakes weighing 849.2 g, concentration D is slightly richer than concentrations A and C. The count of type 2a flakes shows a strong representation of this phase (Table 21). Since Kombewa flakes are absent, we conclude that the original blanks were blocks and plaques. All flakes are less than 60 mm in maximum dimension; this narrow spectrum of flake dimensions (Figure 32, no. 4) indicates that relatively short pieces were knapped. These data, supported by the results of experimental tests, especially tests 2 and 10 (Figure 11), suggest that 4 to 8 pieces were knapped starting with phase 2a. Figure 32 compares the spectra of pale rhyolite flakes (no. 4) and green tuff flakes (no. 3). The green tuff will be discussed in more detail below.

Three whole or fragmentary bifacial pieces were found in concentration D: one preform abandoned during stage 2b, (no. 38, Figure 26); one short fragment of a foliate piece in phase 3 (no. 104); and one short fragment of a point in phase 4 (no. 103), perhaps originating from the same preform as no. 104. It is thus necessary to subtract two or three pieces from the four to

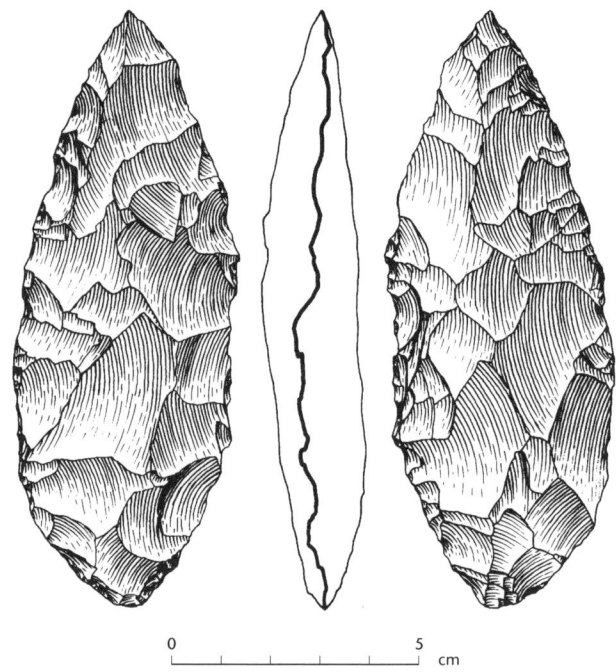

Figure 26. Foliate bifacial piece (no. 38) on pale rhyolite in concentration D. (Drawing by C. Chauchat.)

eight pieces estimated to have been knapped (knapping debris suggests one to six points were actually finished and exported). We again note two poor *Chivateros* bifaces (no. 34 and 40) that were abandoned soon after a few short, hinged removals with hard hammer. These do not affect our calculations.

Green tuff objects are significant in this concentration but have a different spatial distribution. We have discussed their spatial structure here and will present further details in the next chapter.

Concentration B

This is the largest concentration, extending over roughly 50 m², of which 44 m² was excavated. It also contains the greatest number (5189) and weight (4383 g) of pale rhyolite flakes (Tables 22 and 23). The green tuff flakes, which are not very numerous (27 flakes weighing 50 g), were studied along with the green tuff

Table 18. Number and weight of large, medium, and type 2a flakes of pale rhyolite in concentration C.

Concentration C:	Pale rhyolite (total)					
	Large		Medium		Total	
Type 2a flakes	n	W (g)	n	W (g)	n	W (g)
elongated and skewed	6	57			6	57
thick	14	109.6	18	66.2	32	176
cortical	8	58.4	18	66	26	153
Kombewa						
total					64	357.2
all flakes	62	364	209	367	271	730
ratio 2a flakes/all flakes					23.6%	48.9%
Number and dimensions of the largest flakes: n = 2; class 60–64 mm						

Table 19. Numbers, weight, and ratio to all flakes of each raw material variety in concentration D.

Raw material	Number of flakes	Ratio to whole by number (%)	Weight (g)	Ratio to whole by weight (%)
pale rhyolite	815	37.8	1004	22.5
green tuff	1290	59.8	1227	27.6
black quartzite	27	1.3	45	1
gray tuff	9	0.4	9	0.2
brown rhyolite	6	0.3	6	0.1
quartz	6	0.3	5	0.1
quartzite				
miscellaneous	4	0.2	6	0.1
total	2157		2302	

Return to the Archaeological Record

Table 20. Number, weight, and ratio to all flakes of pale rhyolite and green tuff flakes for each dimension category in concentration D.

	Count	Ratio to whole by count (%)	Weight (g)	Ratio to whole by weight (%)
Pale rhyolite				
large	79	9.7	398	39.6
medium	290	35.6	452	45
small	446	54.7	154	15.3
total	815		1004	
Green tuff				
large	99	7.7	441	35.9
medium	454	35.2	566	46.1
small	737	57.2	220	17.9
total	1290		1227	

Table 21. Number and weight of large, medium, and type 2a flakes of pale thyolite in concentration D.

Concentration D:	**Pale rhyolite (total)**					
	Large		Medium		Total	
Type 2a flakes	n	W (g)	n	W (g)	n	W (g)
elongated and skewed						
thick	23		12		35	206.4
cortical	17		34		51	137.2
Kombewa						
total						
all flakes	79	397.6	290	451.6	369	849.2
ratio 2a flakes/all flakes					23.3%	40.5%
Number and dimensions of the largest flakes: n = 3; class 55–59 mm						

Table 22. Numbers, weight, and ratio to all flakes of each raw material variety in concentration B.

Raw material	Number of flakes	Ratio to whole by number (%)	Weight (g)	Ratio to whole by weight (%)
pale rhyolite	5189	90.9	4383	86.3
green tuff	27	0.5	50	1
black quartzite	99	1.7	254	0.4
gray tuff	253	4.4	241	4.7
brown rhyolite	24	0.4	51	1
quartz	21	0.4	20	0.4
quartzite	12	0.2	9	0.2
miscellaneous	81	1.4	71	1.4
total	5706		5079	

Table 23. Number, weight, and ratio to all flakes of pale rhyolite and green tuff flakes for each dimension category in concentration B.

	Count	Ratio to whole by count (%)	Weight (g)	Ratio to whole by weight (%)
Pale rhyolite				
large	263	5.1	1488	33.9
medium	1408	27.1	1943	44.3
small	3518	67.8	952	21.7
total	5189		4383	
Green tuff				
large	7	26	36	72
medium	6	22	9	18
small	14	52	5	10
total	27		50	

objects of concentration D (next chapter). In concentration B we observe two main clusters, one toward the northeast, the other toward the southwest (Figure 27). Because the density of flakes is high in all areas, it is difficult to distinguish isolated knapping localities. However, on the plans they are more clearly visible in the form of trampled zones where flakes were pushed into the sediment by the knappers (Figure 28). In this way we first distinguished four knapping localities from north to south in BT40-41, around BT43-44, in BS46, and in BR48. This latter locality seems to be clearly associated with the block in BQ48. A fifth area is less clearly visible at the southwest extremity, in BO-BP/48-49, while we observe a strong surface density in BP48-49, thus toward the east (Figure 27). The complex situation observed around this block is probably the result of prolonged activity, perhaps by one person who changed position and perhaps even moved the block-seat. There is indeed no indication that the block occupied its current location during all knapping operations. We also assimilated into concentration B numerous flakes found somewhat beyond its limits. Those found in the zone to the west probably belong to the trail of objects displaced by wind from concentrations A and C. Since these are mostly very small flakes, less than 2 cm long, they have very little effect on our quantitative estimations, which consider only medium and large flakes.

Figure 29 is a synthesis of the spatial structure of concentration B with its five main knapping localities, designated B1 to B5 from the northwest to the southwest.

Besides being the largest concentration, concentration B is also the richest. It contains 1671 large and medium flakes of pale rhyolite weighing nearly 3.5 kg. The count of type 2a flakes indicates knapping began from *Chivateros* bifaces (Table 24). Moreover, the nature of the type 2a flakes demonstrates that most of the rough-outs were produced more from fragments of blocks than from plaques. A unique Kombewa flake shows that one rough-out was on a flake blank. The spectrum of flakes closely resembles that of concentration D, but is twice as large (Figure 32, no. 5). It is relatively narrow, with only 7 flakes larger than 60 mm and none over 65 mm. Based on the character of this spectrum and the flake

Table 24. Number and weight of large, medium, and type 2a flakes of pale rhyolite in concentration B.

Concentration B:	**Pale rhyolite (total)**					
	Large		Medium		Total	
Type 2a flakes	n	W (g)	n	W (g)	n	W (g)
elongated and skewed	11	75			11	75
thick	91		80		171	991
cortical	31		91		122	324
Kombewa	1	4.2			1	4.2
total					305	1394
all flakes	263	1488	1408	1943	1671	3431
ratio 2a flakes/all flakes					18.3%	40.6%
Number and dimensions of the largest flakes: n = 7; class 60–64 mm						

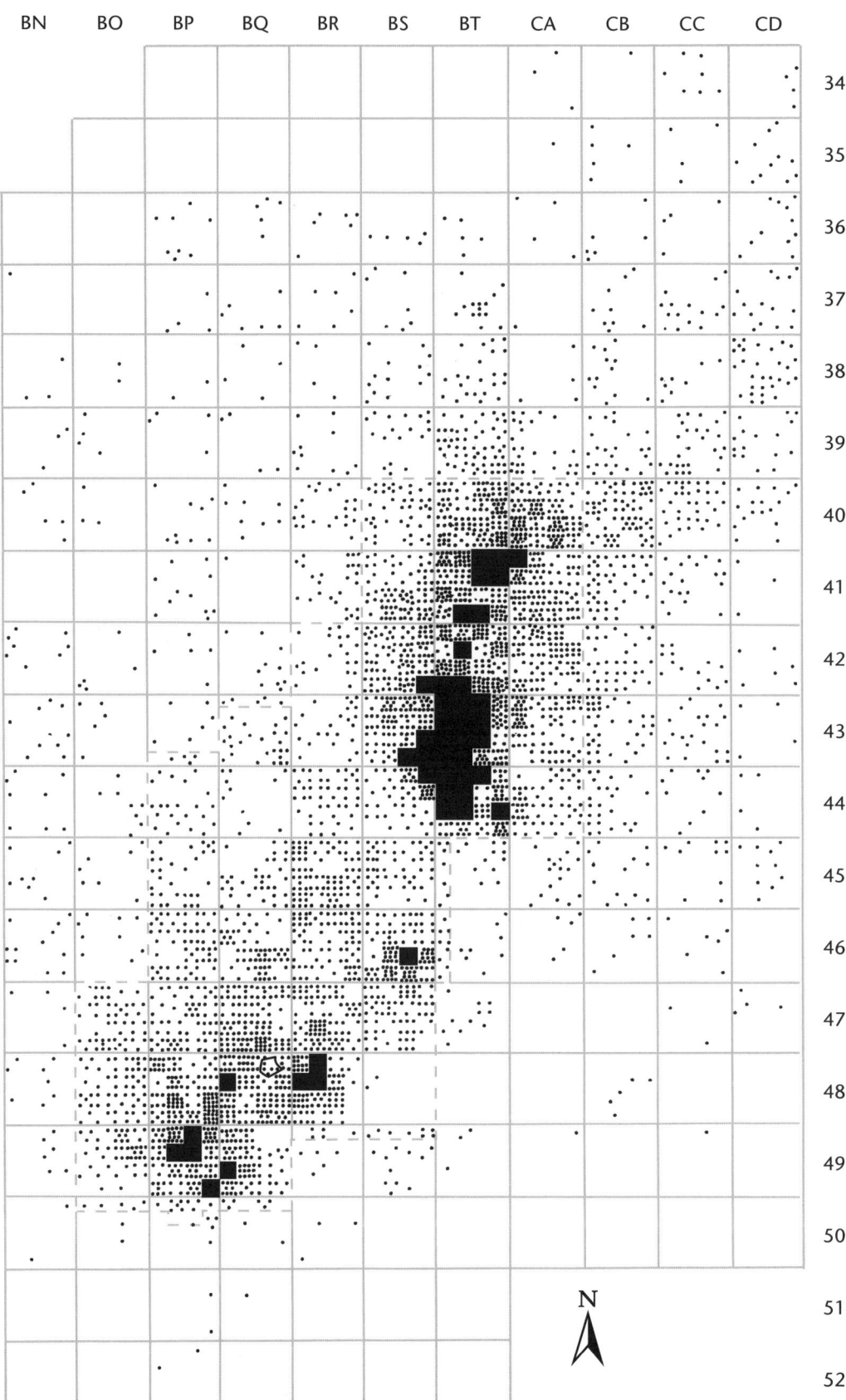

Figure 27. Concentration B; total spatial distribution of pale rhyolite flakes by 25-cm squares.

Return to the Archaeological Record

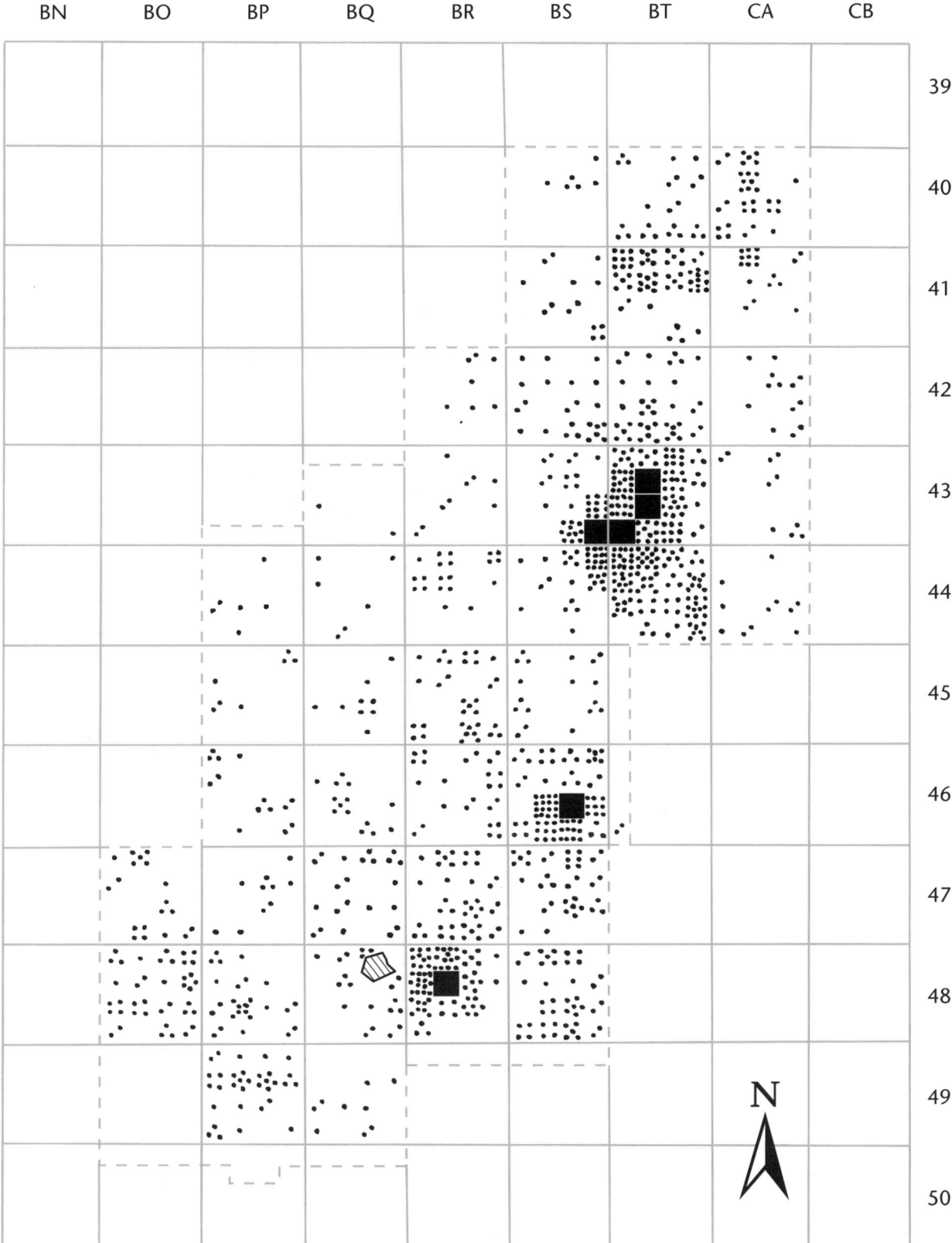

Figure 28. Concentration B; spatial distribution of buried pale rhyolite flakes by 25-cm squares.

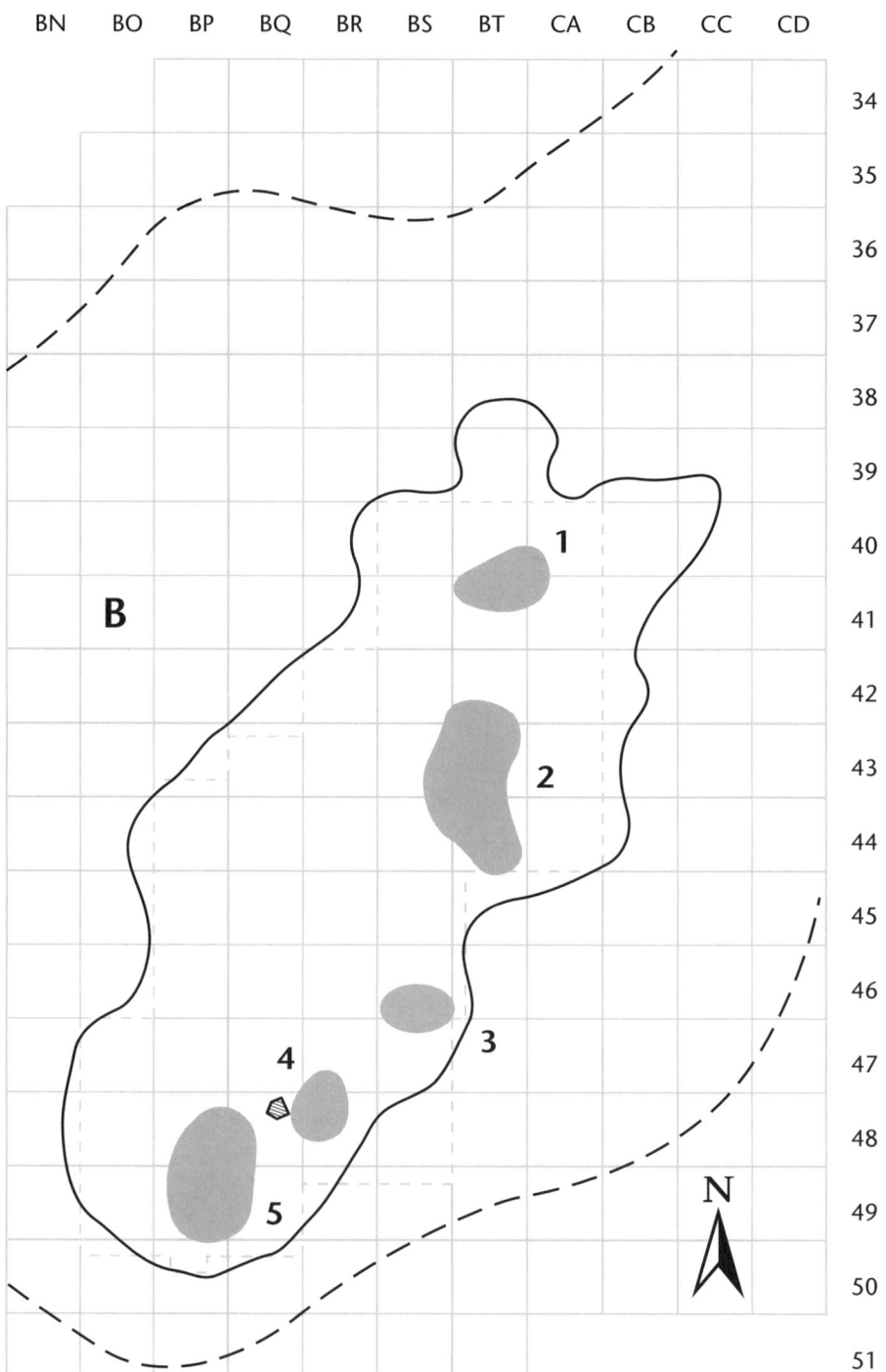

Figure 29. Concentration B. Structure of space and knapping localities no. 1–5 according to the pale rhyolite flakes spatial distribution (Figures 27 and 28).

counts, we estimate that 10 to 20 small to medium pieces were knapped at concentration B.

There are numerous broken pieces in concentration B. No. 7 and 15 are both halves of foliate pieces broken during phase 3. So were three other shorter fragments (no. 14, 61, 72). One thick foliate piece was broken into three fragments at the end of phase 3 (no. 68-77-60). The largest of these fragments, no. 68, was thrown far to the southeast beyond the limits of the plan in Figure 13; the other two remained in place (Figure 30, no. 1). One flake found rather close, in BS45, was refitted to this piece. Two fragments of a point broken during pressure retouch (no. 5-6), which resemble no. 3 from concentration A (Figure 22, no. 1), could also be related to fragment no. 61, which was found farther toward the northeast in BR43. A damaged *Chivateros* biface, slightly less than 10 cm long, was briefly reworked with a hard hammer before being abandoned (no. 75) (Figure 30, no. 2). In total, we must subtract 5 to 7 pieces, which were abandoned, damaged, or broken by percussion or at the beginning of pres-

Return to the Archaeological Record

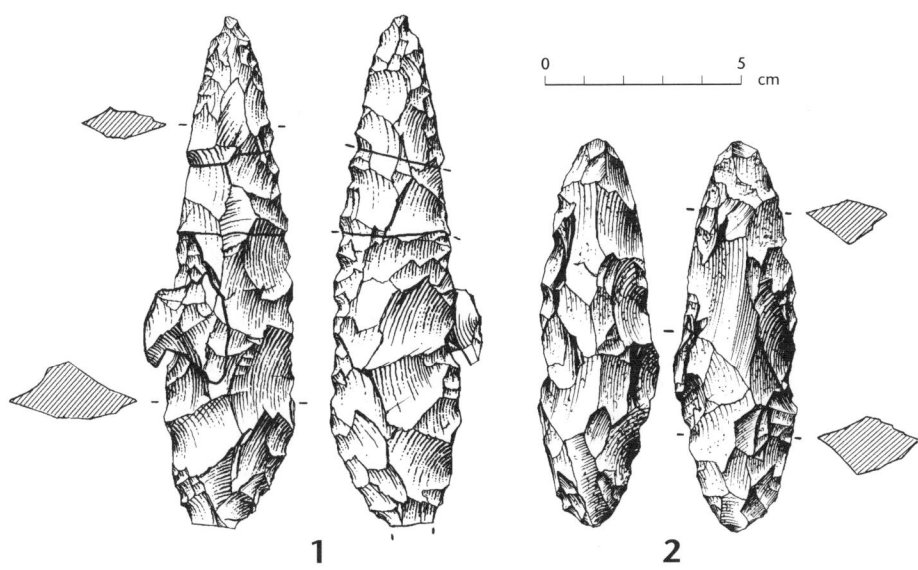

Figure 30. Bifacial pieces in concentration B: **1**, foliate piece no. 68-77-60 and flake from BS45 that refits; **2**, thick foliate piece no. 75. Both pieces are made of pale rhyolite. (Drawing by M. Reduron.)

sure retouch, from our estimation of 10 to 20 pieces knapped at concentration B. The number of pieces finished and exported is thus estimated between 3 and 15.

First conclusions

The estimate that between 18 and 35 pale rhyolite objects were knapped in the workshop stems from a simple addition. Unfortunately, the imprecise number of broken pieces—between 8 and 13—considerably enlarges the range of potentially exported objects to between 6 and 26. This range is a realistic estimate, but the result is at best imprecise. In order to reduce the margin of uncertainty, which for the moment is between 1 and 4, we have attempted to distinguish different varieties of pale rhyolite.

From a spatial perspective, this first analysis isolated 13 knapping localities, the stations where the knappers conducted their work. These are identified by a high density of knapping flakes. However, we must not forget that experimental knapping localities are generally much smaller in area, around 1 m², than some of those recorded on the plans (Kvamme 1997; Newcomer and Sieveking 1980). Therefore, what we observe now actually represents localities that have been disturbed and diffused over the long period they were exposed on the desert surface. Figure 31 is a synthesis of the spatial structure for the whole workshop; it is clear that the disposition of the localities follows an ellipse whose long axis is oriented in a north-south direction and whose northeast quarter is empty. Eolian trails of flakes observed on the site itself confirm that this area corresponds exactly to the zone situated in the path of the trade winds, which are diverted here by neighboring hills. As observed by Binford in his study of the "Mask Site" (Binford 1978) and by Gallay (1991), the disposition of knapping localities we observed is habitual (and easily understandable) when people are seated around a hearth. This disposition thus suggests the presence of a central hearth in the zone of squares BM/BO-35/38. Unfortunately, since there were few lithic objects, we made only surface collections in this zone. No traces of a hearth were visible on the surface. Therefore we do not know if there was a structure or other remains buried underneath.

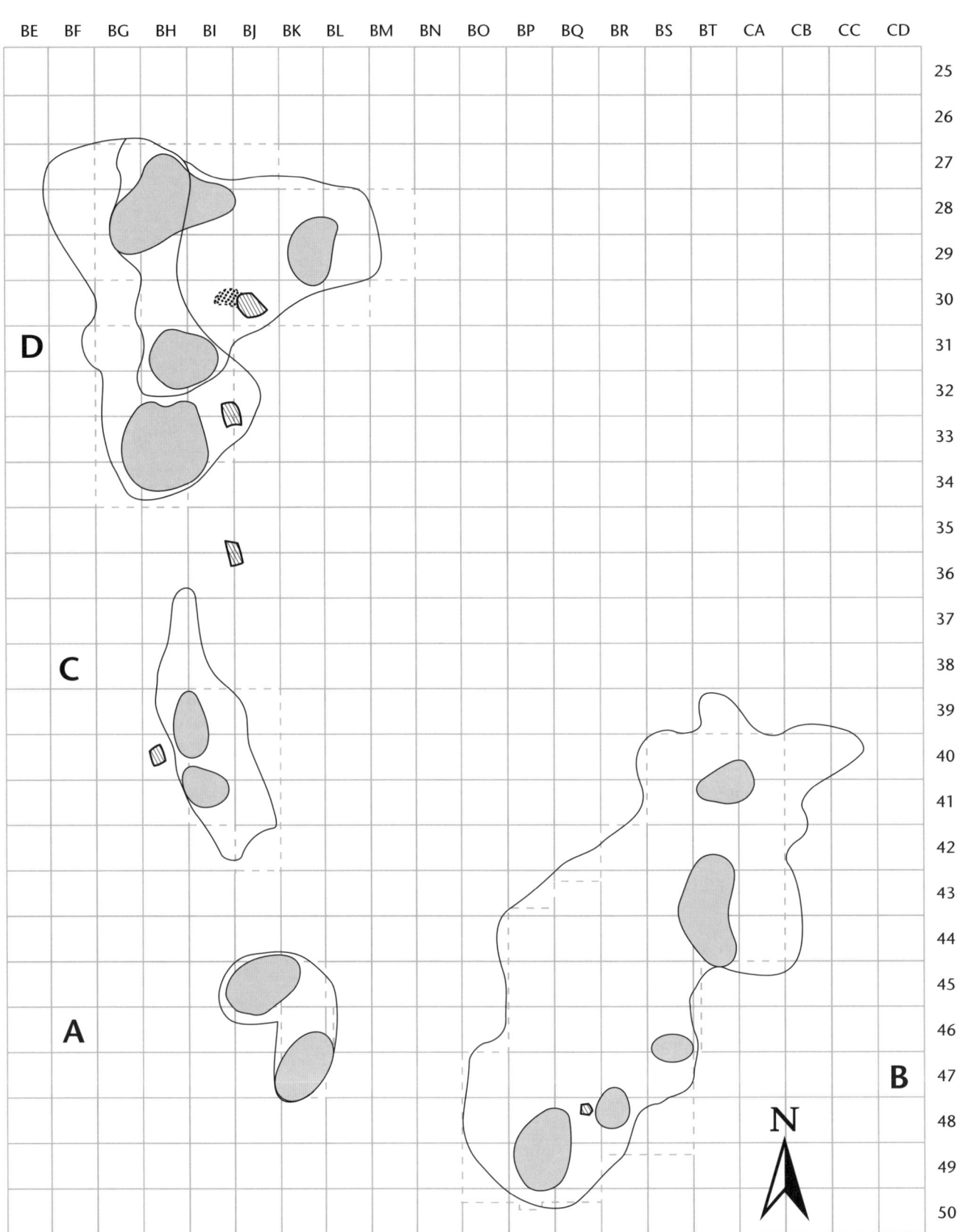

Figure 31. Configuration of the knapping localities and the outlines of concentrations in the workshop of Pampa de los Fósiles 14, unit 1.

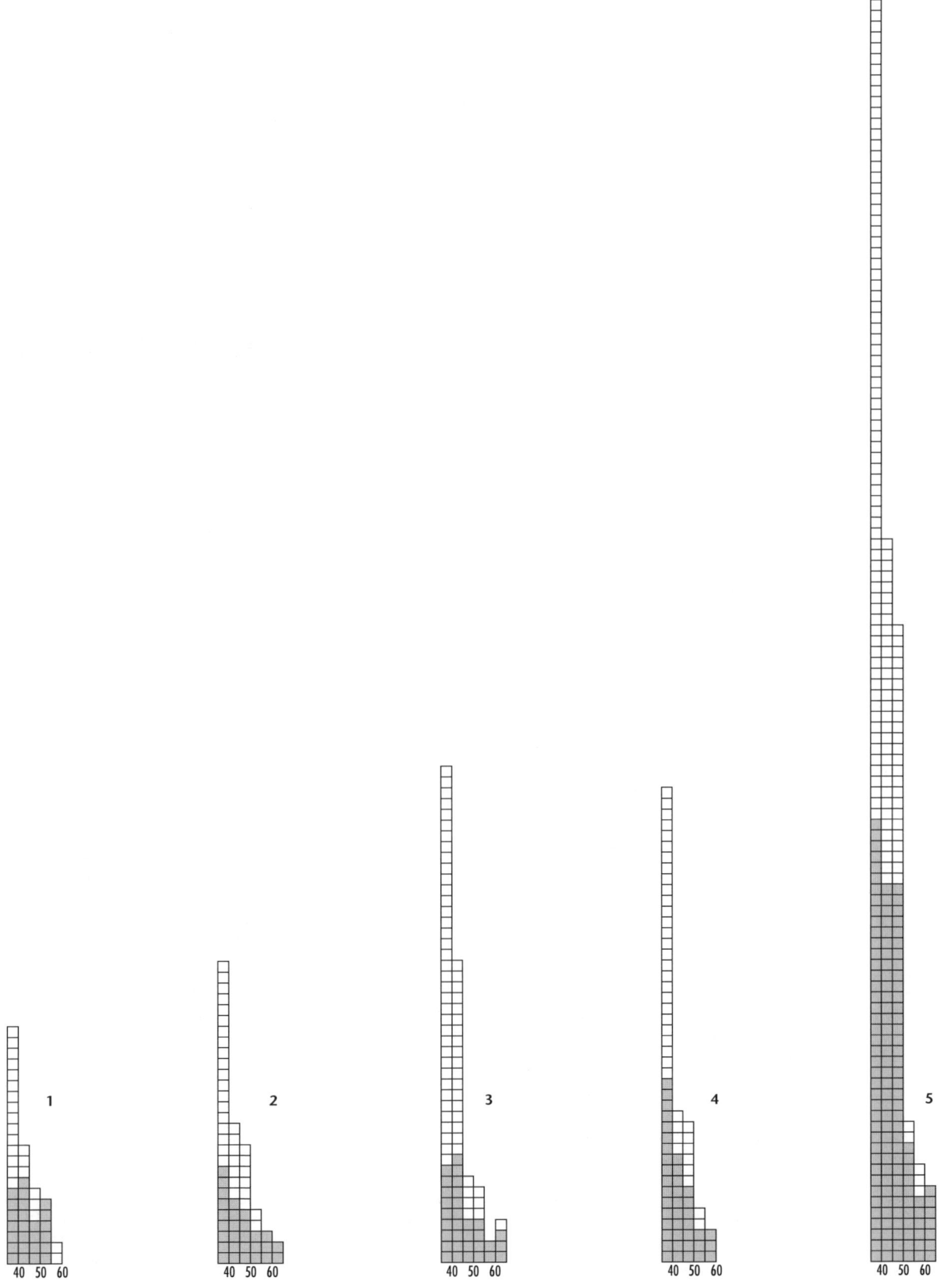

Figure 32. Histograms of large flakes and type 2a flakes: **1** and **2**, pale rhyolite in concentrations A and C; **3** and **4**, green tuff and pale rhyolite in concentration D; **5**, pale rhyolite in concentration B.

Chapter 4
The Raw Material Varieties

Pale Rhyolite Varieties

As we have already noted, during our surveys of the area we identified the main origin of the pale rhyolite knapped at the site as quarry site Pampa de los Fósiles 125, which is located slightly more than 1 km southeast of the site. It consists of a large, steep outcrop (Figures 4 and 12) and a few minor adjacent points. Throughout this area, which was extensively exploited by the Paijanenses, the raw material is rather variable in terms of color, grain, and inclusions. Therefore, following the first phase of our research presented above, we were able to distinguish numerous varieties in the unit studied while continuing the search for fracture and debitage refits. Rather than using numbered codes that are difficult to memorize, we chose qualitative terms in Spanish, which were systematized and conserved in the present description. Note that the greatest variations in this outcrop appear as differences in color. Variations in texture are less pronounced. Within the same block, variations are rarer but do exist; we indicate them where appropriate in the study presented below. The fact that these raw material varieties can be precisely distinguished was of immeasurable help in identifying fracture and debitage refits between flakes, which in turn validated the first distinctions of flake groups made through observation. The refits made between objects from different concentrations are the best illustration.

In addition to the raw material varieties that almost certainly originate from quarry site 125, one other variety almost certainly comes from unit 104 of site 12, located 2–3 km southwest of the workshop, and at least one other originates from an unknown source. Based on the criteria described above, a total of 16 main varieties of pale rhyolite were distinguished. Some varieties are more widespread than others and are found in several concentrations; others are restricted to one concentration. The different varieties will thus be discussed in two separate parts: first, those found in several concentrations; then, those restricted to a single one.

Varieties Present in Several Concentrations

"Ferruginosa" Variety

This is an orange-colored rhyolite that has large rust spots when patinated. We found it in the form of large blocks, not as plaques or flat prisms, at the foot of the northern slope of the main outcrop of quarry site 125. When fresh, it is cream-colored with a bluish tint. It is relatively coarse grained and has numerous pyrite crystals. These crystals are oxidized on archaeologically knapped materials.

This material, accounting for 110 large and medium flakes, constitutes around 60 percent of the pale rhyolite in concentration A. This clearly represents the knapping debris of one thick piece on a block, including several heavy, thick flakes, one clear elongated flake, and several skewed flakes, but few cortical flakes (Table 25). We have already seen that no flake or fragment in concentration A is longer than 60 mm. However, our observations and the data suggest that this piece was rather large. We were able to make six refits between fragments and four refits between flakes, whose spatial distribution is shown in Figure 34.

Table 25. Number and weight of large, medium, and type 2a flakes of pale rhyolite, subvariety *ferruginosa*, in concentration A.

Concentration A:	Pale rhyolite, subvariety *ferruginosa*					
	Large		Medium		Total	
Type 2a flakes	n	W (g)	n	W (g)	n	W (g)
elongated and skewed	6	31			6	31
thick	12	116	10	37	22	153
cortical	1	5			1	5
Kombewa						
total					29	189
all flakes	33	196	77	170	110	366
ratio 2a flakes/all flakes					26.4%	51.6%
Number and dimensions of the largest flakes: n = 2; class 55–59 mm						

These fragments and flakes do not come from the knapping localities already distinguished, but randomly from the entire surface of the concentration. It is thus impossible to know their precise origin. Unfortunately, the distribution of other flakes that could have provided more information concerning the knapping of this variety was not recorded.

In concentration B, *ferruginosa* rhyolite is abundantly represented by nearly 400 flakes, of which around 50 are thick phase 2 flakes (Table 26). Examination (Figure 33, no. 2) and the data suggest that this is the knapping debris of two or three relatively large *Chivateros* bifaces from blocks. The fracture and debitage refits illustrated in Figure 35 show a very clear cluster in the southern part of B5 (cf. Figure 29). Connections also indicate preferential directions fanning from the east/west to the southwest/northeast, which could indicate that the knapper was oriented differently than the knapper in concentration A. There seems to be a trail (clearing out?) extending from B5 toward the west, ending with biface fragment no. 7, onto which a flake from BP47 was refitted.

Table 26. Number and weight of large, medium, and type 2a flakes of pale rhyolite, subvariety *ferruginosa*, in concentration B.

Concentration B:	Pale rhyolite, subvariety *ferruginosa*					
	Large		Medium		Total	
Type 2a flakes	n	W (g)	n	W (g)	n	W (g)
elongated and skewed	5	36			5	36
thick	21	215	28	83	49	298
cortical	1	5	6	9	7	14
Kombewa						
total					61	348
all flakes	66	420	339	509	405	929
ratio 2a flakes/all flakes					15.1%	37.5%
Number and dimensions of the largest flakes: n = 3; class 60–64 mm						

Only 12 flakes were found in concentration C, of which only 3 are large non–type 2a flakes. They are thus too few and too dispersed to represent the knapping of an object. They are primarily located to the east of concentration C, in continuity with those from concentration A. No refits were found (Figure 34). They could thus constitute an eolian trail originating in A. However, the presence of large flakes does not support this theory.

We also found a total of 12 flakes of this variety in concentration D (Figure 37): 8 large flakes, of which 6 are thick (the largest is 57 mm long); and 4 medium thin ones. They may correspond to the beginning of phase 2 knapping. Being dispersed over several square meters, they may represent a clearing out or perhaps the knapping of a piece that was soon broken or displaced. Additionally, four of these flakes found to the north, as well as the group situated around the large block to the east of D4, were lying in gullies. Two of these flakes, as well as two fragments of a third, refit onto each other. Whatever the case, the two dozen flakes from concentrations C and D are not numerous enough to modify our estimations concerning concentrations A and B. Their spatial distribution is not random, since they are oriented in a south/north axis starting from A, but it is difficult to explain. Natural causes, such as flooding along the slope, and the act of a human agent clearing out or throwing the flakes toward the north seem equally likely in this case.

One fragment of a foliate piece (no. 7) from concentration B is made from this *ferruginosa* material. This piece, which has a plano-convex section, was broken during phase 3. Its excessive thickness is evidence of second-rate knapping technique, since this thickness would have been difficult to reduce this late in the knapping process without breaking the piece, which is indeed what happened. One flake that refits onto this fragment was found in immediate proximity to the concentration of *ferruginosa* knapping flakes in B, which yielded 18 of the 23 flake fragments refitted into 11 whole flakes. The complementary fragment was not found; in any case it would have been too short for manufacturing a point. In total, we estimate that three or four foliate pieces were knapped from this material, including one that was broken during phase 3. Note that this series could include a bit of the *naranjilla* variety, notably in the form of several medium-sized flakes. For this reason we will discuss this variety next.

"Naranjilla" Variety

This variety, quite similar to the *ferruginosa* variety, is deeper orange in color, with some lighter spots and fewer rust spots. After a rigorous sorting to distinguish it from the *ferruginosa* variety, nearly 70 flakes were assigned to this variety (Table 27). Even if approximate, this figure corresponds to the knapping of one piece from a thick *Chivateros* biface on a block, indicated by more than 20 thick flakes, of which one overshot shortened the point during the knapping process (Figure 33, no. 3).

Table 27. Number and weight of large, medium, and type 2a flakes of pale rhyolite, subvariety *naranjilla*, in concentration B.

Concentration B:	Pale rhyolite, subvariety *naranjilla*					
	Large		Medium		Total	
Type 2a flakes	n	W (g)	n	W (g)	n	W (g)
elongated and skewed						
thick	15	103	7	28	22	131
cortical						
Kombewa						
total					22	131
all flakes	23	143	45	90	68	234
ratio 2a flakes/all flakes					32.4%	56%
Number and dimensions of the largest flakes: n = 1; class 60–64 mm						

One apical fragment (no. 14) of a foliate piece of this same material, which was broken during or at the end of phase 3, clearly corresponds to this series of flakes. This fragment demonstrates mediocre knapping ability, equivalent to that of the *ferruginosa* rhyolite fragment. The missing fragment was probably not of sufficient length and quality to be reworked into a Paiján point. The majority of *naranjilla* flakes came from the same zone of B5, but were much more dispersed (Figure 35). Seven fragments refit into three flakes, and four flakes refit onto

The Raw Material Varieties

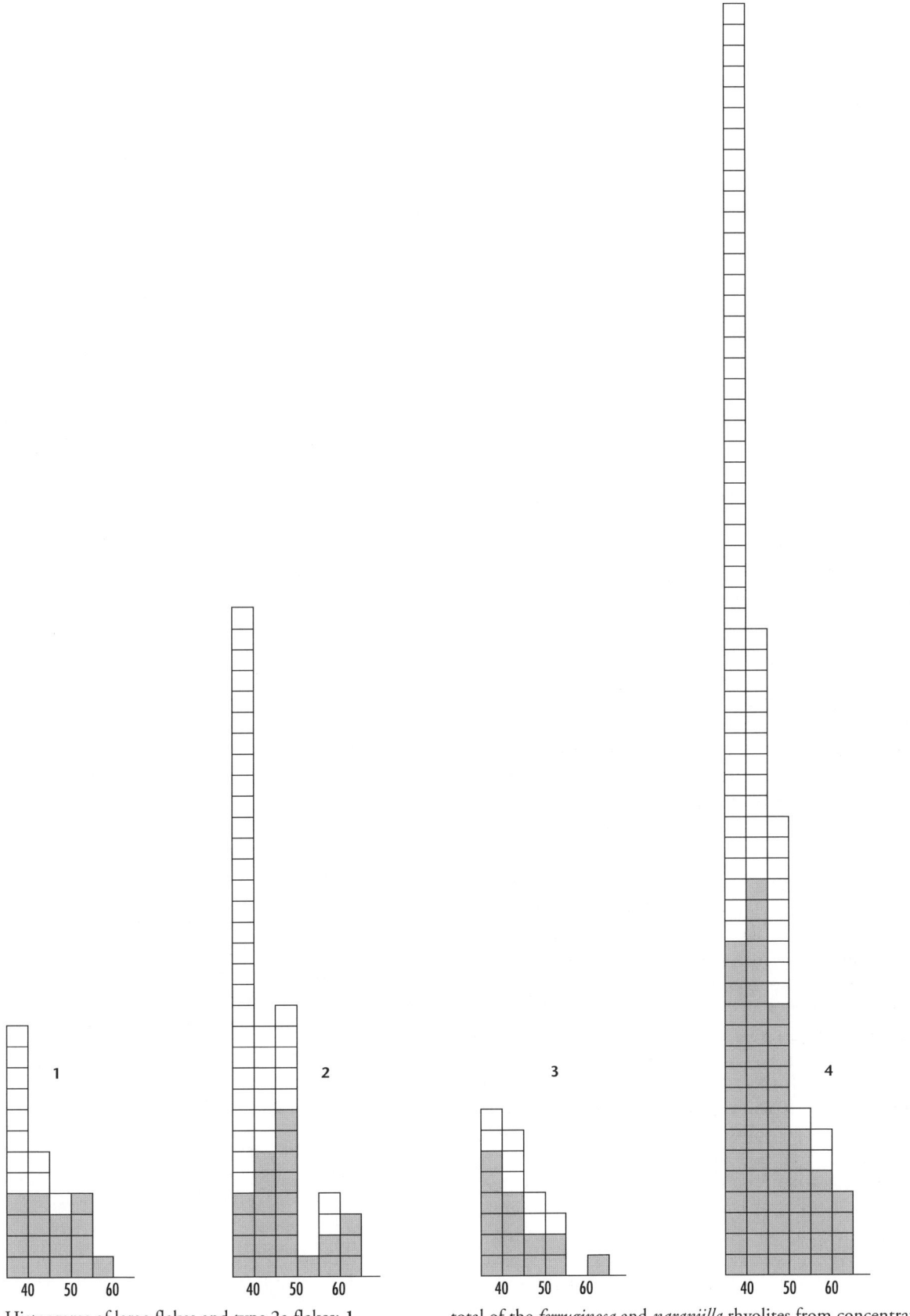

Figure 33. Histograms of large flakes and type 2a flakes: **1**, *ferruginosa* rhyolite from concentration A; **2**, *ferruginosa* rhyolite from concentration B; **3**, *naranjilla* rhyolite from concentration B; **4**, total of the *ferruginosa* and *naranjilla* rhyolites from concentrations A, B, C, D.

each other; piece no. 14 was found about 2 m from this group.

Taking into account the difficulty of distinguishing between the *ferruginosa* and *naranjilla* varieties, we decided to consider them together, adding the series from concentration A and the pieces from concentrations C and D (12 flakes each). According to the totals (Table 28) and the spectrum of large flakes (Figure 33, no. 4), which is similar to the experimental tests of medium length (12–14 cm), we estimate that 4 to 6 pieces were produced from these varieties over the entire workshop. Two of these were broken during phase 3; thus 2 to 4 were actually finished and exported.

"*Puntillada/Floreada*" Variety

This is a pale rhyolite that was clearly distinguishable in the quarries of site 125. It is dotted with fine points ("*puntillada*") or "stars" ("*floreada*"). These two subvarieties, initially distinguished from each other, were later integrated as representing possible variations within the same block.

We can attribute 38 flakes from concentration A to this variety. Considering the small quantity of type 2a flakes, they would correspond to phase 2b or 3 of a small piece (Table 29). Of these flakes, only four refit into two couples (Figure 34).

In concentration C, a few thin flakes that were initially assigned to the *linea rosada* variety may possibly belong to the *puntillada* variety; however, this attribution cannot be confirmed without refits. Other than this one possible convergence, this variety was not observed in concentration C, and only two medium-sized, very fine flakes, undoubtedly displaced by wind, were identified in concentration D.

This variety is most abundant in concentration B, where 102 *puntillada* and 336 *floreada* flakes were identified (Table 30). As with the meager presence of this material observed in concentration A, the quantity of type 2a flakes is too small to represent phase 2a knapping. On the other hand, the number of flakes is great enough to represent the knapping of one or two small pieces. The 38 flakes from concentration A may be the result of discarding part of the knapping debris of these pieces. Even if the *puntillada* variety was clearly identified in concentrations A and B, their combined flakes total only 7 large and 133 medium flakes with a weight of 204 g. Of these, only 6.9 percent by number and 13.7 percent by weight are phase 2a flakes, demonstrating that the piece or pieces were introduced at the end of phase 2a. Only one refit was found in concentration B between two fragments widely separated and well outside the concentration (Figure 35).

If our distinction of the *puntillada* and *floreada* varieties is correct, this latter would form a coherent series in concentration B (Table 31). The number of 2a flakes is just compatible with the execution of phase 2a, especially considering that around 15 of them have cortex. Considering that the pieces were around 12 cm long, suggested by the dimensions of the large flakes, we estimate that the flakes represent the knapping of two or three

Table 28. Number and weight of large, medium, and type 2a flakes of pale rhyolite, subvariety *ferruginosa/naranjilla*, in the whole site.

Concentrations A–D: Pale rhyolite, subvariety *ferruginosa/naranjilla*						
	Large		Medium		Total	
Type 2a flakes	n	W (g)	n	W (g)	n	W (g)
elongated and skewed	11	67			11	67
thick	56	490	45	149	101	639
cortical	2	10	6		8	19
Kombewa						
total					120	725
all flakes	133	839	474	793	607	1632
ratio 2a flakes/all flakes					19.8%	44.4%
Number and dimensions of the largest flakes: n = 4; class 60–64 mm						

Table 29. Number and weight of large, medium, and type 2a flakes of pale rhyolite, subvariety *puntillada*, in concentration A.

Concentration A: Pale rhyolite, subvariety *puntillada*						
	Large		Medium		Total	
Type 2a flakes	n	W (g)	n	W (g)	n	W (g)
elongated and skewed						
thick	2	12	1	4	3	16
cortical						
Kombewa						
total					3	16.2
all flakes	5	24	33	54	38	78
ratio 2a flakes/all flakes					7.9%	20.7%
Number and dimensions of the largest flakes: n = 3; class 50–54 mm						

Table 30. Number and weight of large, medium, and type 2a flakes of pale rhyolite, subvariety *puntillada*, in concentration B.

Concentration B: Pale rhyolite, subvariety *puntillada*						
	Large		Medium		Total	
Type 2a flakes	n	W (g)	n	W (g)	n	W (g)
elongated and skewed	1	3			1	3
thick			1	3	1	3
cortical			2	6	2	6
Kombewa						
total					4	12
all flakes	2	5	100	121	102	126
ratio 2a flakes/all flakes					3.9%	9.5%
Number and dimensions of the largest flakes: n = 1; class 50–54 mm						

Table 31. Number and weight of large, medium, and type 2a flakes of pale rhyolite, subvariety *floreada*, in concentration B.

Concentration B: Pale rhyolite, subvariety *floreada*						
	Large		Medium		Total	
Type 2a flakes	n	W (g)	n	W (g)	n	W (g)
elongated and skewed	1	20				
thick	12	67	15	41	27	108
cortical	1	17	14	26	15	43
Kombewa						
total					42	151
all flakes	33	156	333	374	366	530
ratio 2a flakes/all flakes					11.4%	28.5%
Number and dimensions of the largest flakes: n = 1; class 60–64 mm						

The Raw Material Varieties

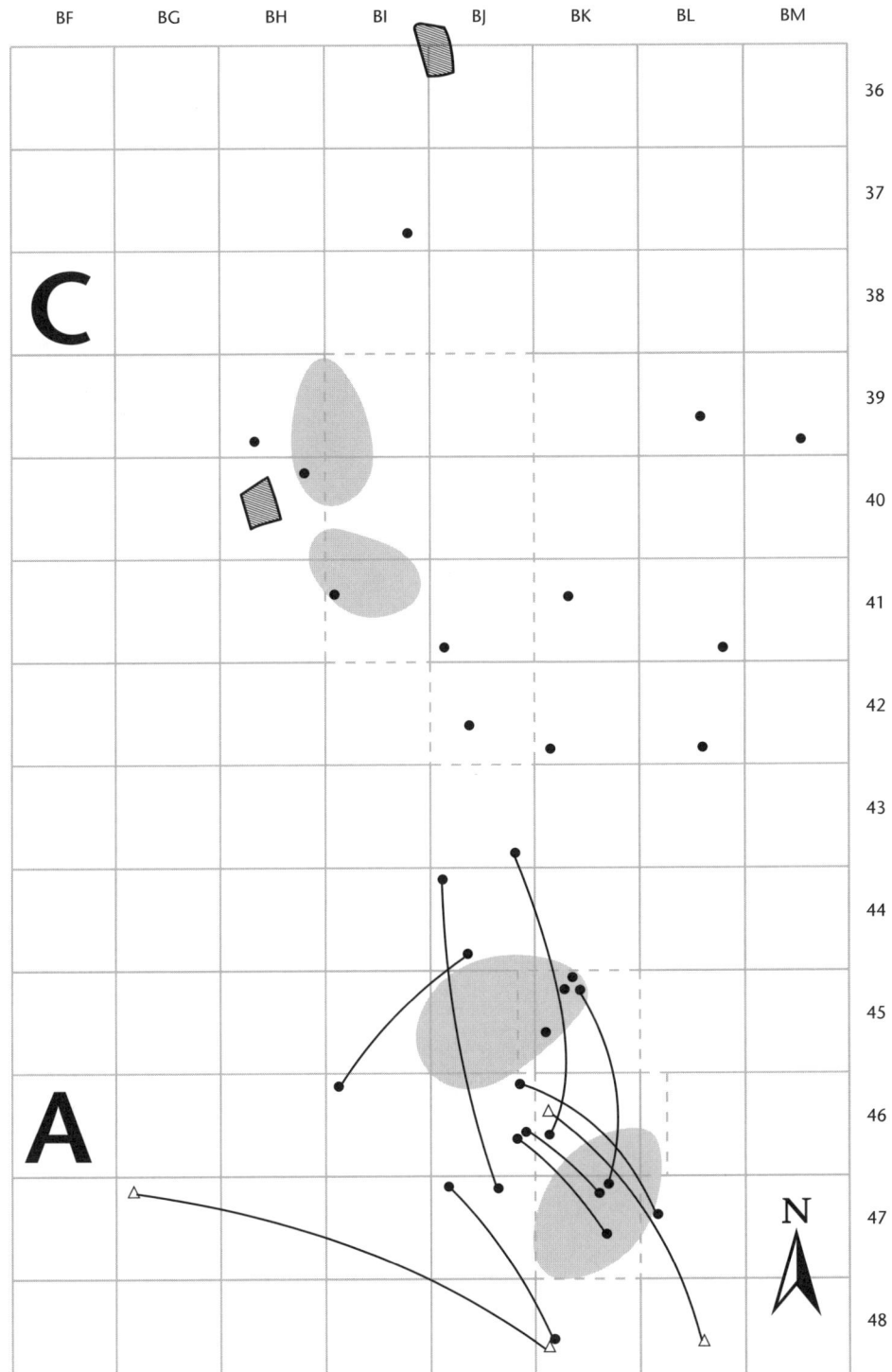

Figure 34. Spatial distribution of fracture and debitage refits of *ferruginosa* (dots) and *puntillada* (triangles) in concentrations A and C. The knapping localities already defined are shaded. Fracture and debitage refits were not distinguished.

points (Figure 38, no. 1). A small handful of darker orange flakes with "stars" comes from the extremity of a piece that was not found. The *floreada* flakes are found dispersed over B, especially in B2 and its immediate proximity. As many as 9 objects were found in each of squares BT43 and 44, as well as in B3, where a cluster of 7 flakes was found in square BS46. Unfortunately, it was not possible to search for refits.

If we wisely combine the *puntillada* and *floreada* varieties, the total from concentrations A and B is 40 large and 466 medium flakes. The number of type 2a flakes remains too small to represent the totality of phase 2a (Table 32 and Figure 38, no. 2). Adhering to the guidelines for medium-length pieces (experimental tests 6, 10, 11, 12; cf. Table 5), we estimate that this set resulted from knapping 3 to 5 pieces.

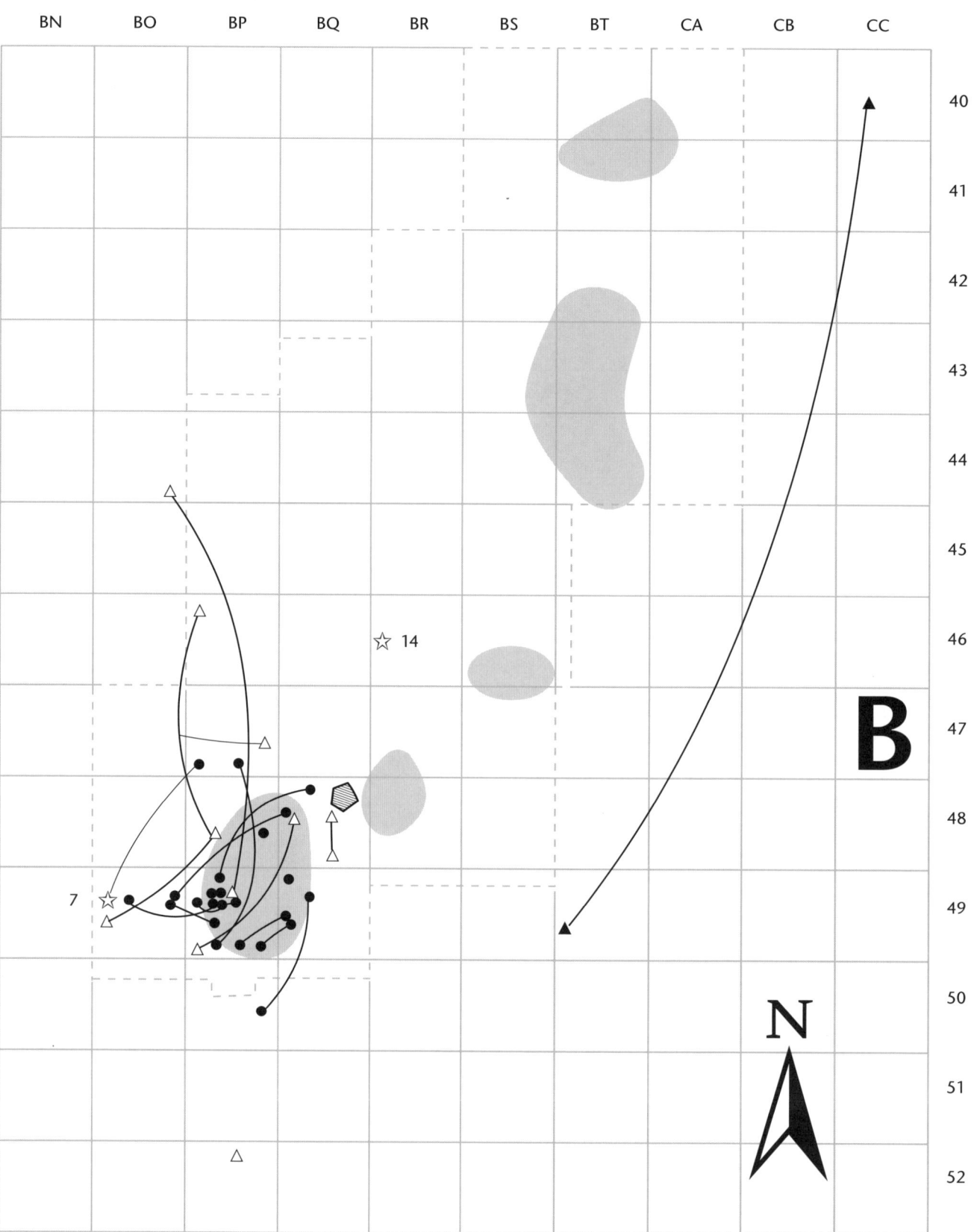

Figure 35. Spatial distribution of fracture and debitage refits of *ferruginosa* (dots), *puntillada* (black triangles), and *naranjilla* (white triangles) in concentration B. The knapping localities already defined are shaded. Debitage refits were distinguished from fracture refits by finer lines. Bifacial pieces no. 7 (*ferruginosa*) and 14 (*naranjilla*) are indicated by stars.

Several fragments of foliate pieces are of the *puntillada/floreada* varieties. One was found at the western limit of concentration B, 2 m from the side of concentration A: no. 5 (mesial fragment) and no. 6 (basal fragment), both found in BN49. This piece was broken at the very beginning of phase 4, when the barb angles were barely formed. It has an oblique flexing fracture of undetermined cause (Figure 22, no. 1). Curiously, three small blows are visible near the initial median fracture. These resemble poor retouch on a reworked fragment, but in this case the piece was fractured again after this retouch. These two refitted fragments may be associated with an apical fragment of the same variety found in concentration A, even though a true refit is lacking. This is the apex of a piece (no. 3) broken at the beginning of pressure retouch (phase 4). It is made of a rhyolite with many small black points of irregular density.

However, there exists another apical fragment that may complete no. 5 and 6, but which again lacks a true refit. This is fragment no. 61, found in BR43 of concentration B. It is the tip of a piece broken by flexing, probably during knapping at the end of phase 3 or beginning of phase 4. It is of medium size, and its section is slightly plano-convex. Its material is compatible with that of fragments no. 5 and 6, but perhaps even closer to the *puntillada* rhyolite of concentration B. We conclude that these 3 fragments (no. 5, 6, 61, 3) probably come from two pieces broken at the end of phase 3 or the very beginning of phase 4. Thus, one to three points of *puntillada/floreada* rhyolite would have been finished and exported.

Finally, one short (9.7 cm) poorly worked *Chivateros* biface (no. 75) was made from this same *puntillada/floreada* rhyolite. This piece apparently suffered from a few final removals by soft-hammer percussion. Its sinuous, crushed edges indicate errors in judgment and accidents in execution. This piece shows the potential variability of this rhyolite on the same blank. One extremity is yellow, then becomes purplish. The characteristics of one face are very typical of the *floreada* variety, while the other face is of a pinkish rhyolite with more intense pink "stars."

"Micro-*Puntillada*" Variety

This variety is mostly, but not exclusively, found in concentration D. It is a cream-colored rhyolite with thin yellow veins, very small, dense black spots that are barely visible, and a few more dispersed larger ones. One extremity of the supposed block is orange/purple in color just under the cortex, becoming more cream-colored toward the center. A brown fissure crosses one face parallel to the long axis of the pieces that appear to have been removed from the block. This material is consistent with the variation in site 125, but it is difficult to distinguish. We attributed 129 large and small flakes to this material, of which 128 were found in concentration D (with 4 fracture refits and 17 debitage refits). Apparently, only one flake, which was undoubtedly secondarily displaced, comes from concentration B (Figure 36).

Before estimating the number of corresponding knapped pieces, we will discuss the fragments of pieces assignable to the micro-*puntillada* variety. An apical fragment of one Paiján point (no. 102) was broken during phase 4 (pressure retouch clearly unfin-

Table 32. Number and weight of large, medium, and type 2a flakes of pale rhyolite, subvariety *puntillada/floreada*, in concentrations A and B.

Concentrations A and B:	Pale rhyolite, subvariety *puntillada/floreada*					
	Large		Medium		Total	
Type 2a flakes	n	W (g)	n	W (g)	n	W (g)
elongated and skewed	2	23				
thick	14	79	17	48	31	127
cortical	1	17	16	32	17	49
Kombewa						
total					48	176
all flakes	40	185	466	549	506	734
ratio 2a flakes/all flakes					9.5%	23.9%

Number and dimensions of the largest flakes: n = 1; class 60–64 mm

ished). This point, which is of mediocre knapping quality, has a twisted profile, an asymmetrical lozenge-shaped section, and a deep transversal hinged flake negative. This piece was almost certainly made from the purple marbled subvariety of this material. This piece may have been reworked after being shortened by 2 cm.

Two other point fragments, one found in concentration D and one in B, can be reasonably attributed to the micro-*puntillada* variety, especially considering that no other groups of flakes at the site seem to be related to their production; moreover, each refits with a flake from concentration D. The first, no. 104, is a short fragment (probably apical) of a point broken by flexing at the end of phase 2 or the beginning of phase 3. It is made of a fine-grained rhyolite with rose-colored marbling and a few red spots. A flake found in BH29, nearly 5 m away in concentration D, refits with this fragment; it was detached just before the piece broke. This material may represent a subvariety of micro-*puntillada*, which it somewhat resembles. The second fragment, no. 72, is the basal fragment of a piece broken during the same phase; it was found in BR44 of concentration B, but refits with a flake found in BI33 of concentration D (very close to fragment no. 104). The flake is made from a fine rhyolite with pink marbling, a few dark spots, and a red cortex, which is also consistent with the micro-*puntillada* material. Judging by their raw material and their technological state, it seems that these two fragments originate from the same foliate preform. There would thus be at least two pieces worked from the micro-*puntillada* rhyolite, which helps us estimate the number of pieces knapped based on the flakes of this material (Table 33).

First of all, there are a relatively small number of 2a flakes with a clear majority of cortical flakes, suggesting the use of one or more plaques as blanks. The quantity of flakes indicates one medium or two small pieces were knapped. We favor the second possibility, since we already have at least two broken pieces of the same material and considering the short length of the large flakes.

A few refits of flakes from phase 2b form four partial half-shells. The width and half-thickness of these two pieces reveal the nature of their sections in the process of manufacture.

1) width 37 mm, thickness 10 mm, rather plano-convex section;

2) width 48 mm, thickness 15 mm, thick or plano-convex section;

3) width 48 mm, thickness 10–11 mm, slightly convex section;

4) non-significant dimensions, flatter removals, including a refit with a flake found on the surface of concentration B (CA44).

In this same material or one quite similar, we identified another poorly made *Chivateros* biface (no. 34). The material is white with very small black spots of medium density. After the

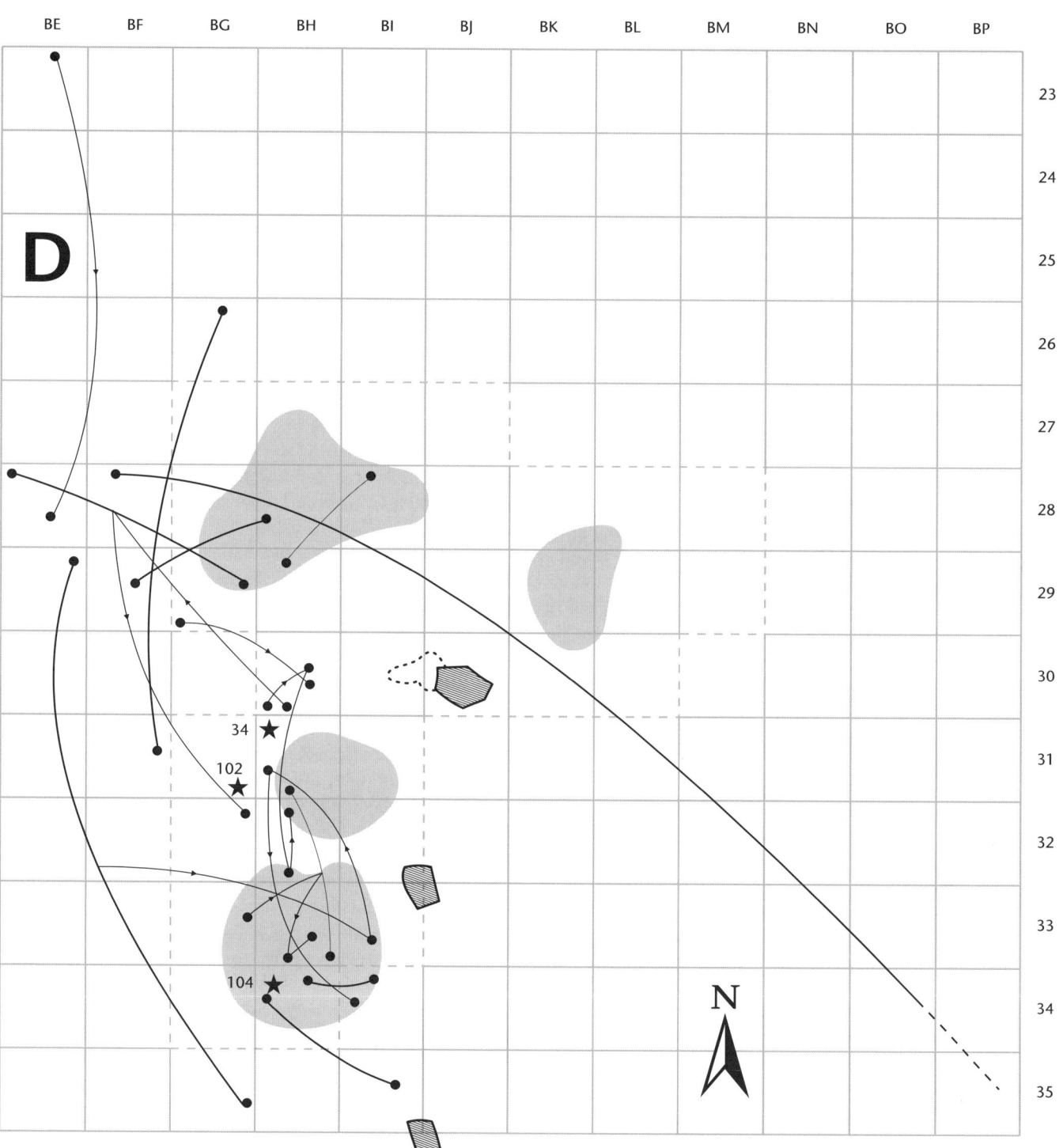

Figure 36. Spatial distribution of fracture and debitage refits of micro-*puntillada* rhyolite in concentration D. Bifacial pieces no. 34, 102, and 104 are indicated by stars. Piece no. 72 is found beyond the limits of this plan in BR44 (concentration B).

tip of this short point was broken, it was further damaged by a few violent and clumsy blows, then abandoned in place (it refits with a thick flake from the same square, BH31). This episode, which can surely be attributed to a young knapper, barely affects the data shown in the table above for the other 128 flakes of this variety in concentration D.

"*Arenosa*" Variety

This is a variety of fine-grained white rhyolite that yellows when patinated. It is punctuated with dense black spots and has a few fine "lines" (which are in fact planes) following several directions. These latter may be responsible for fractures along cleavage planes. Although this material is not very abundant, flakes of it were found in concentrations B (12 flakes), C (9 flakes), and D (57 flakes). We will consider all these flakes together in evaluating this rhyolite variety (Table 34).

Table 33. Number and weight of large, medium, and type 2a flakes of pale rhyolite, subvariety micro-*puntillada*, in concentration D.

Concentration D:	Pale rhyolite, subvariety micro-*puntillada*					
	Large		Medium		Total	
Type 2a flakes	n	W (g)	n	W (g)	n	W (g)
elongated and skewed						
thick	3		1		4	18
cortical	5		17		22	45
Kombewa						
total					26	63
all flakes	17	67	111	171	128	238
ratio 2a flakes/all flakes					20.3%	26.5%
Number and dimensions of the largest flakes: n = 3; class 45–49 mm						

Table 34. Number and weight of large, medium, and type 2a flakes of pale rhyolite, subvariety *arenosa*, in concentrations B–D.

Concentrations B–D:	Pale rhyolite, subvariety *arenosa*					
	Large		Medium		Total	
Type 2a flakes	n	W (g)	n	W (g)	n	W (g)
elongated and skewed						
thick	7	33	4	14	11	47
cortical	3	13	3	8	6	21
Kombewa						
total					17	68
all flakes	29	83	59	90	88	173
ratio 2a flakes/all flakes					19.3%	39.3%
Number and dimensions of the largest flakes: n = 1; class 55–59 mm						

The number of type 2a flakes indicates that this phase is well represented. The number and dimensions of the largest flakes are typical of the knapping debris of a small to medium piece. A 4.5-cm-long basal fragment of a foliate piece (no. 24) found in BJ41 of concentration C can also be assigned to this material; it is in stage 2b. Of the nine flakes or fragments (one large and eight medium, including two refit fragments) of this variety in concentration C, two have been refitted onto this piece and six others are associated with it, although lacking direct refits. This piece was brought to concentration C, where it broke after a few flakes were removed. The piece was undoubtedly first knapped in concentration D, where we find most of the corresponding flakes, including those of stage 2a. Unfortunately, we did not find any refits between the flakes of C and D, although several were found among flakes of the same variety between D and B. We refitted these latter into a partial half-shell, of which the "ghost" is the apical half of a preform in phase 2 (Figure 37). Of the seven flakes constituting this refit, the first and the last, which are large, were found in square BO47, slightly northwest of knapping locality B5. The other five were found approximately 15 m away, somewhat dispersed, but centered by their connections in locality D4. This dispersion is difficult to explain. We find no apparent explanation for the handful of flakes from piece no. 24, which was essentially knapped in concentration D and possibly finished or reworked after its fracture in concentration C; the flakes were finally rejected in B5. The few flakes (four large and eight medium) from concentration B form a rather dispersed group. A thin medium flake from BN39 was found just opposite concentration C, where lie its broken piece no. 24 and the flakes with which it refits or can be associated. Since this material is very particular and recognizable, we can be certain that this flake corresponds to the knapping of this piece, even if we found no direct refit.

"*Linea Rosada/Linea Azul*" Varieties

The "*linea rosada*" and "*linea azul*" varieties, which are typical of the site 125 quarries, were first defined separately, then combined when intermediate aspects were observed on certain pieces. The *linea rosada* material is slightly pink, or yellow before patination, with fine lines in all directions and a few black spots or "stars." The *linea azul* material, more white-colored, is also fine-grained with more or less short fine lines and blue spots. Since both varieties are considered together here, we call them *linea-rosada/azul* for the sake of brevity.

These two varieties are found in all the concentrations, but only two consistent series of flakes are found in concentrations C and B. We will discuss these first, since the small isolated series are too insignificant to change the estimates.

The majority of flakes from the small concentration C are made from this *linea-rosada/azul* variety (245 large and medium flakes). The number of type 2a flakes indicates a strong representation of this phase, which, according to the blade removals (Table 35 and Figure 40, no. 1), started from at least one or two roughouts on rather thick blocks. The dimension of the largest flakes indicates medium length (12–13 cm) rather than short length. According to the counts from concentration C, we estimate that two or three pieces were knapped by percussion. In addition to 3 refits between flakes, we found 15 refits of flake fragments, including one fragment found in A. Six of these are associated with one or two large fragments that reconstitute flakes that were 6–7 cm long before fracture. The distribution of connections among pieces in this concentration indicates the participation of two knapping localities (Figure 39). There are few relations between them, and an extension toward the east in both cases possibly

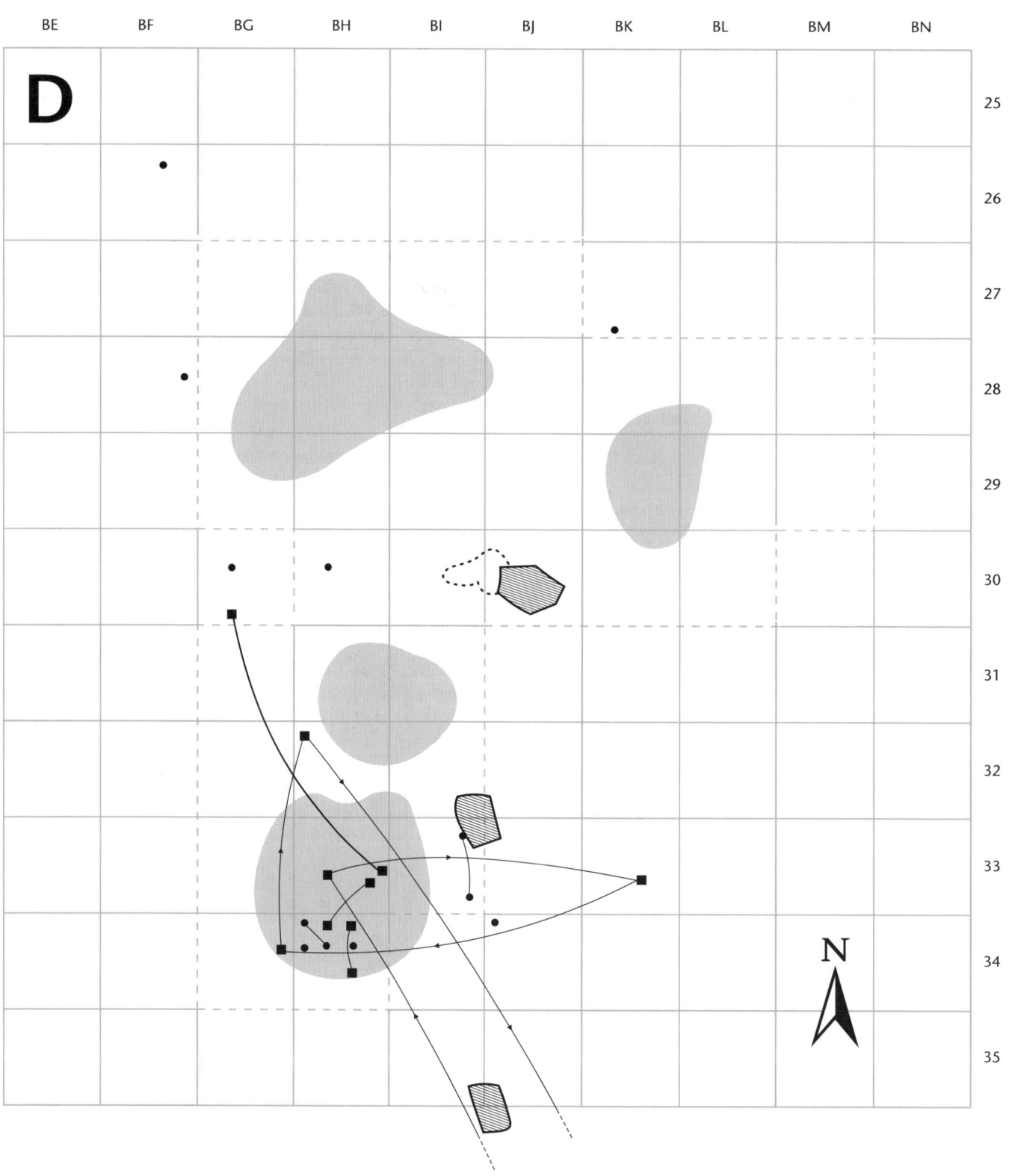

Figure 37. Spatial distribution of fracture and debitage refits of *ferruginosa* (dots) and *arenosa* (squares) rhyolite in concentration D. Two flakes are found in concentration B, beyond the limits of this plan.

represents small clear-out areas in front of the knappers. This distribution supports the idea that at least two pieces were worked in concentration C, each at a single knapping locality.

In concentration B we distinguished eight large flakes that seem to belong to the *linea-azul* variety. Six are type 2a flakes, one Kombewa and five skewed blade flakes, one more than 6 cm long; their total weight is 73 g. These flakes seem to represent an isolated beginning of phase 2a on a thick *Chivateros* biface on a flake blank (Figure 40, no. 3). However, these flakes do not refit together. In concentration A we found nine flakes of *linea-azul*, including one clear and one partial Kombewa. Lacking refits between them, these flakes represent only a small fraction of a phase 2a on a flake blank. In fact, the refitting of one of the flakes from C (BJ41) with one from B (BP46), and this latter with a flake from A (BM47), suggests that these nine flakes in concentration A and eight flakes in B were either transported, abandoned, or resulted from rather complex and puzzling exchanges between several knappers present at the site at the same time.

In concentration D we found seven more flakes with the same characteristics as those from C. Indeed, two of these refit with flakes from C. The other five, which are medium-sized and thin, are scattered over several meter-squares. The two refits prove that some of these flakes were inexplicably displaced after being knapped.

The second significant series of the *linea-rosada* variety comes from concentration B, where more than 100 flakes were identified, especially in B3 and B4. However, it is possible that the series is somewhat contaminated by a few small and medium thin flakes of "*salmón*" rhyolite (presented below). This series includes 111 flakes, with a normal fraction of type 2a flakes (Table 36 and Figure 40, no. 2). The largest flakes are rather short, but their number and weight indicate no more than one piece of small to medium dimensions made on a thick block with a residual cortical face.

One refit was found between a mesial fragment of a *linea-rosada* flake from the concentration B series (CA44) and its proximal fragment in C (BI40), suggesting that we failed to distinguish *linea-rosada* from *linea-azul* in concentration C. In concentration A we attributed seven more medium, rather thin flakes (12.4 g) to *linea-rosada*. This constitutes an insignificant quantity that was perhaps rejected from concentration B.

Table 35. Number and weight of large, medium, and type 2a flakes of pale rhyolite, subvariety *linea-rosada/azul*, in concentration C.

Concentration C:	Pale rhyolite, subvariety *linea-rosada/azul*					
	Large		Medium		Total	
Type 2a flakes	n	W (g)	n	W (g)	n	W (g)
elongated and skewed	6	57			6	57
thick	14	109.6	18	66.2	32	176
cortical	8	58.4	18	66	26	153
Kombewa						
total					64	386
all flakes	58	340	187	328	245	668
ratio 2a flakes/all flakes					26.1%	57.8%
Number and dimensions of the largest flakes: n = 2; class 60–64 mm						

Table 36. Number and weight of large, medium, and type 2a flakes of pale rhyolite, subvariety *linea-rosada*, in concentration B.

Concentration B:	Pale rhyolite, subvariety *linea-rosada*					
	Large		Medium		Total	
Type 2a flakes	n	W (g)	n	W (g)	n	W (g)
elongated and skewed	2	10			2	10
thick	5	41	9	27	14	68
cortical	2	11	8	19	10	30
Kombewa						
total					26	108
all flakes	16	86	95	139	111	225
ratio 2a flakes/all flakes					23.4%	48%
Number and dimensions of the largest flakes: n = 2; class 50–54 mm						

"*Porosa-Rosada*" Variety

This very rare variety is intensely pink in color and has a rather porous texture. It seems to originate from Pampa de los Fósiles 12, unit 104. This would thus be the only variety of pale rhyolite in this concentration with a provenience from outside the large quarries of site 125. We assigned to this material two flakes from concentration A (BK47 and BK48) and two more situated between A and B (BN44 and BO46). It is certain that piece no. 2-23 (Figure 22, no. 2) is of this material. These are the two refitted fragments of a point broken during phase 4. They were found in concentration A separated by 2 m (BK47 and BJ45) and rather close to the previous flakes. The fracture between the basal (missing) and mesial fragments is clean and probably occurred during pressure retouch. It was then reworked by lateral and basal "nibbling" along the long axis that caused the second fracture of the apex. The two fragments found are thus the remains of a large fragment of a point that was collected elsewhere, then soon broke during an awkward attempt at reworking, perhaps by a youth. It is even uncertain that the two or four flakes attributed to this *porosa-rosada* rhyolite originated from this point, since they are much larger than this narrow piece. We did not create a spectrum of large type 2a flakes for this variety.

"*Porosa-Blanca*" Variety

For this variety we have grouped together several small series of flakes and one fragment of a piece. In concentration B we observed a small series of thick flakes and a few smaller, fine ones that we present in a simplified table (Table 37). We did not create a spectrum for this variety.

In concentration D we found five large flakes of *porosa* rhyolite, two of them thick and cortical, dispersed over several squares. One is of a coarse-grained white material; the others have a finer grain and are slightly pinkish in color. In concentration A we note a flake of whitish *porosa* with holes (in addi-

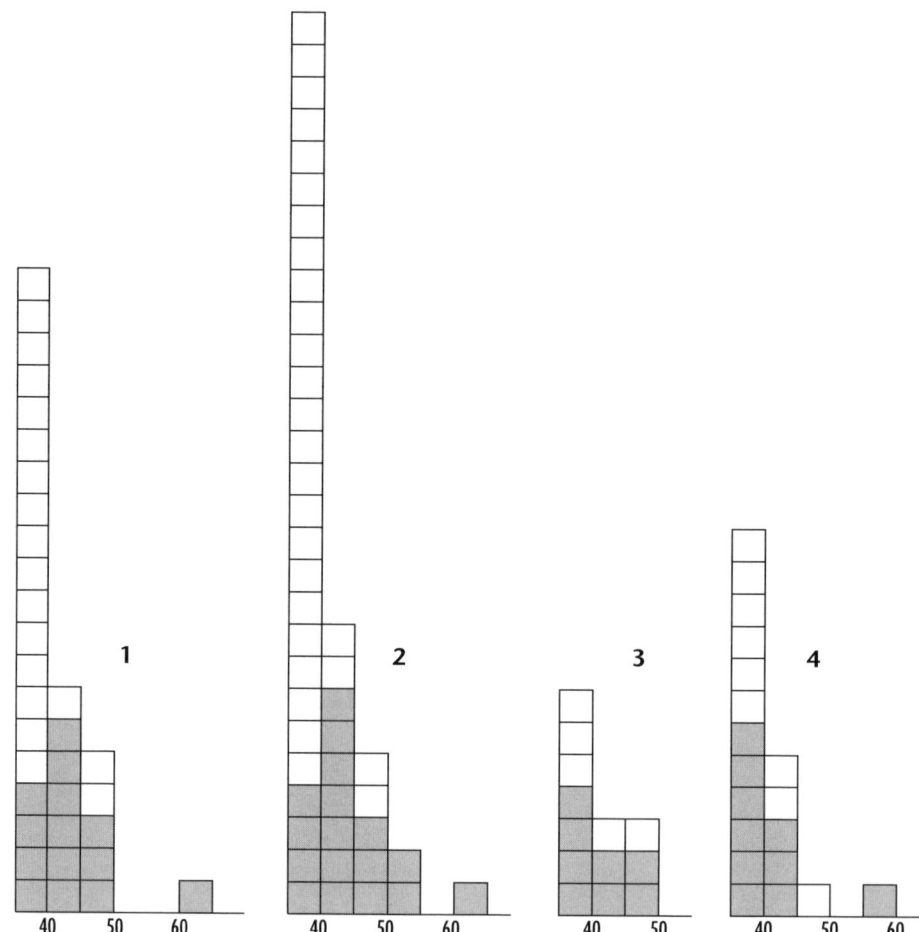

Figure 38. Histograms of large flakes and type 2a flakes: **1**, *floreada* rhyolite from concentration B; **2**, total of the *floreada* and *puntillada* varieties from concentrations A and B; **3**, micro-*puntillada* rhyolite from concentration D; **4**, total of *arenosa* rhyolite from concentrations B, C, and D.

tion to the two *porosa-rosada* flakes already noted). Upon reexamining the small set of 16 pieces and flakes already determined as *porosa* over the whole site, we distinguished three subvarieties of *porosa-blanca*. These are compatible with site 125 (besides the clear *porosa-rosada* related to the quarry of site 12, unit 104).

1) In a subvariety with a whitish, porous texture, we count two flakes from concentration B (two type 2a flake fragments) that can be associated with a large phase 2b flake from D (a white, coarse-grained, light rhyolite), for a total of five flakes.

2) The second subvariety, of a slightly rosy color, may be a more patinated version of the first subvariety. It composes the four other large flakes from concentration D and perhaps the two medium thin flakes from B that were previously tentatively attributed to *porosa-rosada*.

3) The last subvariety is characterized by visible "holes," or small bubbles. To this material we can attribute the refit of one flake from concentration A (BJ49) with four flakes from B that are by-products of mediocre knapping of the base of a piece in phase 2a (all thick flakes, four large and one medium) concentrated in locality B3. A few intercalated flakes are missing from this series. Three other flakes from concentration B, also in proximity to locality B3, can

also be associated with it. Indeed, one piece evokes this last subvariety of *porosa-blanca*, a basal fragment (no. 1, BK48) of a preform from a poorly executed stage 2b, indicated by its excessive thickness. It is clearly of a light, coarse-grained rhyolite without spots except for a few small black spots and vesicles. Its section is plano-convex and rather irregular. The piece would have been difficult to finish after one hinged removal and three others that crushed the edge. If the flakes from B3 originate from this piece, it was undoubtedly rejected in concentration A after it was fractured.

Finally, we include here a small series of 10 flakes from concentration D (one large flat cortical and 9 medium ordinary flakes). These are of a white-gray rhyolite without black spots and with a fine red cortex. There is no evident association between these flakes and others from concentration D, or even from the entire site. They represent the incomplete remains of the knapping of a bifacial piece, or fragment. One of the flakes, which was laterally overshot, again deformed the base in phase 2b. Some of these flakes are missing, but the remaining are not widely dispersed, the majority coming from locality D4. They could represent the reworking of an allochthonous piece by a youth. A fragment of a point or very short base (16 mm long) with a rather triangular section, of a similar nearly white rhyo-

The Raw Material Varieties

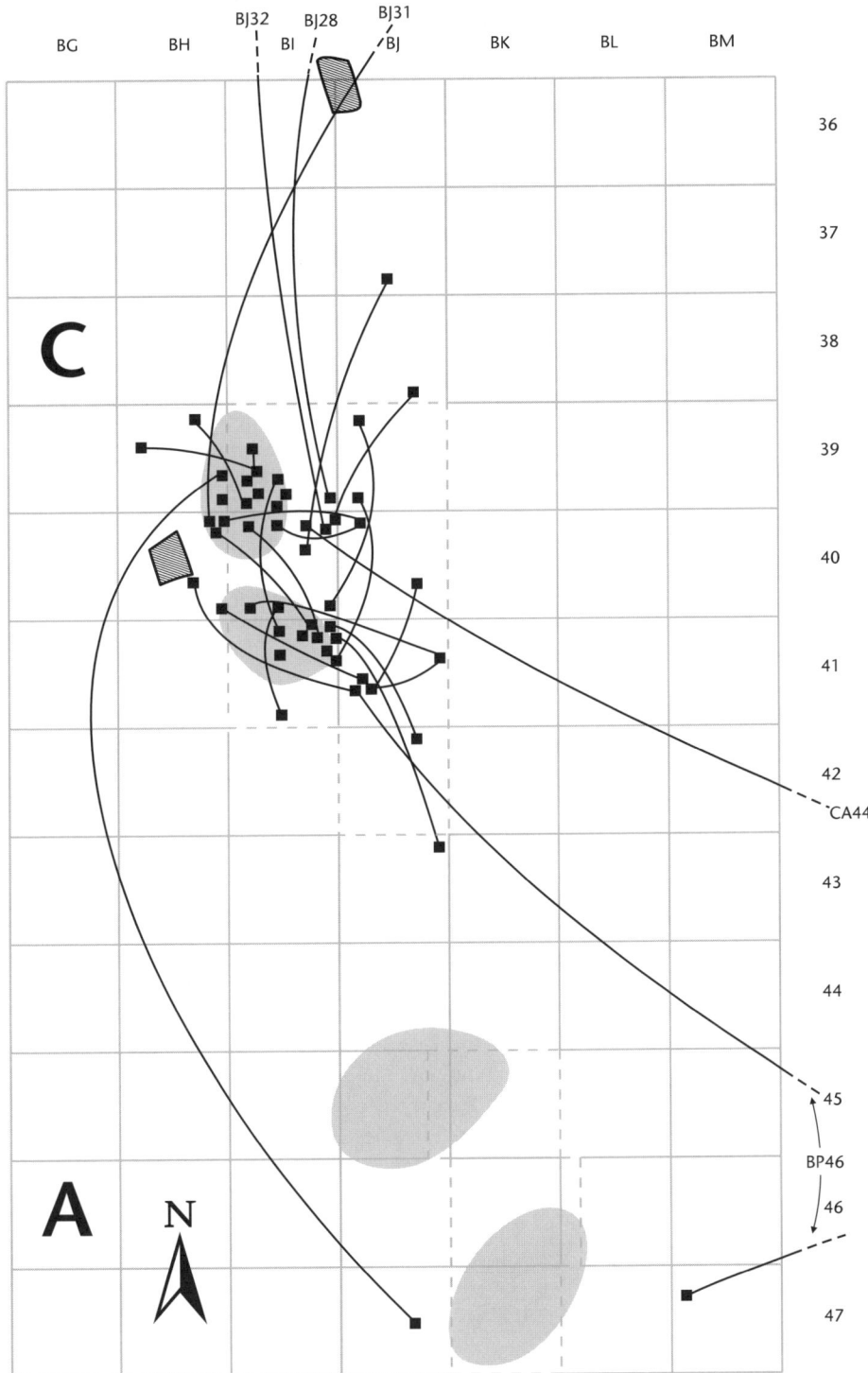

Figure 39. Spatial distribution of fracture and debitage refits of *linea-rosada/azul* in concentrations A and C. Fracture and debitage refits were not distinguished.

lite, could be associated with this residual series of 10 flakes from concentration D. However, this piece comes from square BP49 (concentration B), nearly 20 m from these flakes. Whatever the case, it has very little economic value, since the remainder of the piece, whether or not it is a reworked fragment, was undoubtedly further knapped, even if we could not identify it from its flakes.

In spite of the difficulty of attributing certain flakes to these subvarieties, it is clear that these various flakes of *porosa* rhyolite are insufficient to represent the knapping of the two pink and white *porosa* pieces from concentration A (no. 1 and no. 2-23), or the short fragment (no. 76) described above. Perhaps some fragments were collected nearby, one of which (no. 2-23, of *porosa rosada*) could be from a workshop of site 12, thus below quarry unit 104, and awkwardly reworked and broken by young knappers.

Table 37. Number and weight of large, medium, and type 2a flakes of pale rhyolite, subvariety *porosa-blanca,* in concentration B.

Concentration B:	Pale rhyolite, subvariety *porosa-blanca*					
	Large		Medium		Total	
Type 2a flakes	n	W (g)	n	W (g)	n	W (g)
elongated and skewed						
thick	3		4		7	44
cortical						
Kombewa						
total					7	44
all flakes	6	45	5	13	11	57
ratio 2a flakes/all flakes					63.6%	77.2%

Varieties Restricted to Concentration D

"*Rosada-Verde*" Variety

This is a pink rhyolite with light green veins in parallel bands. It falls within the variations of quarry site 125. Four flakes were refitted onto a whole piece, no. 38, which was abandoned during phase 2b. The piece is 119 mm long, 44 mm wide, and 16–17 mm thick in its central area (Figure 26). The knapping is of average quality. The section is biconvex, with three hinged removals and one edge crushed along 4 cm by scalar-shaped removals (awkward reworking?). The piece remained just finishable until these final accidents occurred. By the end of phase 2a, the piece had already suffered from a lateral distal overshot that removed the tip and shortened the preform by at least 2 cm and a small lateral overshot at the base by a large thick skewed flake. Before these accidents, a cleft had produced a deep "edge-bite" (Whittaker 1994:190) of the lateral edge. The four flakes that refit onto the piece come from very close squares (Figure 41). In addition, four fragments of two flakes were refitted. This variety thus includes a total of 36 flakes and fragments weighing 109.2 g, including one large flake of unclear raw material. Based on the small number of medium flakes, Table 38 is indeed indicative of an unfinished phase 2b and also of an incompletely represented phase 2a. The piece reached the end of phase 2a, which must be taken into account when observing the corresponding spectrum (Figure 47, no. 1). The plan in Figure 41 shows that the distribution is centered in knapping locality D2, with a few flakes dispersed toward the south and a small number carried by the gully to the north.

"*Gris-Fina*" Variety

This is a gray-green rhyolite with small red spots and a fine, smooth grain. Its origin is unknown. We found 45 large and medium flakes of this material, but no piece made from it. This group could very well correspond to the end of phase 2a (four thick flakes and only two with cortex), phase 2b, and perhaps phase 3 of the knapping of a foliate piece of good quality that was perhaps finished elsewhere (Table 39, spectrum Figure 47, no. 2). Many of these flakes are flat and fine, very much in the style of the European Solutrean. They come from a thin biconvex or slightly plano-convex piece. A refit of opposite flakes shows a probable median width attaining a maximum of 65 mm, which is rather wide. It seems that many flakes are missing (exported?), given the few refits found with this relatively easily identified material that has not been found elsewhere on the site. The plan in Figure 42 shows a very clear concentration in D2, as well as some flakes displaced toward the north by a gully and a few others evacuated toward the east. This is a rather marked dispersion compared with an experimental knapping locality (around 1 m square). With its irregular form, this one occupies at least 2 m², which is not exceptional in this workshop. See, for example, the case of D4 and also the particularly jumbled dispersion in all of concentration B (Figure 27). The long period of exposure on the surface is certainly one cause of this dispersion, at least as significant as the activities of the knappers (and children). In concentration D, in particular in D2, the partial superposition of two materials from different origins perhaps implies two successive but separate episodes of activity; if the knapper engaged in two knapping sessions, this may be another possible cause of disturbance.

"*Colorada*" Variety

This purple/yellow/white reticulated rhyolite is very similar to the material of a *Chivateros* biface found in concentration D (no. 40, square BH28). This piece was abandoned after several hinged removals, including one short flake that was detached with a hard hammer and found nearly 5 m away in BI33. With two failed removals, this very short piece was already at a clear technological dead end. It is undoubtedly the work of a young knapper with little experience. Another series, perhaps not quite pure, which may be associated consists of 58 large and medium flakes from concentration D that seem to originate from the limited knapping of a small *Chivateros* biface (Table 40 and Figure 47, no. 3). Two refits of partial half-shells show the "ghost" of a thick piece with a triangular or even lozenge-shaped section. According to Table 40, it seems that some elements are missing from this series or perhaps they represent a very short piece. At the least, they indicate the working of a piece that was probably second-rate (finished or rejected elsewhere?). In addition, the distribution of refits demonstrates a significant dispersal of this

Table 38. Number and weight of large, medium, and type 2a flakes of pale rhyolite, subvariety *rosada-verde,* in concentration D.

Concentration D:	Pale rhyolite, subvariety *rosada-verde*					
	Large		Medium		Total	
Type 2a flakes	n	W (g)	n	W (g)	n	W (g)
elongated and skewed						
thick	3		2		5	40
cortical	2		2		4	11
Kombewa						
total					9	51
all flakes	8	47	28	63	36	109
ratio 2a flakes/all flakes					25%	46.8%
Number and dimensions of the largest flakes: n = 1; class 50–54 mm						

The Raw Material Varieties

material, which can be only partially attributed to the gully. A small majority of flakes was found in knapping localities D3 and D4. Since one flake from D4 refits onto it, the biface that was found in D2 was probably rejected from D4 (Figure 43). It is thus most probable that the knapping of this variety, including biface no. 40, occurred in D4.

Varieties Restricted to Concentration B

"*Granito*" Variety

This variety is not very common, and it is not certain that it originates from the quarries of site 125. As indicated by its name, this material is very coarse-grained. It has a yellow-greenish color that becomes orange when patinated.

One foliate piece made from this material was reconstructed by refitting its three fragments: apical fragment no. 60, mesial fragment no. 77, and basal fragment no. 68 (Figure 30, no. 1). This latter fragment was found nearly 20 m to the southeast of concentration B, beyond the limits of the plans. Two bending fractures with short lips occurred during knapping. The piece has a triangular section. Its knapping quality is mediocre, with several hinged removals on one of its edges. Even before these last awkward removals, it is clear that this piece in phase 3 (129 mm long and 33 mm wide) was too thick to be finished into a typical Paiján point (14.5 mm at the median point, 13 mm at 2.5 cm from the base). Curiously, the basal fragment (found 20 m away) has one crushed edge, as if it had been clumsily reworked by a very young knapper.

A total of 93 flakes attributed to this variety come from a large central zone in concentration B. This identification is confirmed by the refitting of 10 fragments into 5 flakes, the refitting of 8 flakes to each other (including one found in concentration D), and the refitting of one flake onto the basal fragment described above (no. 68) (Figure 30, no. 1). A second flake of *granito* was identified among the flakes isolated in D, 3 m from the first. These 95 *granito* flakes weighing 304 g represent the knapping of a foliate piece from a *Chivateros* biface on a medium-sized block perfectly in accordance with our experimental tests (Table 41 and Figure 47, no. 4). The plan of refits shows a connection between B2 and B3, more precisely between two groups of objects (Figure 44). One is in the southern half of B2, the other to the northwest of B3. The majority of connections between objects occur between the two groups and follow a preferential southwest-northeast direction, which is close to that of the dominant winds. For this reason we confidently propose that the *granito* rhyolite was knapped in B3. Moreover, the refits between flakes all involve objects from B3; and the bifacial fragments are also close to B3, even though this last argument is not conclusive, since the fragments of bifaces are often rejected some distance away.

"*Gris-Violacea*" Variety

This rhyolite is rather fine-grained but not very homogeneous. It has a purplish-gray color that becomes green-brown when patinated. Its source has not been determined. Because it is very

Table 39. Number and weight of large, medium, and type 2a flakes of pale rhyolite, subvariety *gris-fina*, in concentration D.

Concentration D: Type 2a flakes	Pale rhyolite, subvariety *gris-fina*					
	Large		Medium		Total	
	n	W (g)	n	W (g)	n	W (g)
elongated and skewed						
thick	3		1		4	25
cortical			2	7	2	7
Kombewa						
total					6	32
all flakes	13	56	32	47	45	103
ratio 2a flakes/all flakes					13.3%	31.1%

Number and dimensions of the largest flakes: n = 1; class 50–54 mm

identifiable, we were able to attribute a small series of 44 flakes to this material without hesitation. These constitute the remains of the knapping of a small plaque, the flakes showing two areas of cortex on their small sides. No piece or fragment of this exact material was found. One finished point was apparently exported. The figures in Table 42, along with the spectrum (Figure 47, no. 5), suggest that the corresponding piece was very short, around 10 cm long, and made on a thin plaque.

Four fragments were refitted into two flakes, and nine flakes were refitted onto each other. These objects were dispersed over 12 meter-squares in the southern zone of concentration B. A few small flakes (less than 2 cm long) were found in the excavation

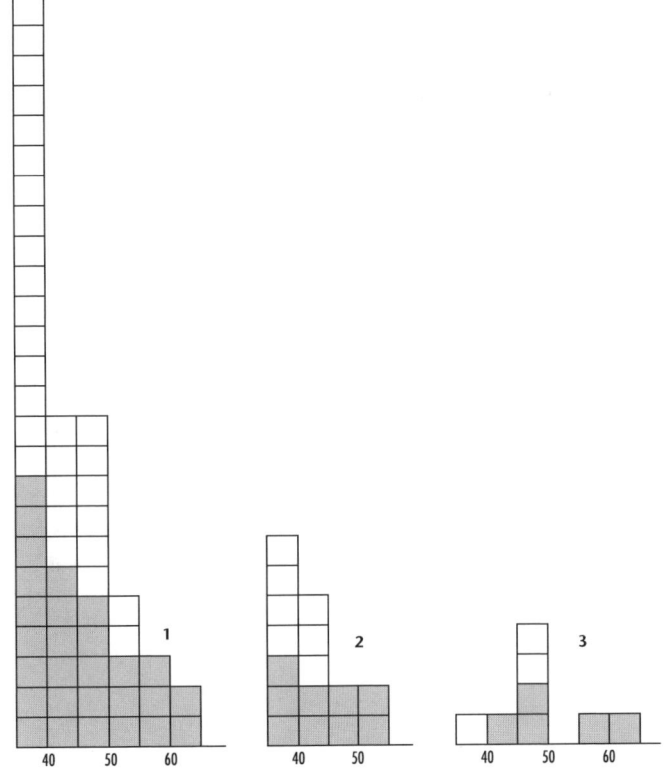

Figure 40. Histograms of large flakes and type 2a flakes: **1**, *linea rosada/azul* rhyolite from concentration C; **2**, *linea rosada* rhyolite from concentration B; **3**, *linea azul* rhyolite from concentration B.

Table 40. Number and weight of large, medium, and type 2a flakes of pale rhyolite, subvariety *colorada*, in concentration D.

Concentration D:	Pale rhyolite, subvariety *colorada*					
	Large		Medium		Total	
Type 2a flakes	n	W (g)	n	W (g)	n	W (g)
elongated and skewed						
thick	2	4			6	20
cortical	5		3		8	34
Kombewa						
total					14	54
all flakes	9	42	49	68	58	110
ratio 2a flakes/all flakes					24.1%	49.1%
Number and dimensions of the largest flakes: n = 2; class 50–54 mm						

of square BP48, probably indicating a knapping locality; the flakes and fragments that were refitted are more dispersed, over about 20 meter-squares. Therefore, this piece was probably knapped in B5.

"*Salmón*" Variety

This variety has a rather fine grain and a homogeneous pink color with no black spots. We attributed a small series of 70 flakes to this material, as well as a fragment of a foliate piece (no. 15) broken at the end of phase 3. This is an apical fragment with a slightly plano-convex section. Its knapping quality is rather good. The series of flakes corresponds to a short phase 2b and a phase 3. One overshot flake slightly shortened the base of its original piece. Almost all were found on the surface and are patinated; it is possible that this is a patinated subset of another variety of rhyolite, but this small series is consistent in itself. Since none of these are type 2a flakes, we summarize them in a simplified table (Table 43). Because of lack of time, the spatial distribution of this variety was not noted with precision and refits were not sought. However, the observations that were made indicate a majority of flakes immediately to the east and southeast of B3 (where piece no. 15 was also found). There is also a possible trail (eolian?) to the north/northeast of B1; since no objects were found between these two zones, they may indicate two different knapping localities. Could this represent two knapping phases of the same object? Only an analysis of refits could have answered this question.

"*Crema/Rayada*" Variety

This material can be difficult to distinguish from the *floreada* variety. However, instead of "stars" it has irregular points, or dispersed "holes" and a few short lines. Its most distinctive characteristics are its pale cream color, for which it is named, and fine texture. We first attributed 129 flakes to this material and 36 flakes to a subvariety that has more short parallel or nearly parallel lines. However, the composition of this group is too unequal (one flake 36 mm long and 35 medium ones including one thick and one cortical) to represent the remains of knapping a projectile point. After observing a clear spatial concordance between these two series, both centered in the northern half of B2, we decided they should be grouped together, even if we did not have time to search for refits between them (Table 44). These 165 flakes show a normal representation of phase 2a (Figure 47, no. 6). In accordance with tests 5 and 14, they could originate from the complete knapping of a piece on a rather large block with residual cortex about 14 cm long. The series lacks a few flakes longer than 60 mm that would confirm this hypothesis (although one fracture refit of a large and a medium fragment reconstituted a flake more than 6 cm long). The series could also be the by-products of knapping two pieces of small to medium dimension, both of which would have been finished and exported since there is no piece fragment assignable to this variety. Once again, unusual circulations of flakes or debris have been noted between different concentrations. For example, one medium thin flake from concentration D, where it was the only object of this variety, was found to refit with four successive refitted flakes from concentration B (with *rayada* characteristics), which were already dispersed over several meter-squares.

"*Morada*" Variety

This is a good-quality homogeneous rhyolite with a purplish-pink (mauve) color. It has very fine reticulated red lines; black spots are missing or barely visible. Its cortex is bright red or dull pink. Because it is relatively easy to distinguish, we were able to refit four

Table 41. Number and weight of large, medium, and type 2a flakes of pale rhyolite, subvariety *granito*, in concentration B.

Concentration B:	Pale rhyolite, subvariety *granito*					
	Large		Medium		Total	
Type 2a flakes	n	W (g)	n	W (g)	n	W (g)
elongated and skewed						
thick	12	101	8	37	20	138
cortical						
Kombewa						
total					20	138
all flakes	25	161	70	143	95	304
ratio 2a flakes/all flakes					21.1%	45.4%
Number and dimensions of the largest flakes: n = 1; class 60–64 mm						

Table 42. Number and weight of large, medium, and type 2a flakes of pale rhyolite, subvariety *gris-violacea*, in concentration B.

Concentration B:	Pale rhyolite, subvariety *gris-violacea*					
	Large		Medium		Total	
Type 2a flakes	n	W (g)	n	W (g)	n	W (g)
elongated and skewed						
thick			1	2	1	2
cortical	7	26	15	25	22	51
Kombewa						
total					23	53
all flakes	8	31	36	45	44	76
ratio 2a flakes/all flakes					52.3%	69.7%
Number and dimensions of the largest flakes: n = 1; class 45–49 mm						

The Raw Material Varieties

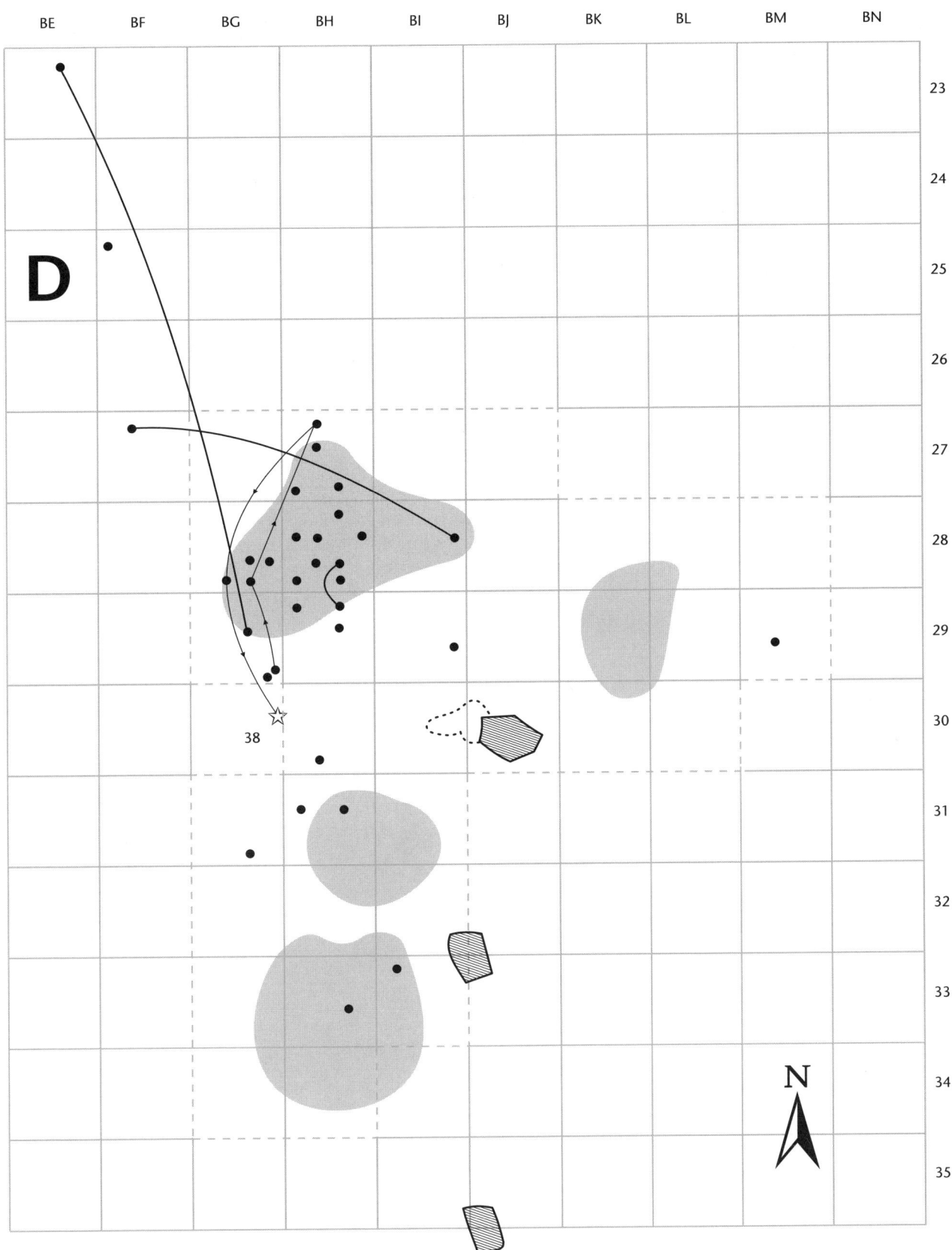

Figure 41. Spatial distribution of isolated flakes and fracture and debitage refits on bifacial piece no. 38 (star) and *rosada-verde* rhyolite (dots) in concentration D.

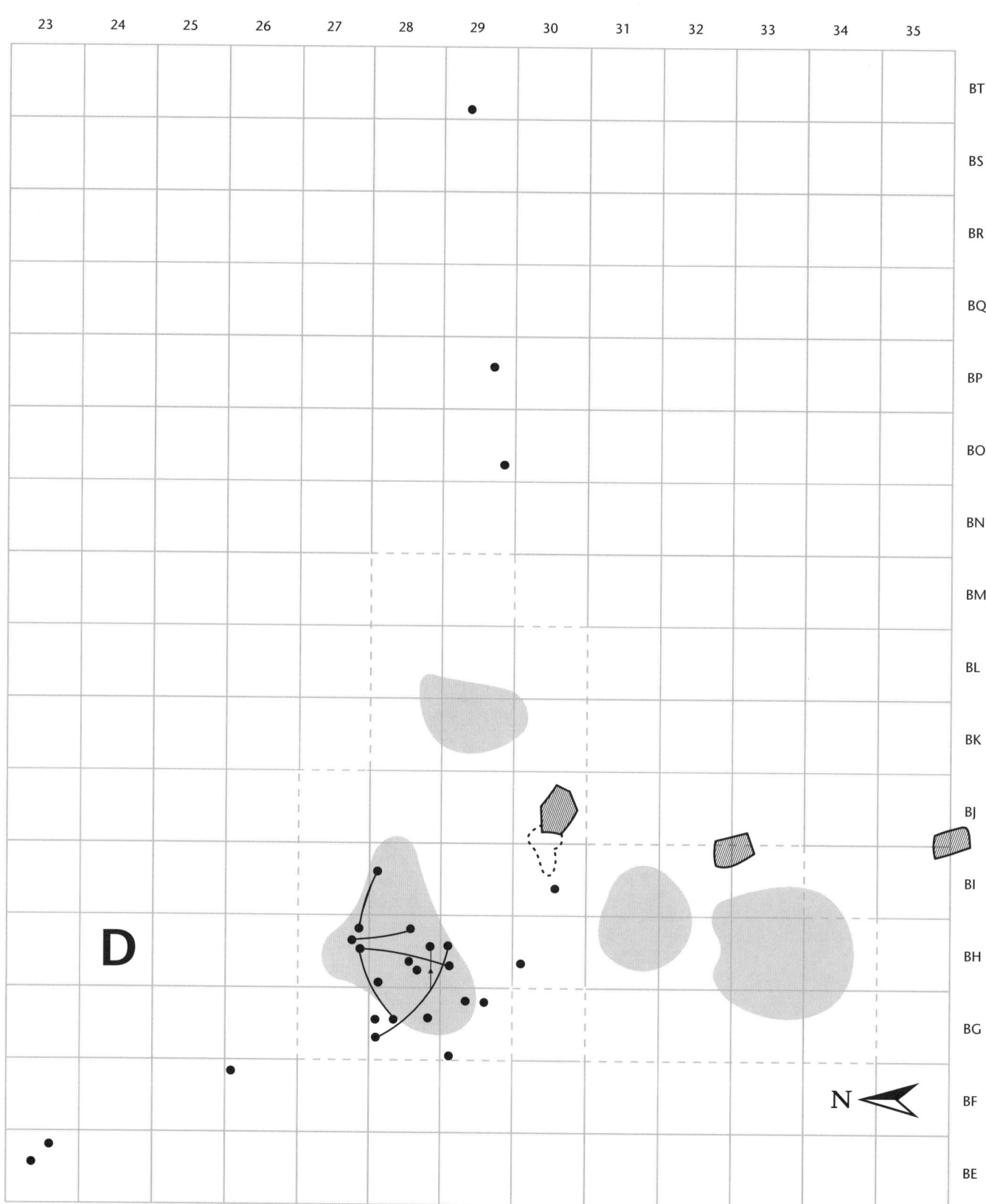

Figure 42. Spatial distribution of isolated flakes and fracture and debitage refits of *gris-fina* rhyolite (dots) in concentration D.

series of flakes (which in turn helped us distinguish the material) out of a total of 110 large and medium ones (Table 45 and Figure 47, no. 7). These series reveal the "ghosts" of two pieces in phase 2 with rather clear plano-convex sections. These figures correspond nicely to the knapping of two small *Chivateros* bifaces. Considering the majority of cortical flakes among the type 2a flakes, at least one of these was made on a thin plaque. They could also indicate the knapping of one large piece, but the refits seem to indicate more than one piece. Moreover, two different color tones can be distinguished, an observation which is reinforced by the refits; one subseries tends to be darker mauve than the other.

The following pieces are attributed to the dark mauve material:

- a convex half-shell formed by refitting seven flakes;
- three couples of flakes from the opposite, almost flat, face of the same shell;
- one flake that does not refit but was definitely associated.

The "ghost" of this set of flakes is a knapped piece, at the beginning of phase 2b, 6.5 cm wide and around 20 mm thick at its median point.

The following pieces are attributed to the light mauve material:

- a convex half-shell formed by refitting nine flakes. The median width of the "ghost" is 45 mm, with a half thickness of 15 mm (during or at the end of phase 2b);
- the half-shell of the opposite face, flatter and with cortex, at an earlier stage of knapping. Two other flat thin fragmented flakes without cortex are also assignable to the knapping of this same face at a slightly later stage. The half-section thus formed is 54 mm wide and 9 mm thick.

These two groups of flakes show the same spatial distribution, concentrated in B4, even though a few fragments were dispersed as much as 4 m to the north and northeast, probably by wind action (Figures 45 and 46).

Miscellaneous Varieties

This category includes flakes that we could not reliably attribute to the varieties defined above, but which very probably belong to them. Fortunately they are not very numerous, and we were able to regroup them into two small ensembles.

The first set of 39 flakes (miscellaneous 1) regroups rather disparate objects; the dominant varieties are of a pink-yellow color that patinates into a red-orange. These are probably the patinated forms of the *salmón, morada, naranjilla,* and *puntillada* varieties. Simplified Table 46 is shown only to illustrate their weak representation. We acknowledge that redistributing these objects into several of the preceding varieties, in particular the *salmón* rhyolite, which is curiously poor, does not change our previous quantitative estimations.

The second group (miscellaneous 2), consisting of 31 apparently non-patinated flakes (buried), is somewhat more homogeneous. The material is mostly a pale whitish rhyolite with small lines and pale pink spots or zones. This group is small and not homogeneous enough to constitute the remains from knapping

Table 43. Number and weight of large and medium flakes (no type 2a flakes) of pale rhyolite, subvariety *salmón*, in concentration B.

Concentration B:	Pale rhyolite, subvariety *salmón*					
	Large		Medium		Total	
Type 2a flakes	n	W (g)	n	W (g)	n	W (g)
total					0	0
all flakes	4	11.4	66	70.2	70	81.6
ratio 2a flakes/all flakes					0%	0%
Number and dimensions of the largest flakes: n = 2; class 40–49 mm						

Table 44. Number and weight of large, medium, and type 2a flakes of pale rhyolite, subvariety *crema/rayada*, in concentration B.

Concentration B:	Pale rhyolite, subvariety *crema/rayada*					
	Large		Medium		Total	
Type 2a flakes	n	W (g)	n	W (g)	n	W (g)
elongated and skewed	1	2			1	2
thick	10	75	7	19	17	94
cortical	3	18	13	24	16	42
Kombewa						
total					34	139
all flakes	23	129	142	199	165	328
ratio 2a flakes/all flakes					20.6%	42.4%
Number and dimensions of the largest flakes: n = 1; class 50–59 mm						

one piece, as is suggested by simplified Table 47. After carefully reexamining the previously distinguished varieties, we deemed it more reasonable to attribute most of this series to the *morada* variety. This attribution does not modify our well-argued estimate of two pieces produced from this material.

Other Observations

Two bifacial knapping flakes were clearly brought to the site, perhaps to serve as knives. In concentration A, the specimen was a large gray rhyolite (?) flake with light inclusions patinated to a greenish color. In concentration D (BG32), the specimen was a large flat yellow or white rhyolite flake. Both these flakes must logically be counted among the *a posteriori* tools, as was actually done in the study of the tool assemblage (see Chapter 3, "The Two Approaches Applied to the Study of the Bifacial Knapping Concentrations").

A small bifacial fragment broken in two was collected in the middle of B2 (no. 110-111). This fragment constitutes two pieces of the lateral-basal edge of a foliate piece or *Chivateros* biface on a plaque (with one remaining cortical face). It was broken along a cleft. The material seems to be a rhyolite from site 125, but the particular variety was not determined. This accident shortened the piece by around 1 cm but very likely had little effect on continued knapping.

Four isolated pieces were found around 15 m northwest of the limits of concentration D within an area less than 3 m in diameter. It is possible but not certain that they are associated with the site studied here. The pieces represent three second-rate

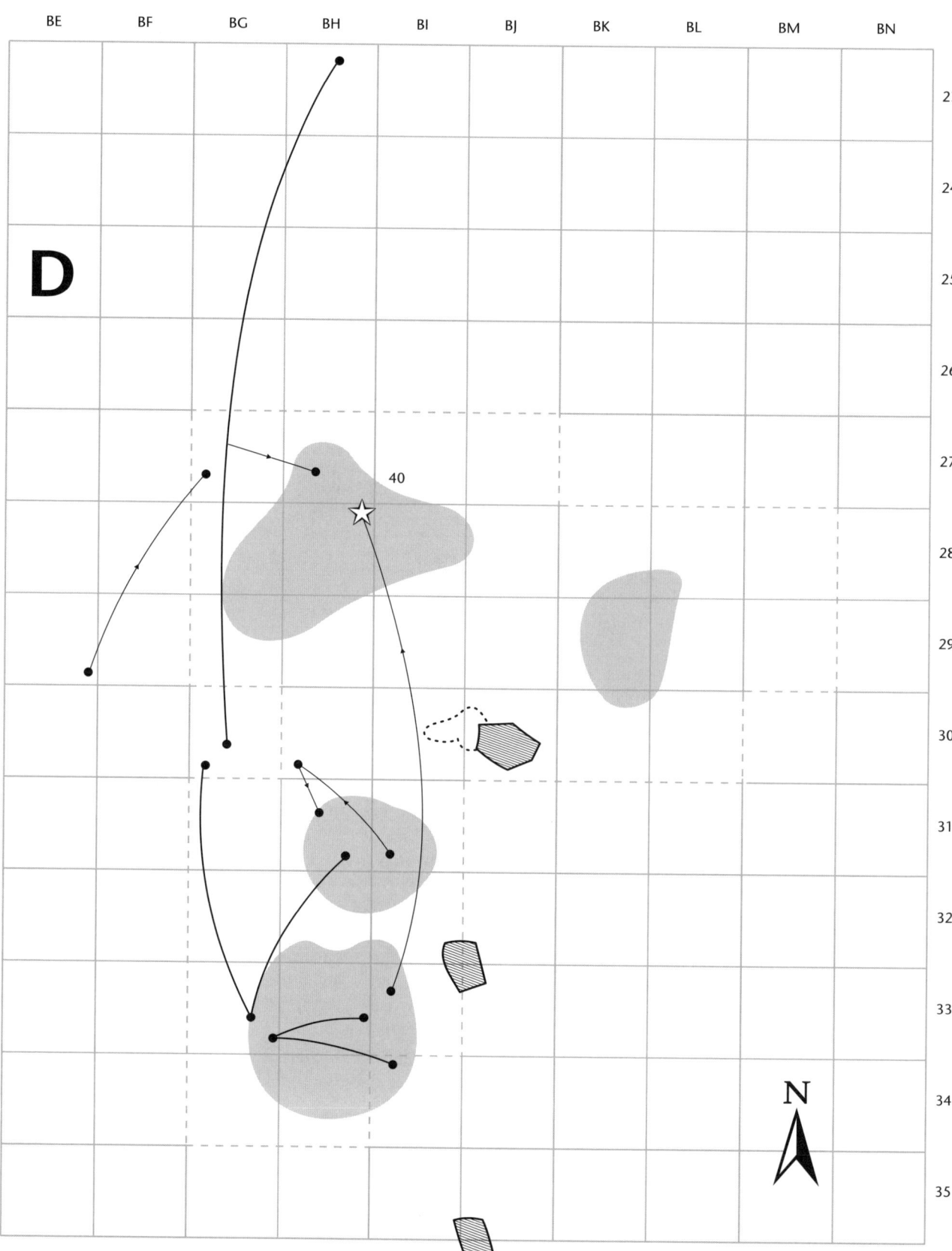

Figure 43. Spatial distribution of fracture and debitage refits of *colorada* rhyolite (dots) and bifacial piece no. 40 (star) in concentration D.

The Raw Material Varieties

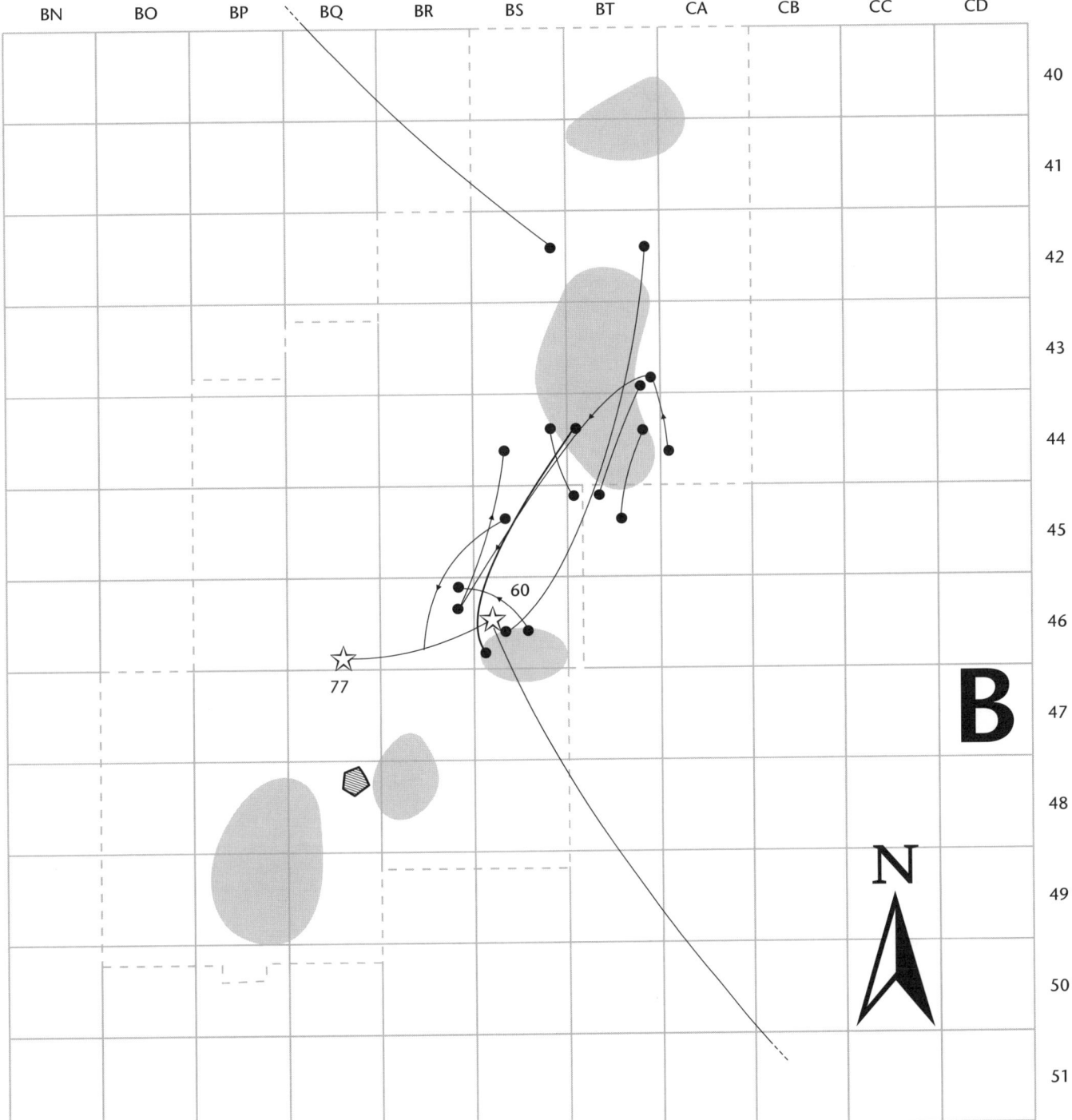

Figure 44. Spatial distribution of fracture and debitage refits of *granito* rhyolite (dots) and bifacial piece no. 60-77 (stars) in concentration B.

Chivateros bifaces or accidents and one fragment of an excellent foliate piece. They are all made of various rhyolites from quarry site 125:

- no. 55 in AO12, a small *Chivateros* biface on a thin plaque,

shows only initial shaping by short bifacial removals. The last blow produced a catastrophic accident, removing an entire edge because of a preexisting cleft. In fact, other visible clefts would have made it impossible to finish the point. It should have been abandoned after testing at the quarry site.

- No. 52 in AQ12 is a *Chivateros* biface on a plaque with a flattened triangular section. Knapping had barely begun when its upper part broke (it was not found). The same comments about the biface above apply to this one.

- No. 53 in AQ14 is a poor *Chivateros* biface on a small plaque with a flattened triangular section. This piece was poorly initiated by hinged flakes removed with a hard hammer. One of the very first flakes removed by soft hammer overshot the flat face and removed all the opposite edge. Knapping was decisively stopped.
- No. 54 in A012 is the basal fragment of a good-quality bifacial piece that was broken at the end of phase 2b.

Not one flake of the varieties of rhyolite previously described refits onto any of these pieces. Thus they represent three mediocre *Chivateros* bifaces damaged by early accidents; all evidence suggests they were put aside by a youth, along with a fragment of a good-quality foliate piece made by one of his elders or collected at another workshop. Because we were not certain that these pieces are part of this site (i.e., were made or collected by the same people that occupied the workshop), they were not considered in the economic study presented below.

Conclusions on Pale Rhyolite Bifacial Knapping

These conclusions are more understandable in table form. Tables 48–50 summarize the results of our detailed analysis of the pale rhyolite varieties for each concentration and for the number of pieces estimated in each case.

Table 45. Number and weight of large, medium, and type 2a flakes of pale rhyolite, subvariety *morada*, in concentration B.

Concentration B:	Pale rhyolite, subvariety *morada*					
	Large		Medium		Total	
Type 2a flakes	n	W (g)	n	W (g)	n	W (g)
elongated and skewed	1	4			1	4
thick	4	24	1	3	5	27
cortical	11	60	26	40	37	100
Kombewa						
total					43	131
all flakes	36	166	110	160	146	326
ratio 2a flakes/all flakes					29.5%	40.2%
Number and dimensions of the largest flakes: n = 3; class 55–59 mm						

Table 46. Number and weight of large, medium, and type 2a flakes of pale rhyolite, "miscellaneous 1" subvarieties, in concentration B.

Concentration B:	Pale rhyolite, miscellaneous 1					
	Large		Medium		Total	
Type 2a flakes	n	W (g)	n	W (g)	n	W (g)
elongated and skewed						
thick						
cortical	2	7	6	6	8	13
Kombewa						
total					8	13
all flakes	3	9	36	39	39	48
ratio 2a flakes/all flakes					20.5%	27.1%

Green Tuff

Green volcanic tuff was knapped in much lesser amounts than pale rhyolite. Its presence is significant only in concentration D, where its extent is clearly different from that of rhyolite (Figures 24 and 25). Elsewhere it is represented only by small numbers of flakes, whose presence is often difficult to explain, and a few rejected pieces (Table 51).

Concentration D

This material includes 95 large and 446 medium flakes (541 total) weighing 991.8 g (Table 52). Of these flakes, 57 are type 2a (31 thick, 24 cortical, 2 clear Kombewa) weighing 274.8 g, or 10.5 percent of the total by number and 27.7 percent by weight. The type 2a flakes thus represent a rather small proportion, perhaps indicating that not all the pieces were knapped beginning with phase 2a at this workshop; possibly phase 2 was begun where the material was extracted, as was observed at the Pampa de los Fósiles 12, unit 104 quarry site (Chauchat et al 1992:109–125). However, this can also be explained by the fact that green tuff seems to exist in the form of plaques whose cleavage planes, barely patinated and just slightly coarse-grained, are not recognized as cortex.

Table 47. Number and weight of large, medium, and type 2a flakes of pale rhyolite, "miscellaneous 2" subvarieties, in concentration B.

Concentration B:	Pale rhyolite, miscellaneous 2					
	Large		Medium		Total	
Type 2a flakes	n	W (g)	n	W (g)	n	W (g)
elongated and skewed						
thick	1	5			1	5
cortical	3	16	1	2	4	18
Kombewa						
total					5	23
all flakes	7	35	24	30	31	65
ratio 2a flakes/all flakes					16.1%	35.4%

Taking this uncertainty into account, the absolute number of flakes alone suggests the knapping of several pieces, *a priori* between 3 and 10 indicated by the tests. The two Kombewa flakes, which do not refit together, suggest one or two rough-outs on large flake blanks.

The spectrum of large flakes (Figure 32, no. 3) shows none greater than 65 mm in maximal dimension, but four in the class just below. These values are similar to the tests of medium dimension on flake and plaque blanks. Therefore the number of pieces knapped is estimated at between four and eight; knapping accidents, which will be discussed below, could have increased the number of medium thin ordinary flakes because of reworking of pieces fractured at the end of phase 2b or the beginning of phase 3.

At first, it is practically impossible to distinguish variants of the green tuff material, since the intensity of patination is more noticeable than the variation of the material in non-patinated pieces. Few refits were found, 16 fracture refits and 12 flake re-

The Raw Material Varieties

fits, showing a significant dispersion. However, it is true that several hundred small flakes (fragments of thin flakes, distal and proximal ends, etc., all less than 2 cm) were not reexamined from this perspective because of lack of time.

The persistent but unsuccessful search for certain refits shows that some large flakes were exported and others were "intrusive." An example of the latter situation is the large flat subcircular Kombewa (or cortical) flake 6 cm in diameter, which was isolated in BL28 (previously presented as part of the tool assemblage) (Figure 15, no. 5). In the same way, several retouched or utilized tools of green tuff were displaced (refit found between concentrations B and D; one burnt flake; other tools impossible to refit). It is thus apparent that green tuff was the preferred material for certain tools, particularly a few non-retouched "knives."

Five fragments of foliate pieces or points made from green tuff were found in concentration D, including two in two sub-fragments originating from at least four pieces.

No. 28-29 forms a large median-apical fragment of a foliate piece broken during phase 3. The first fracture, at 21 mm from the point, probably occurred when an overly deep flake was removed. The plane of the median fracture has a fine nibbling retouch along the entire length (32 mm) of its dihedral edge (75°–80°) formed with one of the smooth faces of the body of the piece. One retouch flake that refits onto the piece is not the last; it is followed by small adjacent removals. It may have been removed after the first fracture, but this is not certain.

No. 46 (Figure 48, no. 4), a basal fragment of a foliate piece in phase 3, is of medium quality. The fracture is a typical "orthogonal" or "perverse" fracture (Crabtree 1972:82–83), which occurred when an overly deep flake was removed. The technological stage, material, and dimensions of this piece are the same as the previous one (not illustrated). These two fragments could have come from the same piece, separated by a median fragment of around 3 cm; the complete piece would have been around 13 cm long.

No. 31 is an apical fragment of a foliate point of medium quality. Its fracture is curious, as if the piece received a shock directly onto its face. Such a fracture could either be voluntary, or the result of an atypical debitage fracture, or the result of the

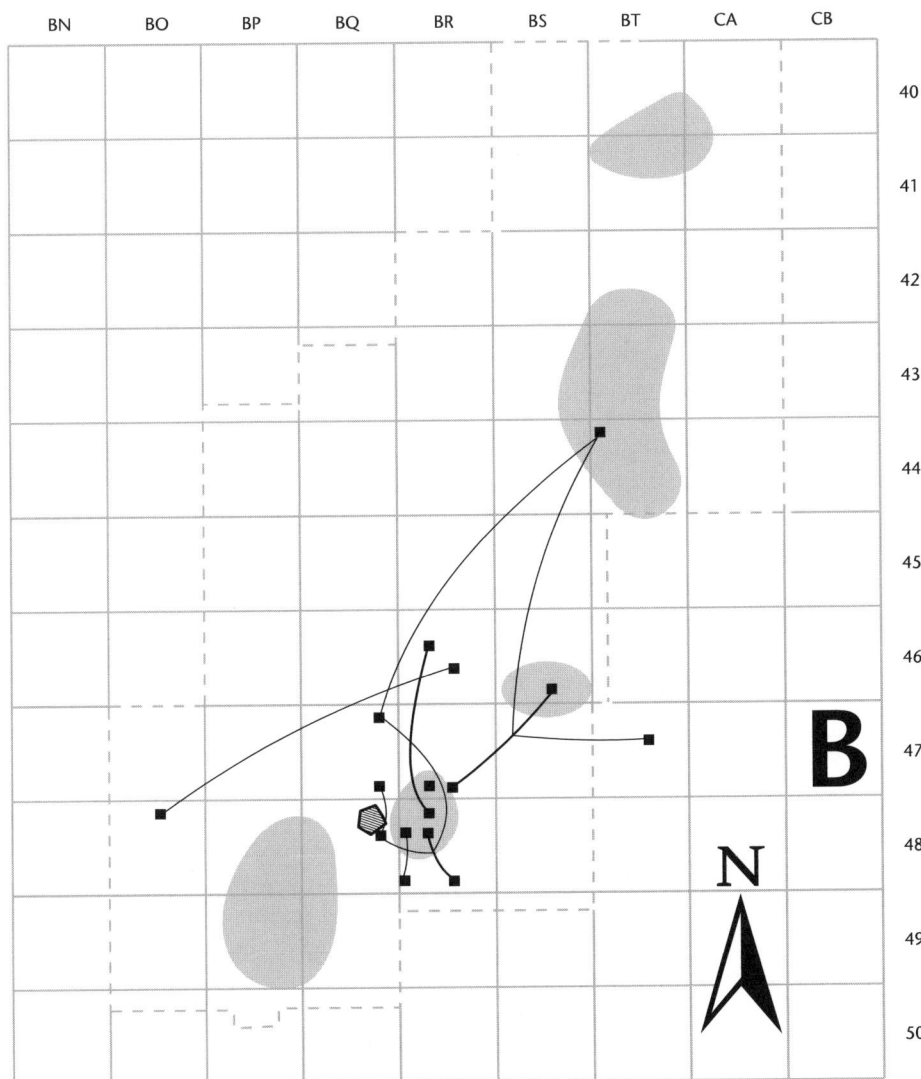

Figure 45. Spatial distribution of fracture and debitage refits of dark *morada* rhyolite (squares) in concentration B.

object falling onto rocks. The dihedral edge between the fracture plane and one of the faces forms a bevel of around 40° and shows fine nibbling removals. This fragment could also be associated with fragment no. 46 and a missing median fragment; the whole piece would have been 12–14 cm long.

No. 106 is the apical fragment of a point at the end of phase 3. It has one possible removal by pressure flaking on one edge. However, this fragment results from a percussion accident; it is the distal fragment of an overly thick flake that was overshot, thus removing the entire tip of the piece.

No. 32-103 is a basal fragment, with a broken and missing stem, and a middle fragment. The two form the basal half of a point at the beginning of phase 4 (Figure 48, no. 3). The stem undoubtedly broke first by flexing. The medio-basal and median fractures have the characteristics of voluntary fractures by direct shock onto the face. These two first fragments are associated with two other fragments, no. 10-105, found far away at knapping locality B4; they form the upper half of a point broken at the beginning of phase 4. The apical fracture has a small lip that is compatible with a knapping accident, but the median fracture is more strongly characteristic of a voluntary fracture. These two latter fragments show a very discrete raw material variation within the ensemble of green tuff, which was also observed on the two first fragments. It has small, barely visible white veins, while the majority of green tuff has very pronounced red dots. The only other piece of this white-veined material is the small basal fragment from BH30 in concentration D.

The history of this point can thus be inferred. During its knapping in concentration D, it first lost its stem at the beginning of phase 4. Immediately after this accident, it was voluntarily broken (because of irritation or aggravation?). Its short apical half was then shortly reworked, perhaps by a young knapper, in concentration B, where it again broke, and its two last fragments were dispersed.

Five other accidents shortened some pieces in the process of fabrication:

1) no. 107 (BJ29) is an overshot flake that removed the extremity of a piece with a triangular section in stage 3, resulting in a loss of 10–15 mm in length.

2) No. 36 is a large overshot flake that removed a thin base, or a still wide foliate piece, from a slightly plano-convex preform in phase 2b, resulting in a loss of 25–30 mm in length.

3) A large flake in phase 2a, under a partial Kombewa flake, removed a 40-mm-wide base at 18 mm from the initial extremity. The piece was only slightly shortened but clearly narrowed by at least 15–18 mm. The refitting of succeeding flakes shows that knapping was continued after the piece was probably turned end for end to compensate for the change in outline caused by this overshot flake (Figure 48, no. 2).

4) No. 41 is the extremity of a rather thick base (phase 2b), 26 mm wide, broken by flexing or tearing during knapping, resulting in a loss of 15 mm in the length of the preform.

Table 48. Summary of knapping bifacial activities: varieties of pale rhyolite present in several concentrations.

ferruginosa	One large piece in A. Two or three medium to large pieces, including one broken in B. Around a dozen flakes rejected in C, and one in D.
naranjilla	One piece in B, broken in phase 3.
ferruginosa/naranjilla	Four to six knapped pieces, including two broken.
puntillada/floreada	Three to five medium pieces, including two broken.
micro-puntillada	In D, two pieces, including one broken and the other rejected or finished but short. One flake and one fragment of a piece rejected in B.
arenosa	The knapping in D of a small to medium piece, broken or reworked in C. Flakes rejected in B.
linea-rosada/azul	Two or three pieces in C. One piece in B. Flakes rejected in D and A.
porosa rosada	Two flakes and one fragment of a reworked and rebroken point in A.
porosa blanca	Two or three fragments of reworked and rebroken pieces.

Table 49. Summary of knapping bifacial activities: varieties found only in concentration D.

rosada-verde	A 12-cm-long biconvex piece, slightly thick, in phase 1b, then damaged and abandoned (Figure 26).
gris-fina	Remains from phase 2b-3 of a well-made, probably finished foliate piece.
colorada	A damaged and abandoned *Chivateros* biface. A mediocre small knapped piece (exported?) A few flakes from B seem to have been rejected in D.

Table 50. Summary of knapping bifacial activities: varieties found only in concentration B.

granito	A medium-sized broken piece, reworked and rebroken (Figure 30, no. 1).
gris-violacea	One small plaque and one short exported piece.
salmón	The knapping from stage 2a of a small broken point.
crema-rayada	One or two exported pieces.
morada	Two exported pieces.

Table 51. Contribution of green volcanic tuff to the knapping waste products of the different concentrations, according to Tables 13, 16, 19, and 22.

Concentration	Count	Ratio to whole by count (%)	Weight (g)	Ratio to whole by weight (%)
A	9	2.9	16	2.3
B	6	1.2	13	1.6
C	1290	59.8	1227	27.6
D	27	0.5	50	1

The Raw Material Varieties

5) An unnumbered flake, similar to (4), found in BH30 is a little shorter; 23 mm wide; loss of length 12 mm.

Considering the difficulty of sorting the mass of knapping remains into raw material varieties and the paucity of distinctive features on the objects themselves, the high number of fracture refits, along with the few debitage refits, can be considered a success. In the interest of maintaining a readable plan (Figure 49), the fracture refits were only mapped if they contributed to a debitage refit. The plan most evidently shows the small number of refits starting from, or finishing at, knapping localities recognized by the presence of green tuff (D1, D2, and D3 in Figure 25), relative to those terminating beyond their limits. In any case, there seems to be a rather distinct group of flake connections starting from D2. It is more difficult to explain the group of five fragments in D1 (plus one other object in proximity) that are linked not only to objects from beyond the limits of this locality in a southwest direction, but also to objects from locality D1 and to another possible group from D3. Finally, the most numerous and dense concentration of objects is found beyond the limits of the knapping localities, between D1 and D2. It is thus possible that this last group is the result of an evacuation from the east of D2 and that the fragment from BL30 is included. This possibility is not sufficient to explain the whole configuration unless we accept that the groupings visible in D1 and D3 are accidental, which cannot be totally excluded. If these groupings are not accidental, there must have been movement of unfinished bifacial pieces among these three knapping localities. This pattern would indicate at a minimum that an individual knapper changed places, at a maximum that several persons present at the same time circulated around the central refuse pit.

Concentration B

In concentration B, 7 large, 6 medium, and 14 small flakes constitute a very small series. Under no conditions could these represent the knapping remains of a whole piece. We summarize the series in Table 53.

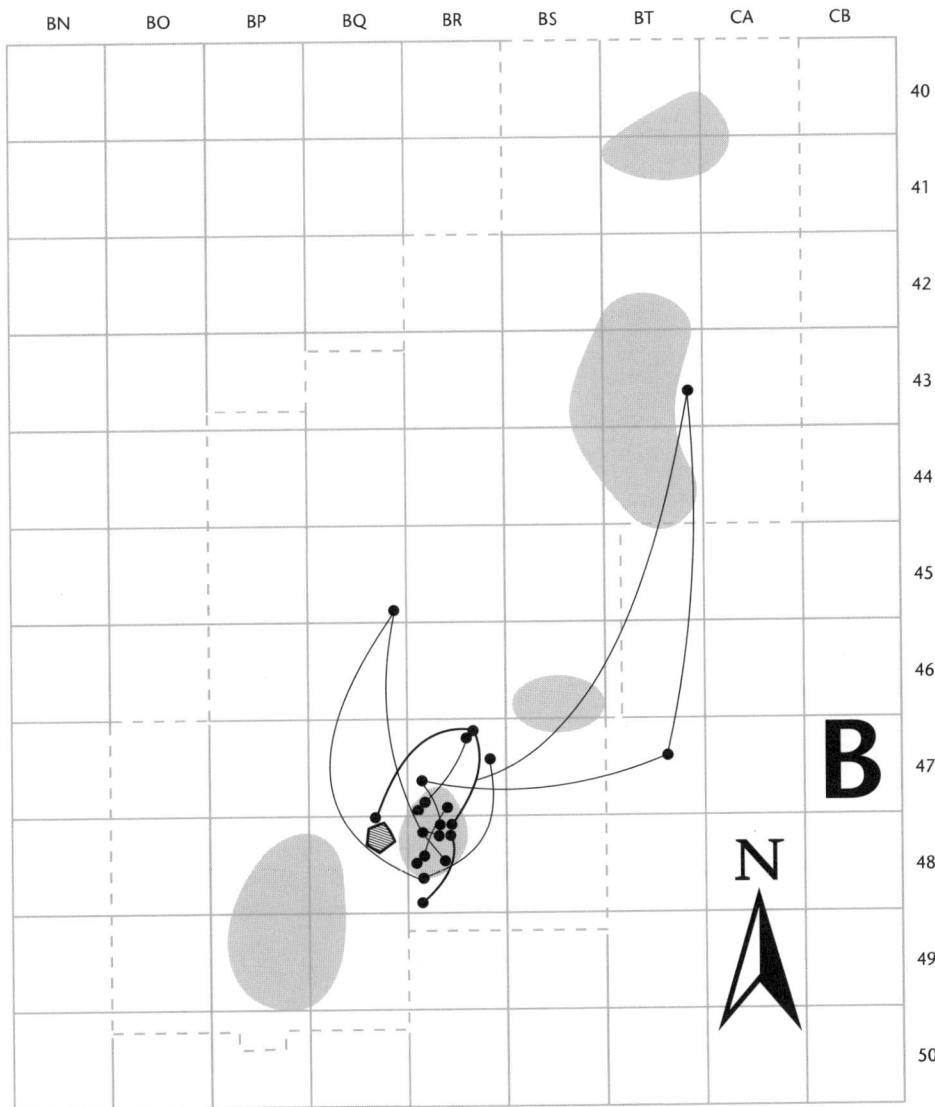

Figure 46. Spatial distribution of fracture and debitage refits of pale *morada* rhyolite (dots) in concentration B.

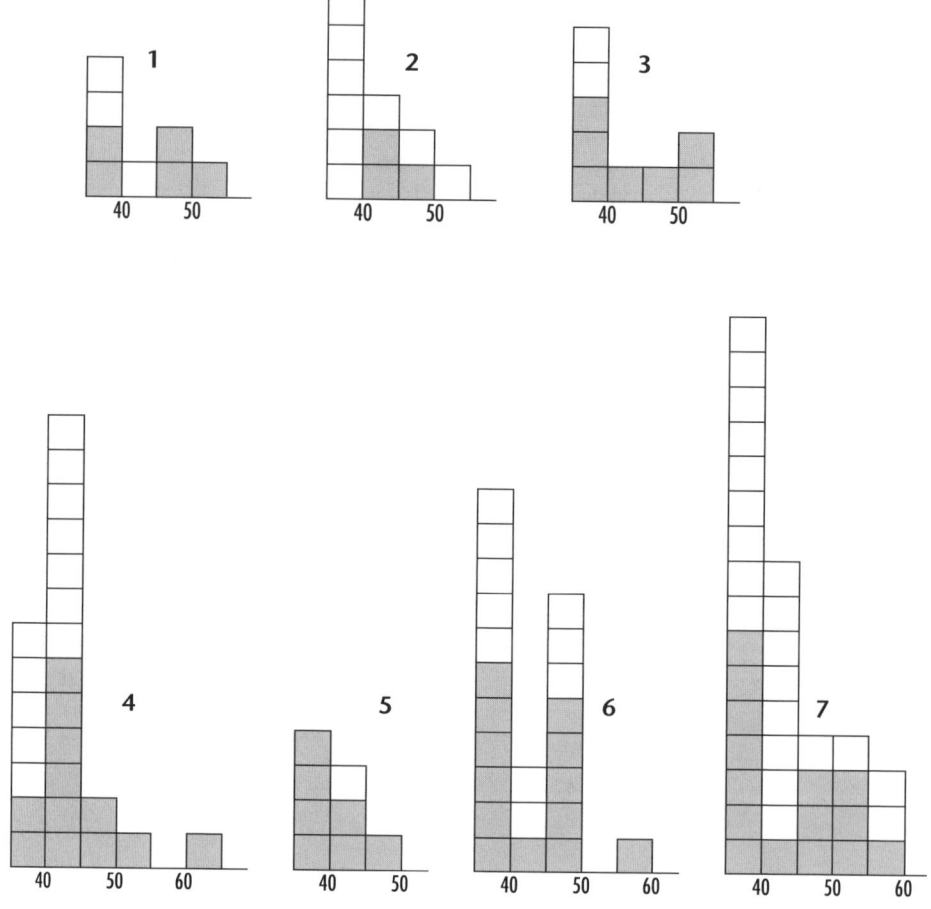

Figure 47. Histograms of large flakes and type 2a flakes. Concentration D: 1, *rosada verde* rhyolite; 2, *gris fina* rhyolite; 3, *colorada* rhyolite. Concentration B: 4, *granito* rhyolite; 5, *gris-violácea* rhyolite; 6, *crema/rayada* rhyolite; 7, *morada* rhyolite.

The small group of flakes from this concentration can be subdivided according to the presence or absence of red spots, as we saw above. None of the small flakes, which yielded one refit, nor two medium ones from the end of phase 3 have these spots. The remaining 11 large and medium flakes do have them and thus appear to have been introduced into concentration B from D. These findings reinforce the following observations on flakes that were considered to be *a posteriori* tools and treated as such in Chapter 3, "Lithic Analysis":

- a large distal fragment of a flake with one sharp edge, found on the margin of B (CD40), which refits with its other two fragments found in D (mesial in BN28, proximal in BK29). This set is illustrated in Figure 15, no. 8;
- another isolated distal fragment was found burned in BT47;
- a large mesial fragment from BQ46 has a probable voluntary fracture, indicating its value as a tool (Figure 15, no. 3);
- a type 2a flake with one utilized edge, which is thus a tool that was abandoned in B; moreover, its color and cortex are slightly different from the rest of green tuff;
- a few remaining flakes that are also dispersed and probably intrusive; red spots indicate they originated in concentration D.

Whatever the case, these 11 flakes of green tuff from concentration B are too few to influence the quantitative estimations presented above for the green tuff of concentration D.

Other concentrations

In concentrations A and C, very few flakes of green tuff were found, 6 in A and 9 in C (including an isolated partial Kombewa flake, no. 62, Figure 48, no. 1). These flakes are dispersed over several meter-squares in each of the concentrations. They very probably result from some sort of unexplained rejection.

Minor Rejections of Flakes

One of the phenomena most difficult to interpret at Pampa de los Fósiles 14, unit 1, is the outlying spatial distribution of small numbers of flakes, usually fewer than 10, relative to most flakes of the same raw material. We briefly alluded to this situation above in the context of the diverse varieties of raw materials. More rarely, these are bifacial pieces or fragments found displaced over vast distances from their supposed knapping location. In order to evaluate this phenomenon better, we will systematically examine each case.

First, it is important to understand clearly the nature of this phenomenon. When classifying raw materials, particularly when

The Raw Material Varieties

identifying diverse varieties of pale rhyolite, we observed that groups of several dozens or even hundreds of debitage flakes belonging to these varieties were usually spatially distributed within one or two knapping localities. However, small numbers of flakes unmistakably of the same material were sometimes found in a different knapping locality or even in a distant concentration. Detailed analyses of these raw material varieties demonstrated that these minority groups of outlying flakes belonged to the main group, since refits often existed between two localities.

Based on these data, several interpretations can be proposed. The first that comes to mind is that a bifacial piece underwent a short phase of knapping at a location other than where the greater part of the work was performed; refits of some of the flakes concerned, which are easier to find among small numbers of objects, would confirm this theory. It would obviously further our understanding of the history of site occupation to identify the knapping phase during which this event took place and determine by the same method if work had resumed at the location where the majority group of flakes was found. If no refits are found among the minority group of flakes, they must be sought among the flakes of the majority group. Other than supposing that the piece itself was carried back and forth between locations while in the process of fabrication, the only other possible explanation is that flakes were thrown or transported from one location to the other during or after knapping. When considering a very small number of flakes, it is pertinent to ask whether they may have served as tools. This is very likely for the Paiján complex (and must be true for other prehistoric cultures), where it has been observed that numerous unmodified, or little modified, flakes were used as naturally backed knives, *tranchets*, or even simple utilized flakes (the "*a posteriori* tools" of our typology: Chauchat et al. 1992:55–57). Effective diagnostic clues for evaluating this possibility are the dimensions of the object, the regularity of its edges, and the presence of use-wear (chips or notches) on the edges. One may also analyze the presence and disposition of abrupt facets that can serve as a back, which may be produced by flake butt, accidental or intentional fracture, flake facet, or cortex.

The minority groups of flakes from Pampa de los Fósiles 14, unit 1, are shown in Table 54, along with the location of their majority groups. In addition, we mapped some of these movements on the plans of the workshop (Figures 50, 51, 52). Following are various interpretations of the phenomenon.

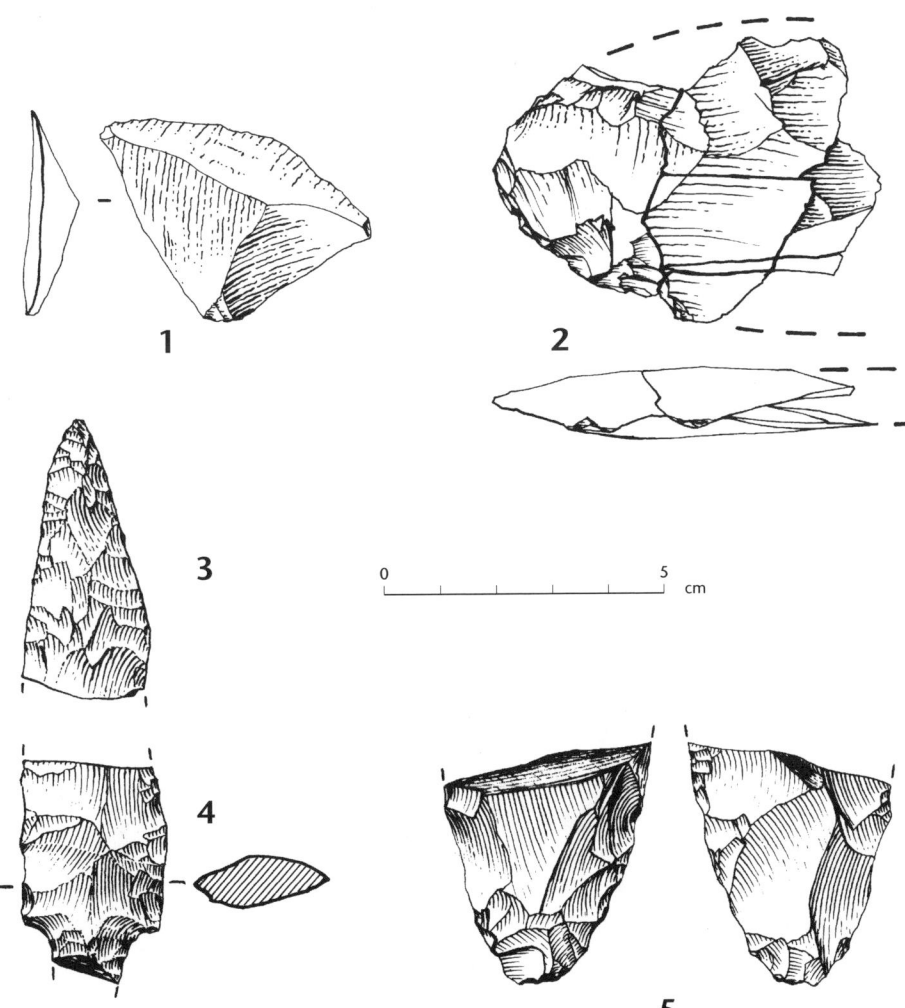

Figure 48. Green tuff objects: **1**, partial Kombewa flake; **2**, refit of an overshot flake and three other flakes onto the base of a biface in phase 2; **3**, apical fragment (in two fragments, no. 19-105); **4**, basal fragment (in two fragments, no. 32-103), very probably from the same point broken during fabrication; **5**, base of a foliate bifacial piece. (Drawings 1 and 2 by M. Reduron; 3–5 by C. Chauchat.)

Reworking a Broken Piece

A half-piece of green tuff was first knapped in concentration D, then reworked in B, where it was rebroken (Figure 50, no. 1).

Displacement during Fabrication

The knapping of one piece of *arenosa* rhyolite in concentration D was continued in C, where it finally broke. It is possible, but less probable, that, like the preceding piece, this was a reworked fragment (Figure 52, no. 2).

One piece of *linea-rosada* rhyolite first knapped in B was probably finished in A (Figure 51, no. 5).

Recuperation of Flakes with a Technical Objective

A few large flakes of green tuff with red dots were collected in concentration D, then transported to B; we can consider them tools (Figure 50, no. 3).

Eight large flakes of *linea-azul* rhyolite, without refits among them, were dispersed between B2 and B3; they very probably came from C (punctuated zone in Figure 51).

Flakes Displaced without an Apparent Reason

- A few flakes of green tuff from concentration D in A and C (Figure 50, no. 2).

- A total of 12 very dispersed flakes of *ferruginosa* rhyolite from A, B, or D in C, without refits among them.

- Complex displacement of *linea-rosada/azul* rhyolite from C in all directions: a few flakes in D (Figure 51, no. 1); 9 flakes in A (no. 2); refit of a fragment in B2 (no. 4); refit of one flake from C to a flake from B (at the limit of the concentration of the 8 large flakes already described), and it onto a flake on the margin of A (Figure 51, no. 3).

- Two flakes of *granito* rhyolite from B in D4 (one downstream in the gully) (Figure 52, no. 3).

- A flake of *crema/rayada* rhyolite from B rejected outside, in the direction of D, around 5 m from this concentration (Figure 52, no. 4).

- Seven dispersed flakes of *arenosa* rhyolite from D4 rejected in B; two of them form the first and last flake of a refit half-shell, the other five come from D4 (Figure 52, no. 2).

- A fragment of a piece of micro-*puntillada* rhyolite from D4 (no. 72) found to the west of B2 may be associated with fragment no. 104, but lacks a true refit (other refits and associations exist between these two zones: see Figure 13); one flake to the east of B2 refits with a series of flakes from D4 (Figure 52, no. 5).

We did not illustrate the case of *ferruginosa* rhyolite because of its particularity. This material was knapped in D4 (probably phase 2a), A, and B5. A group of around 12 flakes with no refits among them was found very dispersed in concentration C. A much more intensive search for refits would have been necessary to determine the knapping locality of origin.

It is difficult if not impossible to attribute all these rejected flakes to rational behavior. Perhaps some are the work of children at play; others may have been transported for a purpose that we cannot determine from the morphology of the flakes. Whatever the case, they testify to the complex history of the site even though it was only briefly occupied, and they seem to confirm that all the concentrations were occupied simultaneously. The three plans in Figure 50, 51, and 52 synthesize the relations among flakes, or minority groups of flakes, and the knapping locations (majority groups) of assumed origin. The three plans clearly show that the majority of flake connections follow a diagonal orientation between B and D, as illustrated by the green tuff and the *granito*, *crema/rayada*, *arenosa* and *micro-puntillada* rhyolite varieties. However, the *linea-rosada/linea-azul* variety shows a different behavior, being knapped principally in C and secondarily in B. Another apparent tendency is that concentration B seems more a recipient than a donor of the minority groups. However, detecting and describing this fact is not the same as finding an explanation for it.

Other Bifacially Knapped Materials

Gray Volcanic Tuff

A small series of flakes found in concentration B at the end of phases 2b and 3 indicates the knapping of a point that was probably terminated and exported. It was made from pale gray volcanic tuff. These flakes are distributed over the entire surface of

Table 52. Number and weight of large, medium, and type 2a flakes of green tuff in concentration D.

Concentration D:	Green tuff					
	Large		Medium		Total	
Type 2a flakes	n	W (g)	n	W (g)	n	W (g)
elongated and skewed						
thick	23	170	8	25	31	196
cortical	9	38	15	25	24	63
Kombewa	1	14	1	2	2	17
total					57	276
all flakes	95	429	446	562	541	992
ratio 2a flakes/all flakes					10.5%	27.8%
Number and dimensions of the largest flakes: n = 4; class 60–64 mm						

Table 53. Number and weight of large, medium, and type 2a flakes of green tuff in concentration B.

Concentration B:	Green tuff					
	Large		Medium		Total	
Type 2a flakes	n	W (g)	n	W (g)	n	W (g)
elongated and skewed						
thick	2	11	1	3	3	14
cortical	2	12			2	12
Kombewa						
total					5	26
all flakes	7	36	6	9	13	45
ratio 2a flakes/all flakes					38.5%	57.8%

The Raw Material Varieties

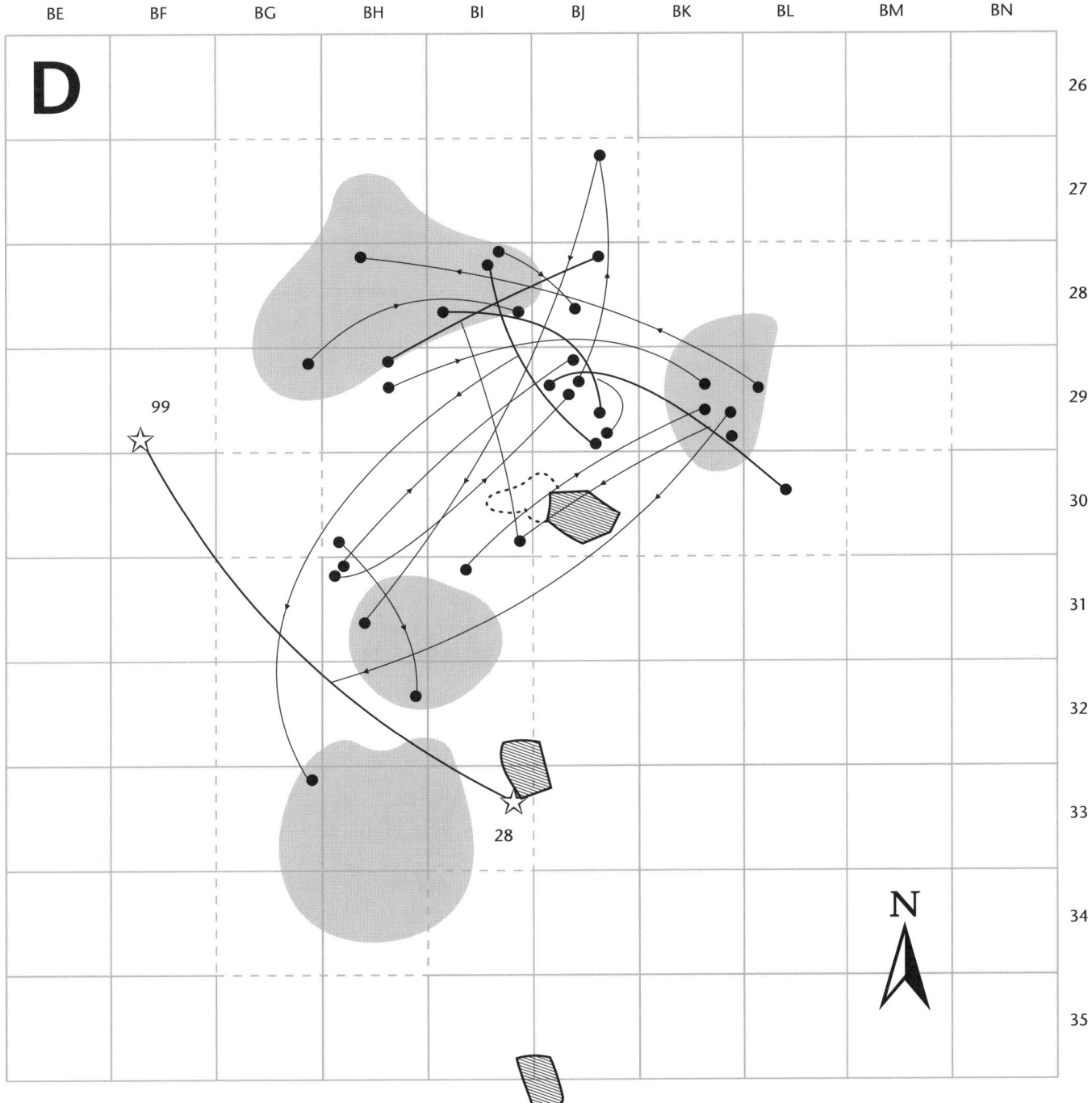

Figure 49. Spatial distribution of green tuff refits (dots) in concentration D; the stars correspond to piece no. 28–99. Only the fracture refits that contributed to debitage refits were figured.

concentration B and even extend slightly beyond its limits toward the margins of A and C. Actually they were separated from the knapping remains of unifaces made from the same pale gray volcanic tuff and which have similar morphologies (see the study of unifaces below). The origin of this material is perhaps close to that of the green tuff, since it is the only other abundant material in the green tuff workshops located a few kilometers to the north; the neighboring hills are formed of stratified volcanic tuffs (cinerites) of different sorts.

We did not look for refits among these flakes, nor did we generate a composition table for them. The absence of type 2a flakes proves that the biface arrived in the form of a foliate piece at least in phase 2a if not 2b. It also possibly indicates that it was exported as a finished point, although we have no proof. The spatial distribution of the flakes is given in Figure 53. A concentration of flakes buried by trampling and by the placement of the knapper was detected at knapping locality B3. These extend slightly into square BT47. There is no evidence against this being the knapping origin of these flakes, which are nonetheless largely dispersed.

This group of flakes, which was very difficult to separate from a larger set that also included uniface knapping flakes, and others whose morphology prevents classifying them into one of the categories pose an interpretative problem. We must not forget that bifacial knapping flakes can be produced from the manufacture of unifaces. This production can occur when an overly thick preform must be thinned by a series of inverse removals in order to form a striking platform more inclined toward the superior face than would be the natural, inferior face of the blank. This production can also occur when the bulb is removed from a flake blank. Thus we cannot dismiss the possibility that this group of flakes resulted from fabricating a uniface. We will examine this hypothesis in more detail in our presentation of this category of tools.

Point Fragments of Exogenous Materials

We identified three projectile point fragments made from particular materials that are clearly not fragments of pieces produced at the site. Rather, they were introduced after fabrication and probably after an episode of utilization.

One short mesial-apical fragment of a Paiján point that was apparently finished was made from rhyolite, similar to the *granito* variety but yellow-green in color and rather fine-grained (no. 81, from BQ47). This fragment is 18 mm long, 12 mm wide, and 6.5 mm thick. Its section is plano-convex (Figure 54, no. 3). The two fractures have pronounced lips, produced by flexing with a notable axial compression. They were certainly not produced during knapping and are characteristic of projectile accidents. Thus this is a point that was broken during utilization, then brought back to the site in the prey that it had penetrated. It is important to note that the edges of this point were clearly blunted before the fracture occurred, which suggests that the final step in finishing a Paiján point was to blunt its edges to reduce their sharpness. We have already noted this polishing of Paiján point edges observed on fragments found in living sites rather than in workshops.

One basal fragment of a Paiján point that was apparently finished or even reworked was made from a material that resembles a gray-red quartzite with a medium grain. This is fragment no. 79, found in BQ46 (Figure 54, no. 1). It is 50 mm long, 25 mm wide with typical small angular barbs, and 7.5–8.5 mm thick. Its section is plano-convex. The stem is 19 mm long and 8 mm wide at its middle. Its shape is somewhat uvula-like. The finishing by pressure retouch is very clear. Curiously, one of the edges is clearly blunted, while the other has a small series of removals by pressure retouch on top of blunting that is identical to that on the other edge, thus removing this blunting along 2 cm just below the fracture. It is possible that this mesial fracture is relatively fresh, but it is dubious that it resulted from this ultimate pressure retouch of the body of the piece. It thus seems that the point fragment was reintroduced into the site and then reworked as an exercise, or that a larger fragment was voluntarily broken after an exercise.

Piece no. 92, found in BP46 (Figure 54, no. 2), is an upper fragment of a Paiján point that was apparently finished. It was made from dark blue tuff found nowhere else on the site. A reexamination of all dark tuff flakes revealed only one tiny pressure retouch flake that is definitely made from this material. It was found very close by, in BP45 (Figure 54, no. 4 and Figure 55). Indeed, one of the edges of the piece was partially reworked by a few pressure retouch removals; the other is blunted. The apical fracture has a short (3.5 mm) pseudo-burin spall that is characteristic of a projectile accident. The mesial fracture is simple, with no notable lip. As with the former fragment, this seems to be a Paiján point that was broken during use and brought back to the site, where it was reworked by pressure retouch before being rebroken.

Figure 55 shows that these objects are not distributed over the entire surface of the unit. On the contrary, they are found in a rather restricted space in concentration B and form a clear trail that seems to begin in knapping locality B4.

Conclusions on Bifacial Knapping Activities

Acquiring Raw Material

We distinguished two varieties of green tuff, one variety of gray tuff, and nearly 15 varieties of pale rhyolite. It therefore appears that lithic raw materials for fabricating Paiján points at this group of workshops were gathered at several sources, rather than by systematically exploiting a particular outcrop.

As we have already stated, an outcrop of green tuff has not yet been located. Nonetheless, this material was largely dominant,

Table 54. Minor rejections or displacements of flakes away from the knapping localities.

Raw material	Location	Rejection or displacement
ferruginosa	A and B5	12 flakes in C, very dispersed, no refits
		12 flakes in D, very dispersed, with a few refits
		possible refits of 2 flakes and 2 fragments of one flake.
		possible beginning of phase A or rejection.
puntillada/floreada	mostly in B2–B3, minority in A	2 very thin medium flakes in D (wind?)
		a few thin flakes in C, but uncertain distinction from *linea-rosada*.
micro-*puntillada*	D4	1 flake in B2
		1 fragment of piece (no. 72) in B2 but refit with a flake from D4
arenosa	D4 (57 flakes)	later knapping phase in C: 9 flakes followed by the breaking of the piece.
		12 flakes in B, with no refits between them but at least 2 with flakes from D
linea-rosada/azul	2 knapped pieces in C1 and C2; 1 piece in B3/B4	7 flakes in D (2 refits with C)
		16 flakes in A (1 refit with C, 1 with B)
		refit of a mesial fragment from B with one proximal fragment from C
granito	B2–B3	2 flakes from D, 1 refitted with flakes from B
crema/rayada	B2	1 flake in D, integrated in a refit of flakes from B
green tuff	D2	a few large flakes in B, one fragment of a piece reworked in B.

The Raw Material Varieties

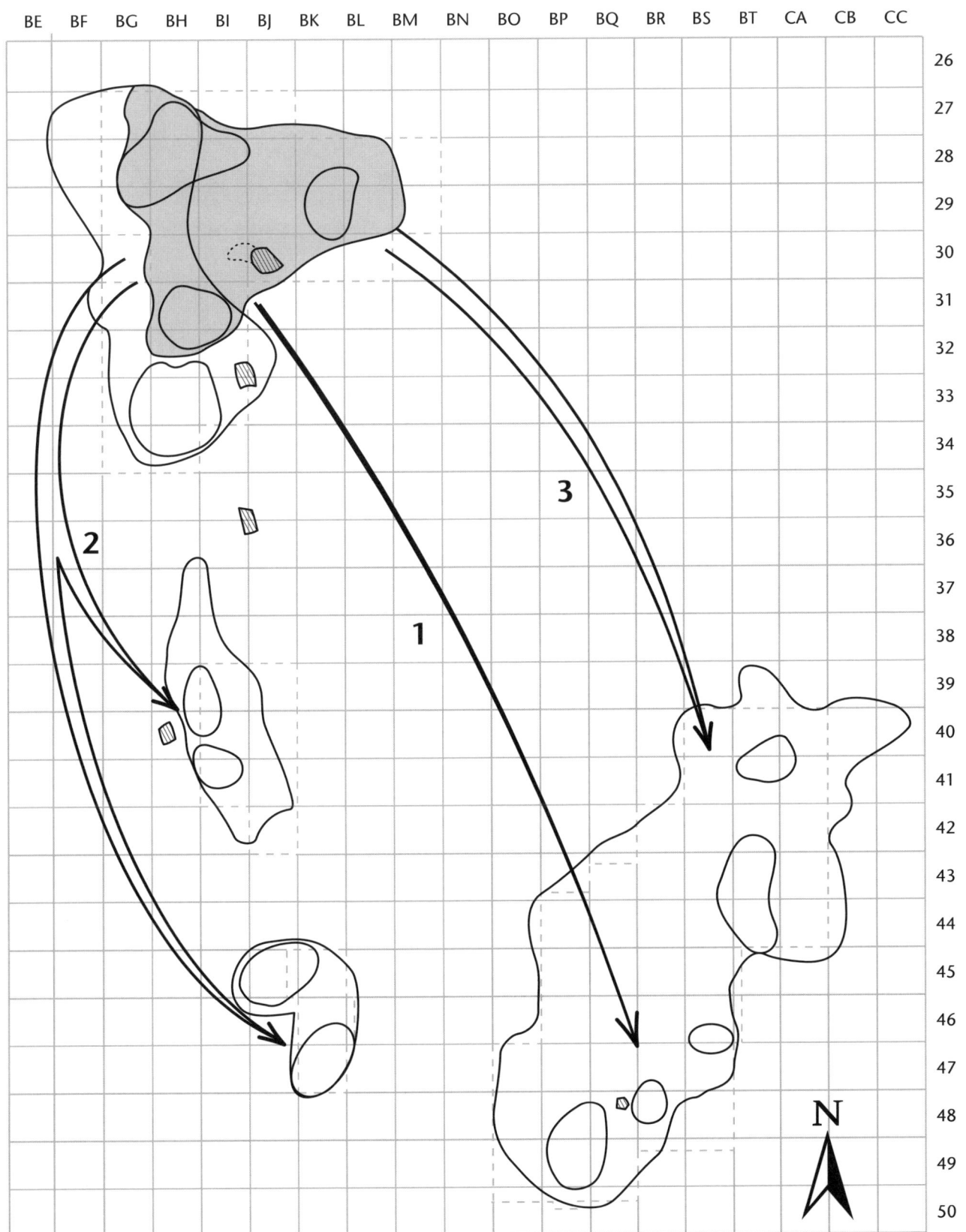

Figure 50. Minority rejections of green tuff flakes. The area of concentration D from which the green tuff comes is shaded. 1, reworking in B4 of a bifacial piece fragment broken during knapping in D; 2, rejected (?) groups of flakes in concentrations C and A; 3, transport of flakes that served as tools to concentration B.

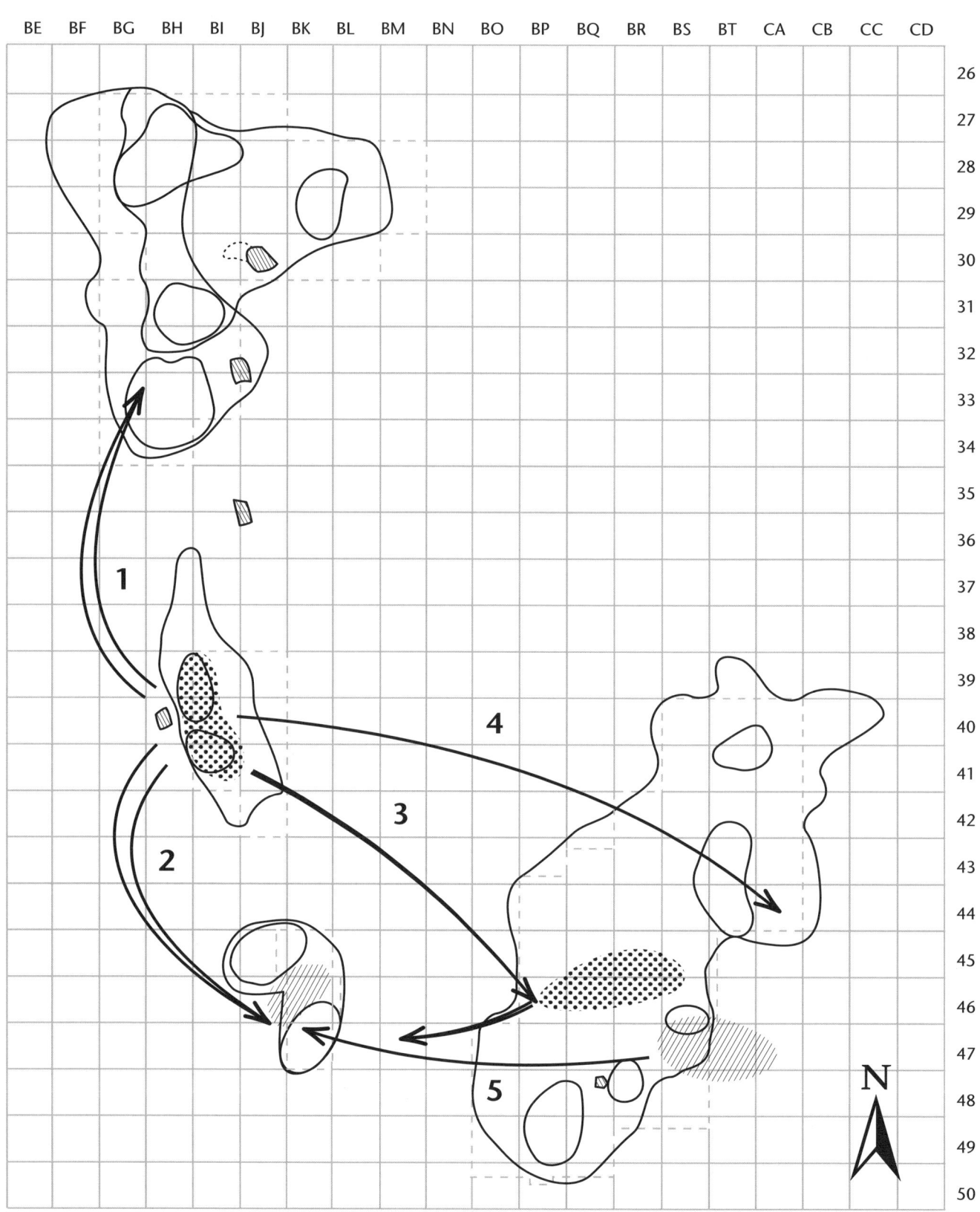

Figure 51. Minority rejections of *linea-rosada/azul* rhyolite flakes. Cross-hatched area: knapping area of *linea-rosada/linea-azul*. Hatched lines: *linea-rosada*. Dots: dispersed *linea-azul* large flakes. **1** and **2**, rejections of flakes toward concentrations A and D; **3**, refit of a flake from C and a flake from B onto a flake from A; **4**, refit of a flake fragment in B; **5**, transport of a piece made from *linea-rosada*, first knapped in B3 and then finished in A.

The Raw Material Varieties

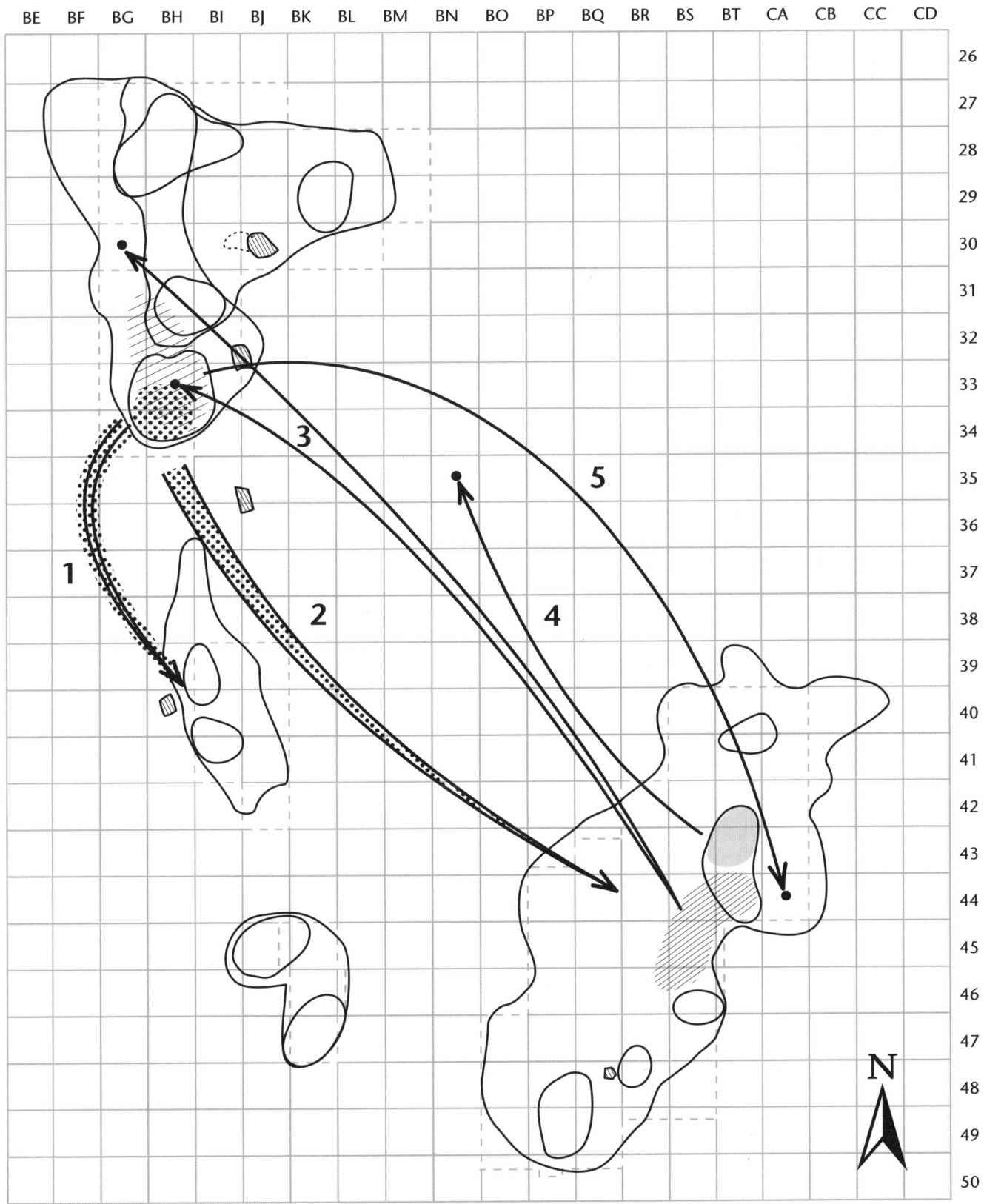

Figure 52. Minority rejections of *arenosa* (dots), *granito* (closely hatched lines), *crema/rayada* (shaded), and micro-*puntillada* (wide hatched lines) pale rhyolites. **1**, *arenosa*: knapping and breaking of a piece in D4, one of the fragments reworked in C; **2**, *arenosa*: rejection of flakes in B; **3**, *granito*: rejection of two flakes in D; **4**, *crema/rayada*: rejection of a flake from B2 north toward D; **5**, micro-*puntillada*: rejection of a flake from D4 in B2.

sometimes as large flakes, among some workshops located a few kilometers north of site 14, unit 1, where we also find pale gray tuff of good quality. This evidence suggests that the source of green tuff is not very far, even if after several surveys we have not found its outcrop, which may have been quite localized.

On the other hand, we have much more knowledge of the outcrops of pale rhyolite. Most of the rhyolite worked at site 14, unit 1, comes from site 125. On two slopes of an easily accessible ridge at this site is a long extension of exposed rock where raw material can be extracted. All evidence shows that this is what the Paiján people did. Within this vast rhyolite outcrop, we observe variations in the nature of the raw material—density and dimensions of spots, fissures, and veins; types of inclusions (pyrites, feldspars, etc.); and texture and color.

Although we could have expected a generous harvest of rhyolite from one good-quality outcrop (a good day's work could yield 10 to 20 *Chivateros* bifaces), the Paijanenses of site 14 were content to collect one to three blanks of a rhyolite variety, i.e., the material from a specific quarrying location. From 20 to 26 bifaces of pale rhyolite were brought to the site, including 3 or 4 of poor quality that were soon rejected. If the rock surface is free of flaws from extraction and previous knapping activities, it is possible to extract small blocks that have been loosened by fissures created by surface exposure; ease of acquisition could thus explain this gathering behavior. This theory is supported by the small number of flake blanks indicated by Kombewa flakes found among the knapping remains. Such flake blanks are produced either when detaching flakes at the outcrop or when trimming large good-quality blocks that are found in the alluvium at the foot of the outcrop. Since blocks are sometimes difficult to detach from the outcrops, any of acceptable quality that had already fallen may have been seized upon by the Paijanenses (as they were by us in our first experimental tests). This trimming at the quarry site implies the use of large stone hammers specially chosen and brought from afar.

The green tuff for four to eight bifaces came from a very different source. The quantity of raw material implies either several trips by a single person, one person coming to the workshop from a different direction each time; or by a more indirect route ultimately arriving at site 14, such as one originating from the north and passing by site 125 to procure bifaces of pale rhyolite. A cache of green tuff bifaces accumulated during a previous passage could be consistent with the first theory of a repeated excursion. The material for the point knapped from pale gray tuff could have originated from the same outcrop as the green tuff. For both these materials, initial knapping could have been done close to this outcrop—for instance, the beginning or all of phase 2a—in order to reduce the weight of the pieces to be transported without making them too fragile. A visual examination of the workshops of this locality indeed showed a predominance of very large flakes that are very certainly by-products of the beginning of soft-hammer reduction. The general attitude of knappers at this site thus appears exploratory and relaxed, without any particular stress in terms of time and productivity.

The origin of the *gris-violácea* and *gris-fina* rhyolites, from each of which one point was made and exported, remains unknown. It is possible that they were brought in an advanced stage of the knapping process; for instance, it seems that the *gris-fina* preform was brought to the site near the end of phase 2a.

Point Fabrication at Pampa de los Fósiles 14, Unit 1

Imported, Abandoned, and Exported Pieces

Table 55 lists the evaluations of the number of pieces according to knapping flakes; evaluations made in comparison with experimental references, first global, then by concentration, then according to raw material variety.

From 25 to 31 pale rhyolite rough-outs (*Chivateros* bifaces) were introduced into the site, of which about two thirds (11 to 19) resulted in finished, functional, and thus exported projectile points. From 9 to 11 pieces were broken or rejected during fabrication (2 in phase 2b, 4 in phase 3, 5 at the end of phase 3 or beginning of phase 4), not counting the 2 or 3 *porosa rosada* and *blanca* fragments that were collected and soon rebroken.

The green tuff was worked much less often and with much less success. Only 4 to 8 rough-outs were brought to the site, of which 4 to 6 were broken at the end of phase 3 or beginning of phase 4. Therefore at most only one or two points were finished and exported, if any at all. According to a small series of fine flakes from phases 2b and 3 that were found in concentration B,

Table 55. Summary count of the number of pieces knapped, broken or abandoned, and finished points, for the different varieties of raw material.

Material	Pieces knapped	Broken or rejected pieces	Finished points
Pale rhyolite			
ferruginosa	(3 or 4)	no. 7	
naranjilla	(1)	no. 14	
ferruginosa/naranjilla	4 to 6	2 broken	2 to 4
puntillada/floreada	3 to 5	2 broken: no. 5–6 and no. 3 and/or no. 61	1 to 3
micro-*puntillada*	2	1 broken: nos. 104 and 72 1 broken/reworked? no. 102	0 or 1
arenosa	1	1 broken: no. 24	0
linea-rosada/azul	2 or 3, + 1		3 or 4
porosa rosada	(1 collected)	(rebroken: no. 2–23)	0
porosa blanca	(1 collected?)	(rebroken: no. 1)	0
rosada verde	1	1 rejected: no. 38	0
colorada	1 mediocre	1 rejected?	0 or 1
granito	1	1 broken: no. 60–77–68	0
salmón	1	1 broken: no. 15	0
crema/rayada	1 or 2		1 or 2
morada	2		2
gris-fina: origin?	1		1
gris-violacea: origin?	1		1
totals			
pale rhyolite	22 to 28	9 to 11	11 to19
green tuff	4 to 8	4 to 6	0 to 2
pale gray tuff	1		1
total bifacial	27 to 37	13 to 17	12 to 22

The Raw Material Varieties

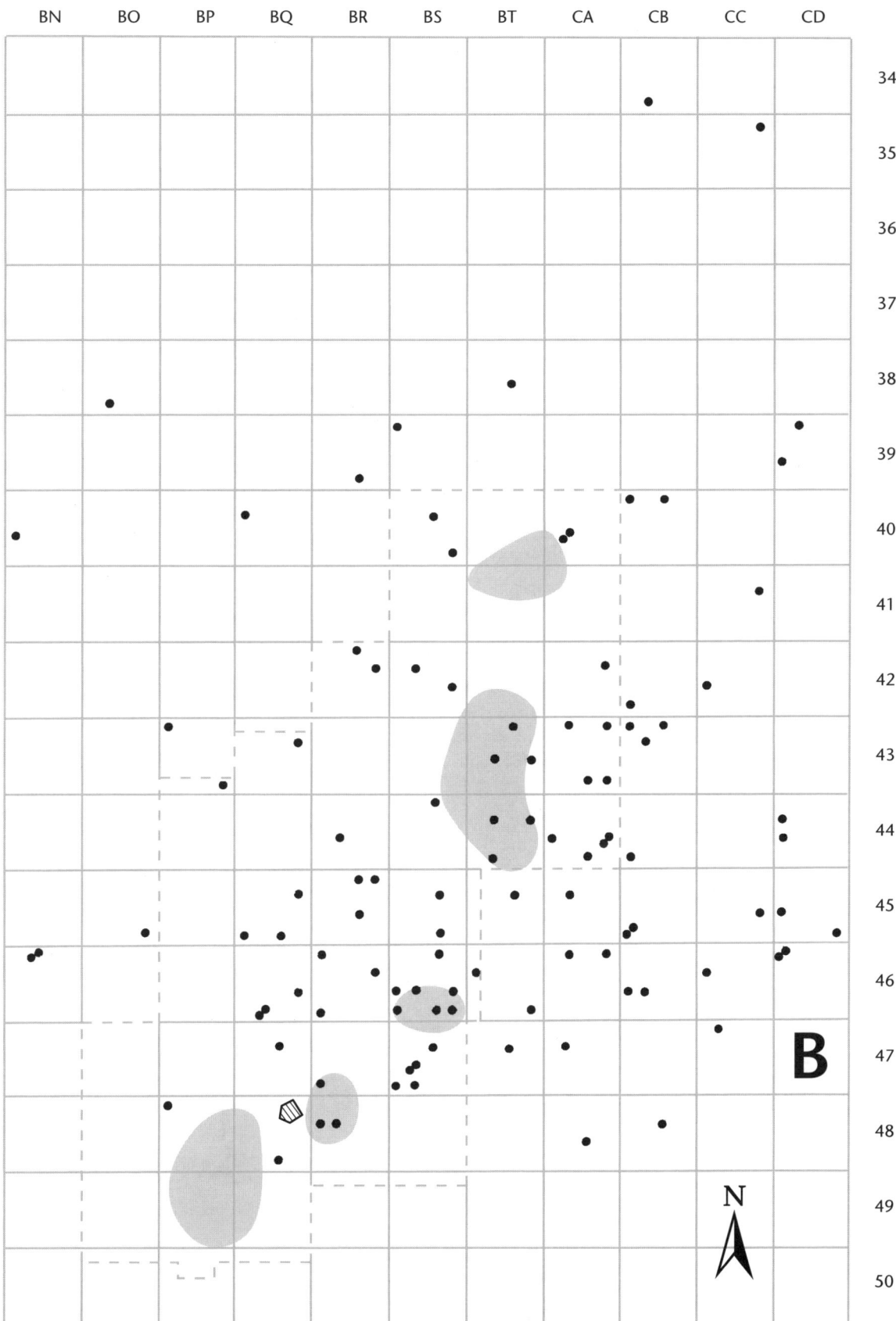

Figure 53. Spatial distribution of pale gray tuff flakes (dots) in concentration B.

one point made from pale gray tuff that was probably finished and exported can be added to this count.

Global Estimate of the Time Devoted to Point Production

The total time spent procuring raw material, including traveling and fabricating *Chivateros* bifaces at the outcrops, can be estimated at 10–15 hours: a few trips of one to two hours each to the various points of quarry 125, and a special trip of a few hours to an outcrop of volcanic tuff.

On the basis of our experimental tests (Pelegrin and Chauchat 1993, and Table 3), we propose to make generous estimates of the time devoted to bifacial knapping at the site itself. This is contrary to what we would have proposed, had acquisition and production proved to be more systematic. We will also suppose that points were relatively small, in accordance with the dimensions of the pieces that remained in place. For each point, we thus propose approximately one hour for percussion knapping and one hour for phase 4 pressure flaking. This estimate results in the following figures:

- 2 pieces abandoned or broken in phase 2; 20–30 minutes each, for a total of 40–60 minutes;
- 5 pieces broken or rejected in phase 3; 40–60 minutes each, for a total of 200–300 minutes;
- 6–8 pieces broken at the end of phase 3 or beginning of phase 4; 60–80 minutes each, for a total of 360–640 minutes.
- following the hypothesis of the lowest number of finished pieces, we add at least 80 minutes for one point with a short apical fracture in phase 4 and possibly abandoned, and 60 minutes for one second-rate foliate piece (indicated by the absence of refits) that was possibly abandoned.

The number of finished and exported points can be estimated at between 12 and 22, at 120 minutes each, except for the point of gray tuff at 80 minutes, and twice 120 minutes for the *gris-fina* point and the short *gris-violácea* point. This gives us a total of 1,360 to 2,560 minutes, to which we add 20–30 minutes for the reworked fragments of *porosa blanca*. We thus arrive at a global working time of 2,120 to 3,590 minutes, or 35 hours and 20 minutes to 59 hours and 50 minutes. To this total we must add time for the few blows made on rejected *Chivateros* bifaces and for a little pressure retouch on two of the broken points brought back to the site (nos. 79 and 92). Therefore we can reasonably estimate that 35–60 hours were devoted to knapping at the site, in addition to the 10–15 hours spent procuring rough-outs at the outcrops.

For a single worker, this total of 45–75 hours would thus represent one to two weeks of nearly exclusive activity. However, there is no reason to believe that the acquisition and knapping activities were not much more extended in time over the rather long occupation period of the site, nor that there was only one knapper involved. On the contrary, certain observations that we will now reexamine suggest that several individuals participated in fabricating Paiján points.

Qualitative Aspects: Skill Levels

Certain behavioral differences are rather easy to detect in the context of Paiján point production at the site. These largely correspond to different levels of knapping skill, unless we consider that an individual's efficiency may have fluctuated according to his physical or mental condition. The latter hypothesis, while conceivable, is not very convincing given the conditions of Paiján point fabrication that we were able to reconstitute through the archaeological data. The knapping of Paiján points was an important activity, necessitating a long period of apprenticeship and intense mental concentration. This situation is reflected, for instance, in the separation of most workshops at some distance from the living sites. Whatever the type of prey sought by the Paiján people, projectile point production played a vital role in acquiring animal protein for the group. It is thus highly plausible that the knappers not only dedicated the time, but also created working conditions conducive to maximizing the yield from their knapping activity. This interpretation means that this work was practiced in a manner that assured completion of the *chaîne opératoire* and yielded a functional Paiján point whenever

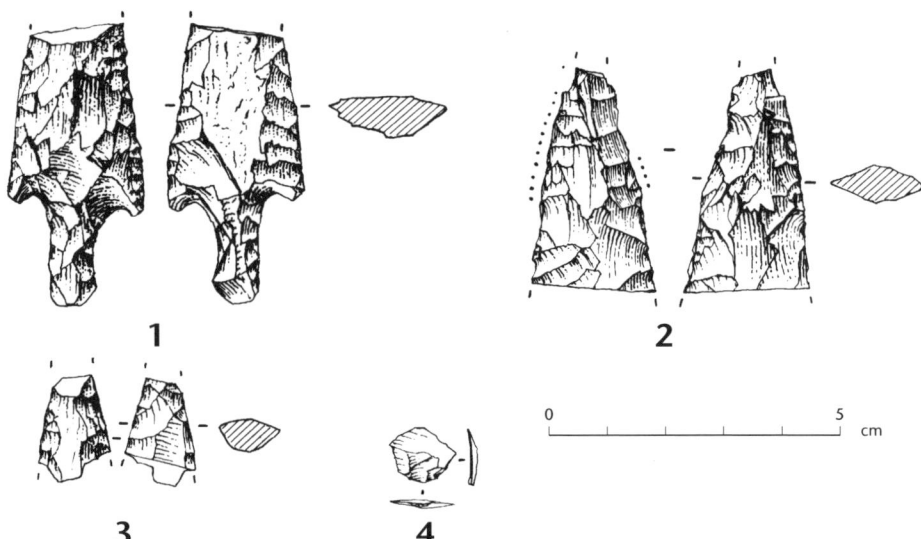

Figure 54. Objects of exogenous materials: **1–3**, projectile point fragments no. 79, 92, 81; **4**, small flake probably knapped from piece no. 92. (Drawings by M. Reduron.)

The Raw Material Varieties

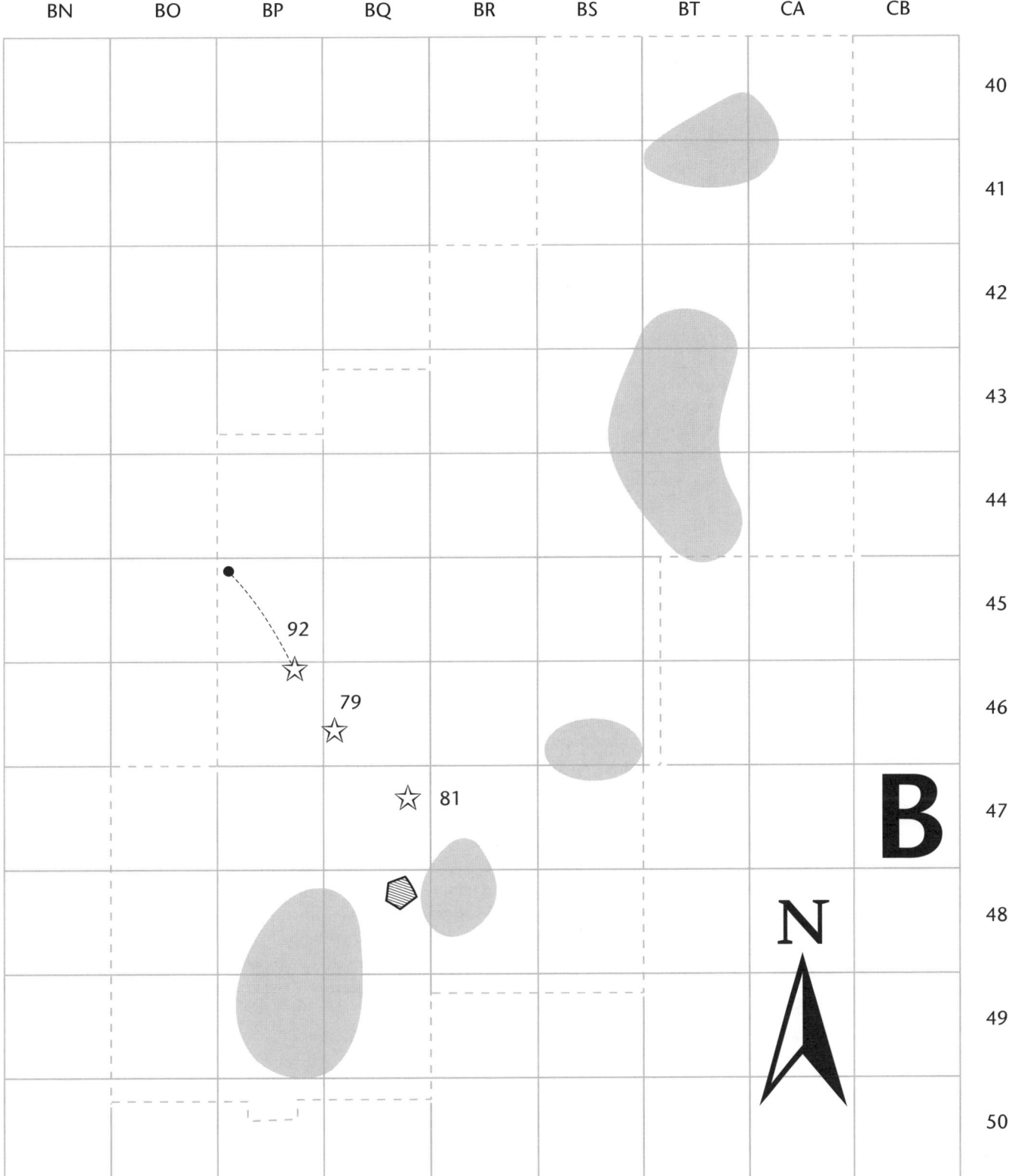

Figure 55. Spatial distribution of projectile points fragments (stars) and knapping flake (dot) of exogenous material in concentration B. The dashed line shows the association between the flake and piece no. 92. No direct refit was found.

possible. A broken or defective point observed in the archaeological assemblage thus very probably indicates a less than optimal level of expertise. The observed defects indicate knappers who had not yet mastered knapping techniques or who incompletely understood the sequences and strategies that are critical at different stages of manufacture.

The required high level of expertise implies an evolution in the apprenticeship of the knapper. This evolution probably continued throughout childhood, adolescence, and into adulthood, culminating with mastery of the skills associated with knapping. At this stage the knapper would almost always succeed, by appropriate execution along the entire *chaîne opératoire*, at transforming carefully selected blocks or flakes into functional projectile points. Being functional, these points disappeared from the archaeological record, leaving only the remains of their production as evidence of their existence.

It is thus possible to distinguish the different levels of expertise corresponding to individuals at different stages of apprenticeship at the time the workshop was occupied. These levels of expertise certainly corresponded to different age classes: child, adolescent, adult. Because of individual idiosyncrasies, we cannot dismiss the possibility that skill levels varied in spite of uniform maximum levels of apprenticeship. However, assigning an expertise level to the individual responsible for knapping a given group of flakes is a much more difficult task. Moreover, we must not give undue significance to the terms "child," "adolescent," and "adult," which are employed as equivalents of the associated skill levels, not as a measure of biological age. We know that life expectancy was short; an individual could have been considered an adult at 15 or 16, but we do not know if knapping skills were mastered at this age or later.

By definition, the knapping of exported points is performed by one or several skilled, thus mature knappers. The good-quality series of phase 2 flakes created as by-products of these points are the most readable evidence of this optimal skill level. For instance, the refitted half-shells of *morada* pale rhyolite, the well-prepared flakes of *gris-violácea* and *gris-fina* rhyolite, and even the fragments of some pieces broken at the end of phase 3 or beginning of phase 4 are without technical or morphological flaws. The projectile points fragments brought back to the site already knapped (nos. 79, 81, 92) are also the final products of a competent knapper, but the failed reworking of two of them (a simple exercise in pressure retouch) are surely not by the same hand.

On the other hand, some behaviors seem to us to be the work of children or young adolescents just beginning to acquire the difficult skills involved in the fabrication of Paiján points:

- a few short second-rate *Chivateros* bifaces soon abandoned after a few awkward blows;
- a collection of fragments of pieces made from *porosa* rhyolite (no. 2 and 23), whose clearest example is the *porosa-rosada* biface from the quarry unit 104 of site 12. These were probably found at adjacent workshops and rapidly broken here (implying that a few workshops from at least site 12, 2–3 km to the southwest of site 14, already existed);
- reworking of fragments of foliate pieces from the site itself.

These were subject to a few short hinged removals before being dispersed or rebroken (e.g., fragment no. 68 of a piece made from *granito* rhyolite, Figure 30, no. 1, and no. 5-6, made from *puntillada*, Figure 22, no. 1).

We are still tempted to distinguish an intermediate level between these two extremes, which would be the level of an adolescent capable of performing some bifacial shaping but still lacking the skills necessary to thin the piece. A few pieces rather clearly represent this level, particularly the above-mentioned *granito* rhyolite piece broken at the end of phase 3 (no. 60-77-68, Figure 30, no. 1) before fragment no. 68 was reworked by a child. The same can be said for piece fragments no. 7 (*ferruginosa*) and 14 (*naranjilla*); both have triangular sections and are much too thick at this stage to be finished by pressure retouch, that is, they were broken because of overly late attempts to thin them. A good knapper would have avoided arriving at this point of "sub-deviant" pieces (Chauchat 1991). Even beginning with difficult *Chivateros* bifaces, he would have taken fewer risks by attempting earlier, during phase 2b, to thin the body to 10–11 mm and the base to 8 mm. Otherwise, finishing the piece by pressure retouch would become practically impossible.

Considering the low level of success, the four to six fractured green tuff foliate pieces (most if not all the imported rough-outs of this material) could also represent the activity of a knapper of an intermediary skill level. However, we are more inclined to attribute these pieces to a rather competent knapper. Most of them, if not all, were broken in normal progression of the *chaîne opératoire,* during the ultimate phase of reduction by percussion (phase 3) or at the beginning of pressure retouch, both of which necessarily imply a significant degree of risk. Unfortunately, since we were unable to locate the source(s) of green tuff, we could not experimentally test the raw material. The number of fractured pieces might be explained by the difficulty of adapting to this material by knappers accustomed to working rhyolite. However, there are problems with this theory. We could understand the breakage of the first piece, the first attempt to work green tuff, which requires modifying the techniques used to work rhyolite. However, it is more difficult to accept the repetitive breaking of material that was imported from some distance and thus *a priori* had an invested value. Whatever the case, each of the rough-outs has a satisfying section—biconvex, not too thick, and not too unbalanced.

It is also possible, although impossible to prove, that this lack of success at knapping green tuff reflects the impatience of a young knapper already possessing a certain degree of skill but still lacking self-control. We can further hypothesize that the voluntary fractures seen on several fragments, resulting from shocks directly onto the faces, are evidence of a frustrated and angry knapper. We agree with N. Pigeot (1987) that self-control is the last lesson learned on the road to becoming a mature knapper.

In summary, we can distinguish three main levels of expertise or competence, based on the data from this workshop. Level A is that of the most effective knapper, who succeeds at following the majority of knapping operations to their end and thus, except in the case of rare accidents, produces functional points that disappear from the archaeological record. Level B represents the knapping apprentice who is still frequently unsuccessful at the necessary thinning operations and thus rarely produces finished points. The pieces are either abandoned when they become too narrow relative to their thickness or are broken by overly violent or awkward blows. Level C is that of the child who is not yet capable of correctly evaluating the faults of the material, nor of mastering the knapping techniques necessary for performing operations other than reworking pieces abandoned by elders. This situation often results in the truly deviant pieces defined elsewhere by Chauchat (1991). Undoubtedly finer distinctions can be made starting from these three levels. Moreover, within a group occupying a workshop, more than one person could have attained a given level of expertise.

In the case of the green tuff pieces, we could thus hypothesize a slightly lower level of competence characterized by a lower degree of self-control. This level, which we could define as A′, describes the knapper responsible for the accidents who is nevertheless generally capable of finishing points made from rhyolite. However, presence of the theoretical A′ knapper means that there need not have been a level A knapper on the site, since the rhyolite pieces could have been produced by A′. The existence of a level A′ knapper is necessary to account for the fractured green tuff pieces and could also be associated with the successfully finished rhyolite pieces. The presence of a level A knapper is thus possible but not necessary. It is therefore simpler not to attempt to distinguish between the manifestations of these two levels.

The data presented below are taken from Tables 55, 56, and 57, and from Table 54, with the addition of the work duration and classification according to the three main skill levels. To the last two columns of Table 56 we added the provenience of the majority of flakes of each variety (knapping localities) according to previous analyses. The first column represents the main provenience; the second, the minority provenience.

Keeping in mind the reasoning described above, the manifestation of a given skill level is evidence of at least one representative knapper. We thus have evidence of at least one or two adults (level A-A′), one youth or adolescent at level B, and one child at level C; therefore the minimum size of the group is three or four persons. From a quantitative point of view, the most efficient work was performed by the one or two good knappers over a total of 30 to 50 hours. They produced the great majority, if not all, of the finished points as well as the pieces broken in an acceptable state—made from green tuff and *puntillada* and *salmón* rhyolite. If we estimate an average of 6 hours of work a day, an arbitrary figure that corresponds to what a knapper can accomplish given the requisite effort and concentration (Pelegrin and Chauchat 1993:377), these 30 to 50 hours correspond to a total of from 5 to more than 8 days of work. For two adults, the estimated time falls to between 2½ and 4 days. These estimates do not account for displacements to the quarry (at least for site 125) and acquiring raw materials there, which could have occurred before arrival at the workshop. It also cannot account for the traces of activities related to unifaces (numerous episodes of utilization marked by rejuvenating several pieces), which will be discussed below.

On the contrary, the activity of the level B knapper(s) occupies only six to nine hours, or a little more than one day for one

Table 56. Classification by level of expertise.

Raw material variety	Broken or rejected pieces	Finished pieces	Level	Duration (minutes) min.	max.	Knapping location
gris-violacea		1	A	100	100	B5 or B4
ferruginosa		2 to 4	A or A′	240	480	A and B5; phase 2a in D, reject in C
crema/rayada		1 to 2	A or A′	120	240	B2n and B?
puntillada/floreada	2 broken: no. 5~6...3, no. 61	1 to 3	A or A′	240	520	B2 and A; a little in B3 and B5
pale gray tuff		1	A or A′	80	80	B3
salmón	1 broken: no. 15	0	A′	40	60	B3 or B1
morada		2	A or A′	240	240	B4
linea-rosada/azul		3 to 4	A or A′	360	480	C and B3; 4rejections from C in A, B, and D
gris-fina		1	A or A′	100	100	D2
green tuff	4 to 6	0 to 2	A′	240	720	D1-3
arenosa rejected in B	1 broken: no. 24	0	A, A′ or B	20	30	D4 then C2; some flakes from D
granito	1 broken: no. 60~77~68	0	B	40	60	B3 and B2s? 2 flakes rejected in D
porosa blanca	collected and rebroken: no. 1	0	B	20	30	B3 and D4? one rejected flake in A
ferruginosa	1 broken mediocre: no. 7	0	B	40	60	B5
naranjilla	1 broken mediocre: no. 14	0	B	40	60	B5
rosada verde	1 rejected: no. 38	0	B	20	30	D2
micro-puntillada	1 broken and reworked: no. 102	0 to 1	B	80	120	D4
micro-puntillada	1 broken: no. 104+72	0	B	40	60	D4; no. 72 rejected in B
colorada	1 rejected?	0 to 1	B	60	120	D4 or D3
porosa rosada	collected-rebroken: no. 2~23	0	C			A2
floreada	mediocre *Chivateros*: no. 75	0	C			B? thrown in CA43
micro-puntillada	mediocre *Chivateros*: no. 34	0	C			D3
colorada	mediocre *Chivateros*: no. 40	0	C			D4

person, unless we consider that the work at this level proceeded more slowly or perhaps intermittently. We thus tend to believe that level B is represented by only one person. The estimate of zero to two finished pieces is low although quite possible at this intermediate level, where the knapper rarely finishes a piece. We conclude that the duration of activity could be extended to two days. Other behaviors are also possible—absences or participation in other activities, two subgroups arriving at the site at different times, etc.

The activity of level C is very different because it is integrated only in appearance into the *chaîne opératoire*. Indeed, it can be considered intrusive behavior—importing poorly chosen or tested pieces, collecting pieces previously abandoned. All of this results in working time that seems to be very low. There is no reason to believe that one or several children could not have been present at the workshop at least part of the time. Given the relatively high number of common tools found, which are characteristic of subsistence activities at the camps, we believe that adult females were also present at the site rather than at a separate camp as is generally the case in the area. This interpretation also helps explain the presence of a garbage pit containing food remains, an uncommon occurrence at Pampa de los Fósiles workshops.

Spatial Distribution of Knapping Activities

In concentration D we find the knapper(s) of level A-A′ essentially at the knapping localities of D1, D2, and D3. Here one piece made from *gris-fina* rhyolite was finished and 4–6 green tuff pieces were worked, most of which were broken, a maximum of two being finished. These operations could be the work of a single person. To this same level A′ knapper we could attribute the piece made from *rosada-verde* (Figure 26, no. 38), which was also knapped and abandoned in D2. This piece was thinned insufficiently relative to its width during phase 2, but could have been continued by a good knapper. However, the last few blows to the mesial area (left edge of the right face in Figure 26) produced step-like hinge terminations that irremediably prevented its completion. This failure shows lack of control by a knapper who was not confident at a moment of high risk.

On the other hand, it seems that knapping locality D4 was primarily occupied by a level B apprentice who was responsible for the pieces made from micro-*puntillada* (no. 103 and 104-72, broken, but perhaps also a finished piece), *colorada* (possibly one piece rejected and one finished), and *arenosa* (no. 24, broken). We also have evidence of a child at this locality (after the departure of the apprentice?) who briefly reworked then abandoned a fragment of micro-*puntillada* that had been abandoned by the apprentice, and two *Chivateros* bifaces (no. 34 and 40). In addition, the *arenosa* piece, first knapped in D4 (phase 2), was later reworked in C2, where it was broken. For an unknown reason, a handful of flakes from this operation were dispersed in the southern part of B.

Concentration B is much more difficult to understand. A piece of *salmón* rhyolite knapped in B1 was further worked in B3, where it was broken (no. 15), even though it is attributed to a level A knapper. In B2 and its environs we find *crema/rayada* rhyolite material from which one or two finished points were made, as well as *puntillada/floreada* material. This latter material, represented by two broken pieces, also seems to have furnished one to three finished points. Despite the dispersion of flakes, a pale gray tuff piece seems to have been knapped in B3, finished, and exported (however, we will see below that this could be a uniface). This gray tuff probably has the same origin as the green tuff. The *granito* variety was also knapped in B3 by a level B knapper (piece no. 60-77-68). Despite the level A attributed to the knapper of the gray tuff and *salmón* rhyolite (broken piece no. 15), this group is not very impressive. Given the results, it probably corresponds to the level A′ already seen in association with concentration D. In the zone between B3 and B4 we find the *linea-rosada/azul* variety already seen in concentration C. The existence of several pieces of the same variety of material knapped at two locations far from each other perhaps indicates that two knappers exploited the same quarry location before working the imported pieces separately (perhaps simultaneously). This interpretation would be an additional argument for the presence of at least two adults at the workshop. The *morada* rhyolite was knapped exclusively at B4, resulting in two finished pieces assignable to level A.

The *ferruginosa/naranjilla* variety of rhyolite is attested in B5 by two pieces that were clearly too thick (no. 7 and no. 4, level B?) and broken in phase 3, as well as three projectile points produced in the same area but not found, thus *a priori* considered to be finished. Were they really finished? If so, by a more competent knapper? Or were they broken by the same level B knapper and rejected farther away in the nearby ravine, possibly after being reworked by a child? The behavioral possibilities are numerous, and none can be favored. One piece of the *gris-violácea* variety was also knapped in B5 by a level A knapper.

From the beginning of this study, the spatial distribution of knapping flakes has permitted us to distinguish what we have called knapping localities in each concentration. However, we must remember that these knapping localities have been disturbed and dispersed during their long period of exposure on the surface. Moreover, in certain cases they may have been produced by several persons working close together.

We reclassified the data of Table 55 according to the knapping locality that is the source of the majority of flakes of each variety. We have thus simplified somewhat in most cases by not considering minority groups of flakes secondarily distributed in different knapping localities. Thus Table 57 has only one of the last two columns of Table 56.

One of the first conclusions we can draw from Table 57 is that there is a general mixture of skill levels in the different knapping localities. There is no apparent spatial segregation between levels A and B, thus no evident hierarchical distinction between good knappers and apprentices. Evidence of these latter is present all over in association with the remains of level A knappers. However, our analysis did not always enable us to separate each locality. Therefore D1, D2, and D3 are treated together, as are B3 and B4 and concentrations A and C. Moreover, we do not have enough data on locality B1. In D1, D2, and D3, level B is present for a duration of 20–30 minutes; in B3 and B4 it is present for 60–90 minutes; in B5 it is present for 80–120 min-

The Raw Material Varieties

Table 57. Classification by knapping locality and number of knapping episodes in each locality. In the attribution of knapping localities, the slashes indicate a location between two knapping localities, while the commas indicate that the location is situated in several localities. Total of knapping episodes for the entire unit is from 30 to 39 plus 3 short ones (less than 5 min. each).

Knapping locality	Raw material	Broken or rejected pieces	Finished points	Level	Duration (minutes) min.	max.	Knapping episodes
A	porosa-rosada	collected-rebroken: no. 2~23	0	C			1
A2	ferruginosa		1	A	120	120	
	puntillada	broken: no. 5~6...3,	0	A	60	80	1-2
C	linea-rosada/azul		2 to 3	A	240	360	2-3
D1, D2, D3	green tuff	no. 99-28, no. 46, 31, 106, 32~103: 4 to 6 pieces	0 to 2	A'	240	720	4 to 6
D2	gris-fina		1	A	100	100	
	rosada-verde	rejected: no. 38	0	B	20	30	2
D3	micro-puntillada	mediocre *Chivateros*: no. 34	0	C			1 (short)
D4	arenosa	broken: no. 24	0	A or B	20	30	
	micro-puntillada	broken: no. 104~72; reworked?: no. 102	0 or 1	B	120	180	
	colorada	rejected?	0 or 1	B	60	120	5
	colorada	mediocre *Chivateros*: no. 40	0	C			+1 (short)
B2	floreada		1 to 3	A	120	360	
	crema/rayada		1 or 2	A	120	240	
	puntillada	broken: no. 61	0	A	60	80	3 to 6
	puntillada	mediocre *Chivateros*: no. 75	0	C			+1 (short)
B3	porosa-blanca	collected and rebroken: no. 1	0	B	20	30	
	pale gray tuff		1	A	80	80	
B1, B3/B4	salmón	broken: no. 15	0	A'	40	60	
B3/B4	linea-rosada/azul		1	A	120	120	
	granito	broken: no. 60~77~68	0	B	40	60	
B4	morada		2	A	240	240	8
B5	ferruginosa		1 to 3	A	120	360	
	ferruginosa	mediocre broken: no. 7	0	B	40	60	
	gris-violácea		1	A	100	100	
	naranjilla	mediocre broken: no. 14	0	B	40	60	4 to 6

utes. Most level B activity took place in D4, with an estimated time of 200–330 minutes, or an average of 4 hours and 25 minutes. We thus observe that level B activity is present but with a shorter working time when it is associated with level A activity. This observation implies not only the association of a mature knapper with an adolescent, but also that the adolescent either worked only part of the time when the adult was present, or worked intermittently or much more slowly. Only in D4 did an adolescent work alone.

An alternative interpretation could be that, at least in certain cases, the manifestations of level A and B at the same knapping locality are the work of the same knapper. This knapper would sometimes but not always be able to produce finished points. The minority durations of level B knapping that we observe would be due to the lowest level manifestations of this knapper, except in the case of locality D4 where only level B is present. However, the morphologies of the abandoned bifacial pieces do not support this hypothesis. In most cases the overly thick and narrow sections, series of awkward blows, etc. are not isolated accidents in a well-mastered reduction process but serious faults that can only be attributed to an incomplete apprenticeship. The sole clear exceptions are the green tuff pieces and also the *floreada/puntillada* piece no. 5-6...3 (Figure 22, no. 1), which have been grouped under level A'.

Duration of Occupation and Number of Knappers

Table 58 is an even further simplified version of Table 57. We totaled the main data for levels A and B only. In the last column we list in hours and minutes the average estimated duration of activity for level A, dividing the units of analysis by the number of known localities. We did the same for level B in knapping locality D4. For instance, we divided the average obtained for B3 and B4 by two, and by three the average obtained for the group D1, D2, and D3. We obtain figures on the order of slightly more than 3 hours to almost 6 hours. Locality B2, one of the largest of the site, is an exception, for which we do not obtain a duration consistent with this range of values unless we divide the average by two. It is interesting to note that this is not the case for the group D1, D2, and D3, in which D2 is also very vast and

Table 58. Synthesis of work done in each knapping locality for levels A and B.

Knapping locality	Level	Abandoned pieces	Finished points	Duration min.	Duration max.	No. localities	Average duration per locality (hours, minutes)
A2	A	1	1	180	200	1	3h, 10m
C	A	0	2–3	240	360	1	5h
D1, D2, D3	A	5–7	1–3	340	820	3	3h, 15m
	B	1	0	20	30		
D4	B	3–4	0–2	200	330	1	4h, 25m
B2	A	1	2–5	300	680	1	8h, 10m
B3, B4	A	2	4	480	500	2	4h, 20m
	B	2	0	60	90		
B5	A	0	2–4	220	460	1	5h, 40m
	B	2	0	80	120		

includes two main categories of raw material. If we consider that this group contains four knapping localities, we attain a very low average for each (2 hours 25 minutes), from which we conclude either that D2 must be considered a single locality or that one of the other localities was occupied during a much shorter duration. *In summary, by associating knapping activity duration with the knapping localities revealed by the spatial distribution of flakes on the surface, we can confidently assign for each locality a value for duration of knapping activity of between 3 to 6 hours.* Locality B2 is an exception and may have a double value (Table 58). We have indicated elsewhere (Pelegrin and Chauchat 1993:377) that making a Paiján point is hard, tiring work, especially the final pressure retouch phase; figuring a daily average of about six hours of work, the output of a knapper would very likely not exceed two or three points per day. This experimental result is not very far from our estimate of the average duration of work in the knapping localities of the workshop.

In conclusion, it seems quite feasible that each knapping locality corresponds to the occupation of one knapper for the approximate duration of one work day (from 3 to 6 hours), taking into account the other tasks that he must have been required to accomplish during this same time period—utilizing unifaces, subsistence activities, etc.

The true occupation of the site depends on factors that are not available for us to analyze. We were able to estimate the activity of the knappers at 35–60 hours, which seems to be distributed between 30–50 hours for level A knappers and 6–9 hours for level B knappers. Of course, the actual duration of occupation depends, first, on the number of persons involved in the knapping activity, and second, on whether this activity was continuous or intermittent. We know that numerous unifaces were utilized and resharpened, that one or several meals were consumed, and that some activities of an unknown nature were performed, attested by the presence of common tools and knapping remains of rare stones (unifaces, rare stones, and food remains are treated in detail in following chapters).

The 35–50 hours of work at level A-A' represents from 6 to more than 8 days of work at an average of 6 hours a day, and 11–16.5 days at an average of 3 hours a day. This latter duration appears to be a minimal average for an activity as important as fabricating points.

In the case of one day's occupation at the site, we must assume the presence of from 6 to more than 16 level A-A' knappers. The hypothesis that one day's work equaled 6 hours implies the presence of one level B knapper. However, this knapper would have moved among several localities, indicating a level of restlessness far greater than that of his quasi-immobile elders. In general, the more level A-A' knappers we estimate at the site, the shorter is the duration necessary to accomplish the work indicated by the archaeological data. The results of these calculations are presented in Table 59. If we consider that the level B knapper worked for 2 days (totaling 6–9 hours) during which time other knappers were also at work, we see that these same values are attained by 4 or 5 level A-A' knappers in the case of the minimal hypothesis (a total of 35 hours for level A-A' activity), and by at least 6 knappers in the maximal hypothesis (total of 50 hours). A count of 4 to 6 level A-A' knappers is the most probable. However, if we consider that the level B knapper did not work as long as the others, they could have remained longer at the site; and we can accept a lower number of level A-A' knappers, for instance, three to four. In contrast, if two level B knappers were present, the work time of each could be reduced to 3–5 hours, which leaves only one day of presence at the site and requires a greater number of A-A' knappers. Given the

Table 59. Low and high estimates of site occupation duration for one to six persons, based on low and high estimates of average work days.

Knappers	Total hours	Total days 6 hours/day	Total days 3 hours/day
Low estimate			
1	35	5.8	11.6
2	17.5	2.9	5.8
3	11.6	1.9	3.9
4	8.8	1.5	2.9
5	7	1.2	2.3
6	5.8	1	1.9
High estimate			
1	50	8.3	16.7
2	25	4.2	8.3
3	16.7	2.8	5.6
4	12.5	2.1	4.2
5	10	1.7	3.3
6	8.3	1.4	2.7

behavioral complexities already exhibited by the spatial dispersion of the material and the various levels of expertise shown by the group of knappers, it is very difficult to argue convincingly in favor of one or another estimation. *We can only surmise that four to six level A-A' knappers and one level B knapper seems an average and likely estimate.*

In summary, at the end of this long and complex analysis, we have obtained few solid results. More often, we have reached only plausible possibilities that cannot be confirmed. In general, the regular disposition of the concentrations, and especially the knapping localities, on the perimeter of the ellipse seems to indicate that most if not all of them were occupied at the same time. Moreover, it is evident that knappers of different skill levels worked at closely spaced localities; in several cases the evidence implies an apprentice working alongside a mature knapper. However, it is difficult to explain the very short working time of these apprentices. If we accept the number of four to six level A-A' knappers that we calculated above, we could infer that each one moved a limited number of times within one concentration. If we divide concentration B into two localities with a limit between B2 and B3, as can be done with concentration D according to the raw materials, we also arrive at five to six concentrations, each including two to three knapping localities that could have been occupied during one work day or part of one.

Chapter 5
Other Observations

Unifaces

From the beginning of research on the Paiján period, tools similar to European Paleolithic *limaces* ("slugs") have been observed (Ossa 1973:121 and Figure 68; Chauchat 1976: plate XXXVI). Similar objects also existed in the other great lithic tradition of the central Andes, the Lauricochense (Lavallée et al. 1985:122–124), and are generally characteristic of all the Paleoindian industries of the Americas. We have called these tools unifaces (Chauchat 1976, 1988, Chauchat et al. 1992:56–60) in contrast to bifaces. An obvious similarity between these two types is that both are made by soft-hammer percussion, creating in one case a unifacial tool, in the other a bifacial tool. In the zone of Pampa de los Fósiles, only site 27 and the workshop studied here, site 14, unit 1, possess a significant proportion of unifaces, although their number is still modest. Except at these two sites, unifaces, although always rare, are usually found in the context of projectile point knapping workshops. There are numerous indications that, at the time of manufacture, these tools are usually wide and massive; after several phases of intensive utilization their dimensions are greatly reduced by preferential retouching on the two long sides. Since the maximum thickness cannot be reduced proportionally, the section becomes progressively thicker until the stage is reached where the two opposed edges become steep. In this way the object eventually attains a morphology very similar to that of the European Mousterian *limaces*. At this point the uniface is abandoned and appears in the archaeological record. We alluded to the unifaces of site 14, unit 1, in the introduction to this study.

Seven unifaces were found in this workshop, including one that was exploded by thermal shock, and one isolated fragment. Three are made from pale tuff, including one of a laminated variety. The others are made from quartzite or dark-colored tuff (gray-black to black) with a fine homogeneous grain.

As with the bifacial pieces, our objective is to describe the unifaces and to determine their technological state (degree of reworking and cause for abandonment) and also to identify the flakes associated with them in order to determine their technological history. Just as with projectile points, "ghosts" of unifaces not found during collection and excavation, and thus probably absent from the site, can be detected by the presence of series of refitted flakes.

Methods of Analysis

Starting with the first classification in 1988, the small or medium retouch flakes thought to be associated with unifaces were distinguished by two characteristics:

1) a smooth and flat butt, often reduced in size or spindly, typically forming an angle of 60° with the superior face.

2) raw material different from materials utilized for Paiján points (rhyolite and green tuff at Pampa de los Fósiles) and for domestic tools, although these latter are also sometimes made from black quartzites.

We performed a second, very rigorous sorting to group elements of the same raw material and confirm their technological attribution. Our objective was to clarify the "history" of unifaces at the site through evidence of their rejuvenation during the course of utilization, which is represented by retouch flakes. Refits were sought over the entire site in order to detect possible displacements of the same uniface among different concentrations. This operation was difficult, since the flakes are often very small and patination can alter the color and texture of the material. However, several refits demonstrate that most raw material varieties remain clearly identifiable and thus make it possible to associate flakes that do not directly refit but very probably come from the same tool.

Description

Unifaces are made from several varieties of volcanic tuff (except green tuff) and black quartzite. Their spatial distribution is indicated in Figure 18. No. 74 is the only piece whose location was not precisely recorded, since it was collected when the site was discovered in 1970. However, this piece comes from the southern zone of the site, close to the alluvial terrace slope, where five other unifaces were also found. Only one was found in the northern zone, in D4. In fact, three of these pieces (nos. 78, 84 and 16-116-108) come from the zone between B2 and B4, near the possible block-seat associated with this latter knapping locality. One of the fragments of the piece was fractured by thermal shock (no. 16-116-108) and rejected at some distance in BF46, beyond the limits of concentration A. It is possible that piece no. 74 was originally found in proximity to the three previous ones, since this concentration was noted at this moment. Therefore, four of seven unifaces were associated with locality B4, a fifth was found barely 2 m away, between B2 and B3; and only two, no. 22 and 27 (Figure 56, no. 2 and 3), were found beyond this zone, in A and D4 respectively.

Uniface no. 17 (Figure 56, no. 1) is somewhat unusual because of its thickness, the irregularity of its edges, and its carefully shaped pointed tip. This tool seems to have been abandoned, since it is practically beyond rejuvenation. It is short and still somewhat wide but very thick. Its lateral edges are affected by hinged removals due to the more or less successful removal of small flakes by hard-hammer percussion. Of 29 retouch flakes or fragments that could be refit onto this uniface, around 10, in the area about the tip, seem to have been removed with a soft hammer. The uniface comes from the south of B2, but the flakes associated with it are dispersed in a trail several meters long oriented to the north, between the western margins of B2 and B1. A few objects are more isolated either toward the west of the uniface or toward the northeast beyond B1. The origin of this trail, which may have been caused mainly by wind, is in the northern half of B2. Figure 57 shows the disposition of connections between refitted flakes and the predominance of their di-

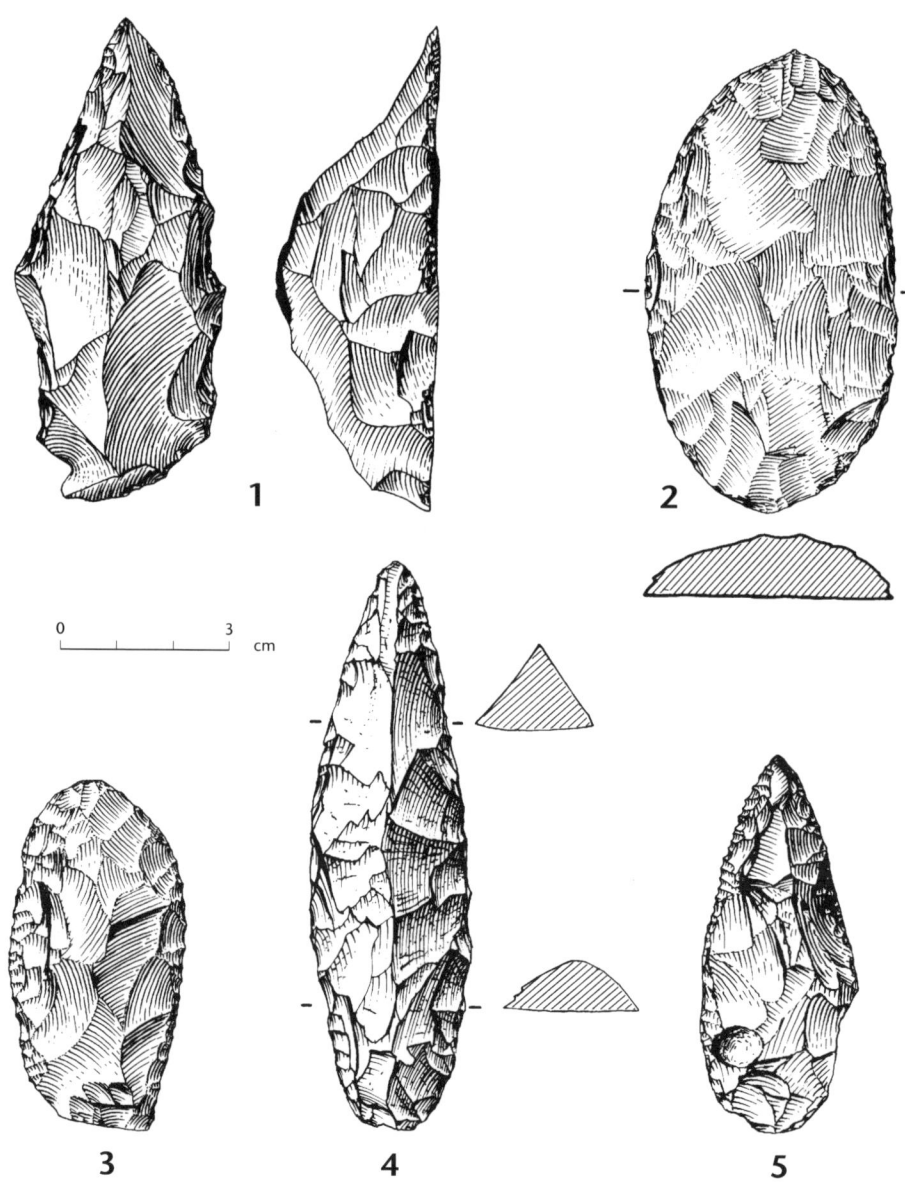

Figure 56. Unifaces from workshop Pampa de los Fósiles 14, unit 1: **1**, no. 17 from concentration B; **2**, no. 22 from concentration A; **3**, no. 27 from concentration D; **4**, no. 84 from concentration B; **5**, end fragments no. 16 and 108 from concentration B and medium fragment no. 116 from west of concentration A. (Drawings 1, 2, 3, and 5 by C. Chauchat, 4 by M. Reduron.)

Other Observations

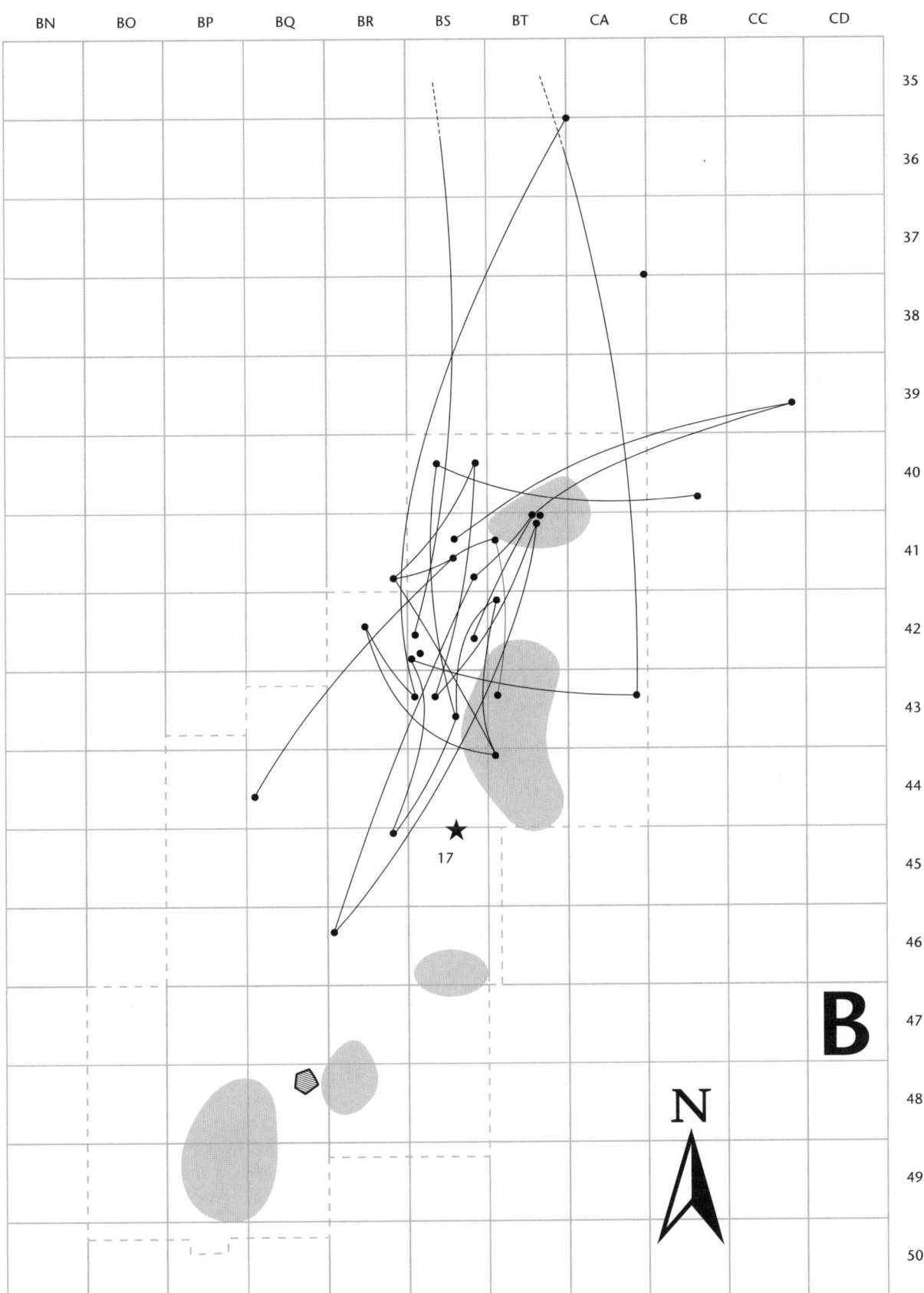

Figure 57. Spatial distribution of resharpening flakes (dots) from uniface no. 17 (star).

rections toward the north and northeast; those in the east-west direction are clearly fewer.

We were able to refit three small series of flakes of this same material from concentrations A and B (Figure 58), although they do not refit with the 29 flakes described above. It is possible that these three series of flakes, each representing the retouch of a flank or basal extremity of a piece with a smooth, flat face, come from the same missing uniface. This would have been a thick tool made from black quartzite, analogous to uniface no. 17. Considering the identity of the raw material, uniface no. 17 and the missing uniface may have originated from two halves of the same large black quartzite cobble that was broken in two; or perhaps both were made from flakes removed from the same block or from two fragments of the same large flake. Alternatively, these three series may have come from a previous state of the same uniface when it was much larger. This last hypothesis is much more complex and less probable than the former (which supposes two different unifaces) because it implies that the uniface was subjected to several phases of irregular retouch with a stone hammer before being abandoned in place. One of these series seems to be centered in locality B2 with a significant dispersion toward the west and north; another occupies an empty space between A and B; and the third is situated in A. All these flakes form a diffuse trail oriented from the southwest to the northeast. However, the elements are grouped so that each set of refits is well localized without overlapping into others. Other small flakes, with a few refits of two or three flakes, could also have originated from the two previous pieces. A few of the thinner ones seem to have been detached with a soft hammer.

In concentrations A, B, and C, these black quartzite flakes are distributed over a band more than 12 m long, beginning in A and widening in B (Figure 58). This very loose distribution is completely different from that observed for the bifacial tools. It suggests that unifaces were worked while walking between concentrations A and B, which could be the case if a uniface was shared among several people working simultaneously in A and B. Moreover, we observe that many of these flakes are found all around the main concentration of flakes from uniface no. 17 but few within. In concentration D, we observe a few flakes of this material that could have originated from no. 17 or its missing twin uniface. The distribution is essentially over localities D2 and D4 (Figure 59).

In addition, a large flake and a fragment of a flake of black quartzite found in a disturbed context (in the small gully to the northwest of the site at the margin of concentration D) are of a material similar to that of uniface no. 17 and the missing uniface. These objects demonstrate that black quartzite cobbles were knapped at or near the site, or that flakes or fragments with flat faces were brought to the site. This black quartzite, which is often found in the form of cobbles at Paiján sites, comes from the alluvium of Quebrada de Cupisnique, about 10 km to the north. It is particularly easy to knap large flakes from these cobbles and to create good-quality cutting edges.

Unifaces no. 22 and 27, as well as no. 74, whose location was not precisely recorded, are all rather similar. They are wide and oval, although at least one extremity is more angular than rounded. No. 22, collected between A1 and A2, is made from a light green patinated tuff that is somewhat coarse-grained. It has a small amount of inverse flat retouch toward the proximal extremity of the flaking face, which no doubt served to remove the bulb of percussion. Four small flakes of the same material found nearby in A2 could have originated from this tool (Figure 58). Despite the absence of direct refits, we can suppose this tool was finally resharpened in A2. No. 27 is a small uniface made from finely laminated tuff with a multicolored patination. A slight denticulation on its edges is similar to no. 16-116-108 described below. This tool comes from knapping locality D4; only one other small flake of this material was found in BK47 (thus clearly in locality A2). These two objects do not directly refit, but are very likely associated.

Two other pieces have the typical *limace* form: narrow, pointed, with steep edges (no. 78 and 84). These two pieces were found barely 1 m from each other near locality B4. No. 78 is a fragment broken in its mesial part and missing the tip. Its mesial fracture is somewhat difficult to explain. A lip on the ventral face shows that the body of the piece was broken by dorsal flexing, which is different from a retouch accident. The tip could have been broken during resharpening, since the fracture has a superior lip of the type that can be produced by an accident during direct retouch. The missing fragments (tip and basal half) were not found. No flakes were refitted to this fragment, although some flakes of the same black quartzite variety were found in concentration B. No. 84, found near locality B4, is a typical whole uniface. It has a triangular section and a narrow but unpointed end (Figure 55, no. 4). It is made of dark laminated tuff. Its edges have a straight delineation with semi-abrupt covering retouch until the median line of the superior face, and a later passage of discrete *Quina*-type retouch (stepped, scalar retouch). Five small retouch flakes of this same material found grouped in locality D4 (Figure 59), as well as two others found in the space between B1 and B2, could have originated from this tool, but no direct refit was found.

One uniface, no. 16-116-108 (Figure 56, no. 5), was reconstituted from several fragments: . It is made of pale gray tuff and apparently was burned. Its edges show very regular micro-denticulation produced by pressure retouch at a frequency of around six teeth per centimeter. This type of retouch is unique among all the known Paiján unifaces except perhaps for no. 27 (Figure 56, no. 3), on which it is much less clear. This serration is especially visible on the left edge, perhaps because the right edge was abraded by use. No refits were made to this piece.

Flakes of several other raw material varieties that originated from unifaces could not be refitted to any piece found at the site. These flakes are thus evidence of the retouching of pieces now missing from the site because they were exported:

- one series of five flakes of fine black quartzite (different from that of the unifaces found at the site) found around locality D2, resulting from reworking a lateral edge (Figure 59);

Other Observations

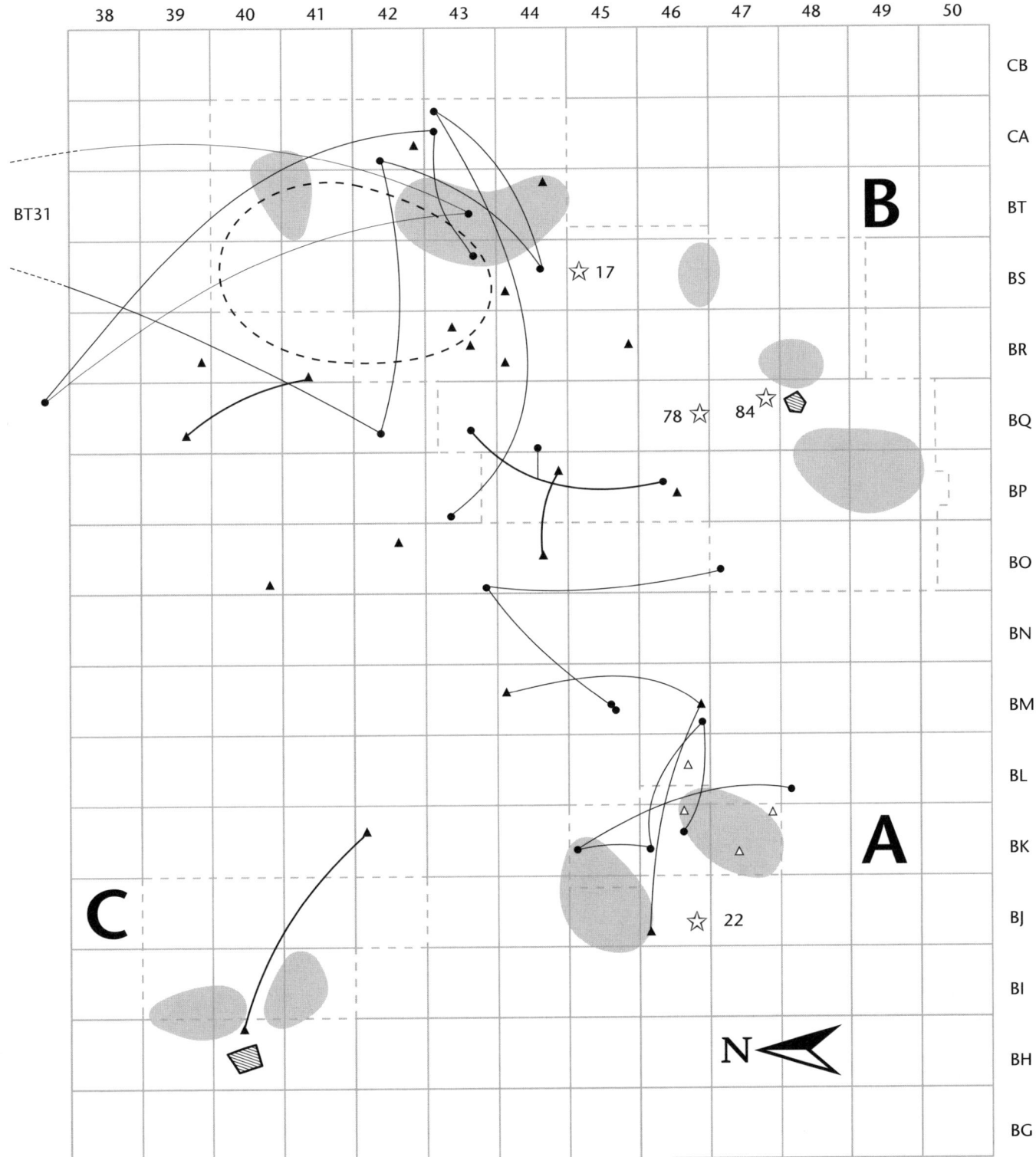

Figure 58. Spatial distribution of resharpening flakes from the "ghost" uniface made from a black quartzite identical to no. 17 (dots); other resharpening flakes from a uniface missing from the site, made from a black quartzite different from that of no. 17 and its twin "ghost" uniface (black triangles); and pale gray tuff flakes from uniface no. 22 (white triangles). The oval zone delimited by the dashed line designates the main group of flakes from uniface no. 17.

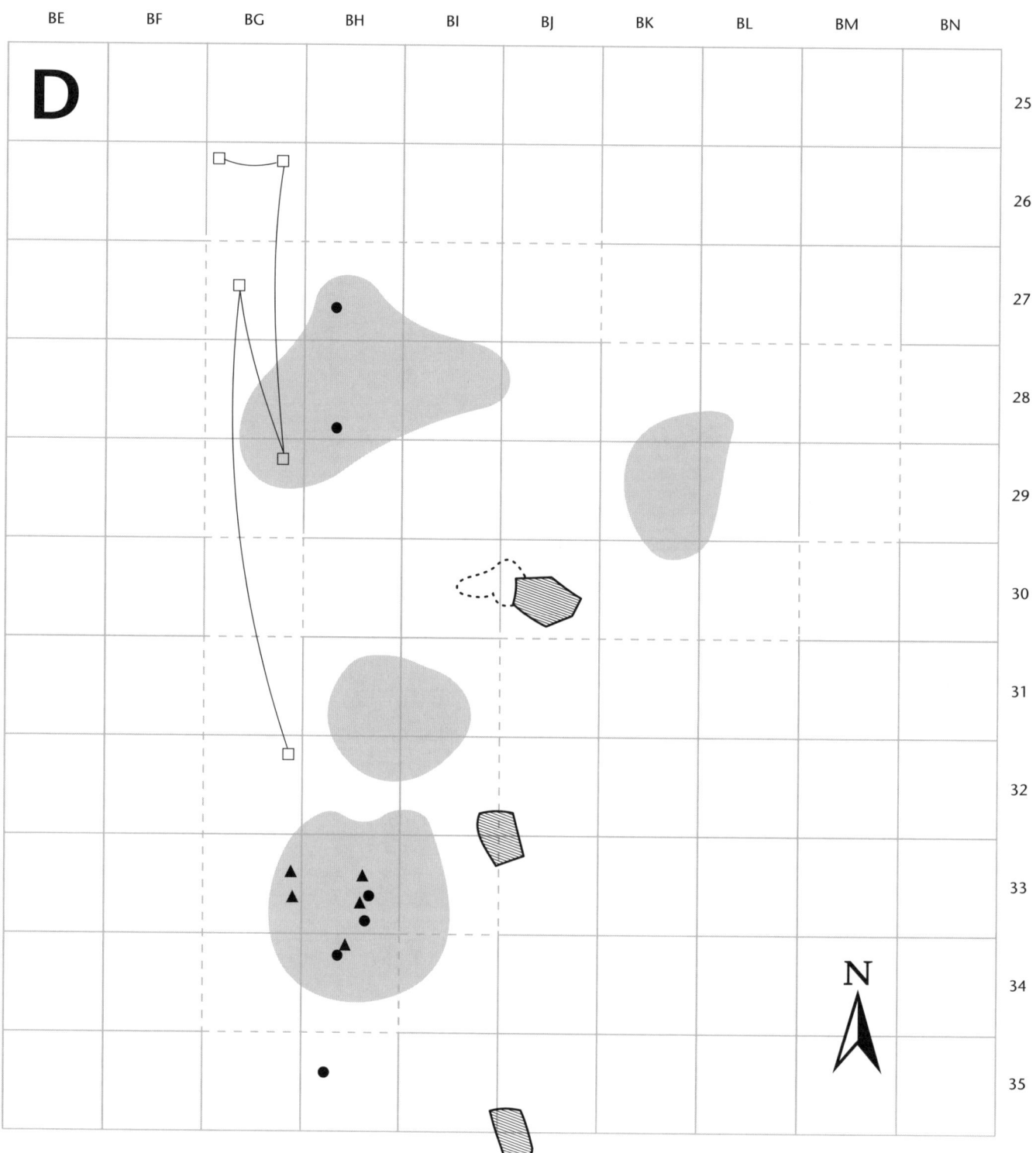

Figure 59. Spatial distribution of uniface resharpening flakes in concentration D. Dots: fine black quartzite of uniface no. 17 or of its twin "ghost." Triangles: dark laminated tuff of uniface no. 84. Squares: black quartzite of a uniface not found at the site.

- one isolated flake of coarse-grained laminated tuff, the only example of this material found in BP48 (locality B5);
- two isolated thin flakes, one of which is in two fragments, of very fine grained volcanic tuff found in the zone between concentration A and C;
- a group of eight patinated and six non-patinated flakes, made of pale blue tuff, dispersed in concentration B;
- two interesting small flakes made from pale green tuff slightly patinated to beige: one bladelet with a smooth butt originating from the front of the tip of a uniface; and the

- two refitted fragments of a small retouch flake found between D2 and D3;
- 11 flakes made from dark-colored slightly laminated tuff, identical to the material of the naturally backed knife no. 25 (Figure 15, no. 1), found largely scattered over the zone between B, C, and A, with one small group of four objects, including one refit, found in locality B2, plus a twelfth isolated flake found to the east of D4.

To conclude the subject of unifaces, one group of small and medium thin flakes of pale gray tuff from concentration B poses a problem. Because of their faceted butts or the presence of flat opposed negatives (originating from the opposite edge of a necessarily thin piece), around two thirds of these flakes were reasonably attributed to the fabrication of a Paiján point (end of phase 2 and phase 3 of a small piece that was not found, probably finished and exported). For this reason we have already treated them in the category of bifacial knapping (see above). However, certain unifaces also have plano-convex bifacial retouch. One such tool, also made of pale gray tuff, was found at site 27 of Pampa de los Fósiles (Chauchat et al. 1992: Figure 132, no. 10). In this case the flat face was probably initially worked by removing a few very flat flakes. In the present case, the characteristics of approximately 100 flakes in question correspond more closely to finishing a point.

However, there remain around a dozen of these flakes without opposed negatives, or fragments without butts, that could have originated from retouching one or several unifaces of the same material. Nonetheless, they are scattered in the same manner as those that were classified in the bifacial knapping category (Figure 53) and are grouped in an identical manner near locality B3. The unifacial knapping flakes thus seem to have been produced at the same time and in the same manner as the supposed bifacial knapping flakes. Moreover, we already have noted that uniface rejuvenation flakes are very widely dispersed, and it is troubling to observe that the supposed bifacial knapping flakes of pale gray tuff are similarly dispersed, which is not the case for flakes of almost all varieties of rhyolite. This difference in dispersion, for which we have no explanation, favors an association of these flakes with unifacial rejuvenation more than with bifacial knapping. It is therefore important to remember that there is some uncertainty concerning this set of flakes. The clearest implication is that the Paiján point of pale gray tuff, assumed to be finished, may in fact not exist, and that flakes supposed to be associated with it may actually have originated from a uniface. Considering the current state of data collected at the site and our knowledge, it is impossible to choose between these two possibilities.

These above-mentioned groups of flakes, which do not correspond to any of the unifaces abandoned at the site, thus imply the rejuvenation of six to eight unifaces that were exported at the end of the knapping activities. There remains uncertainty about the existence of two pieces: first, the twin negative of no. 17, from which the flakes might have originated, since they may as well have originated from a previous state of 17; and second, the mysterious piece of pale gray tuff that was counted as a point in the last chapter, but which could just as well be a uniface.

Conclusions

The unifaces of Pampa de los Fósiles 14, unit 1, were manufactured from raw material varieties rarely employed for fabricating points. These are pale and dark gray volcanic tuffs and fine-grained black quartzite. In other sites of the region, unifaces made from green tuff were observed, but this is not the case here.

The morphology of the unifaces, as we observed here and at other Paiján sites in the region, implies a particular type of knapping by-product. These are most often detached by a soft hammer; material is always removed from the dorsal face, the opposite one remaining smooth. These flakes thus have plain, flat butts. Moreover, the characteristic plano-convex section of unifaces results in a high incidence of flakes with very curved profiles. On uniface no. 17 we observed an awkward, rather coarse retouch by hard stone percussion, resulting in a thick piece with an irregular outline, which was eventually abandoned in place. This behavior can certainly be associated with that already revealed in the context of bifacial knapping, showing a low level of technical maturity that can perhaps be attributed to a young apprentice.

Our technological and spatial analysis of unifaces reveals that the series of flakes that refit, or that are assignable to the same piece, are very few in number, from two or three to a dozen (not considering the exceptional behavior associated with piece no. 17). Therefore the unifaces were not manufactured on site from flakes, blocks, or preforms. In fact, the small series of refitted flakes often originate from one edge of the piece and not its whole perimeter, implying the rejuvenation of this edge. At another site we found two massive oval-shaped unifacial pieces that had been carefully knapped by soft-hammer percussion. They had evidently been cached and could represent unifaces in their original state, for we usually find these tools in an exhausted and unusable state. We thus propose that unifaces were in fact multi-purpose knives or scrapers whose edges were resharpened by soft-hammer percussion each time they became dulled by use. Since utilization apparently most often affected one of the long sides of the piece, resharpening increasingly narrowed the piece. Moreover, the fact that retouch is unifacial makes it difficult to thin the piece accordingly, resulting in a morphology that is similar to that of Mousterian *limaces*. These same factors also increase the steepness of the retouch. Incidentally, it is highly probably that European Mousterian *limaces* underwent a similar reduction process of alternate use and rejuvenation (Dibble 1984, 1987, 1988).

In addition to the seven unifaces collected at the site, our analysis of flakes that could be assigned to this tool type revealed the presence of six to eight other pieces, which were not abandoned at the site but were apparently exported by the knappers. One piece could have been at least partially manufactured on site, if we accept the hypothesis that some (or all) of the pale gray tuff flakes originated from a uniface and not from a bifacial piece. One other piece is dubious, since it may consist of an earlier state of no. 17. The knappers thus arrived at the site with 13 to 15 unifaces, one of which was perhaps barely in the rough-out stage. Seven of these unifaces must have already been significantly reduced and were abandoned at the site, and the others were exported. We note that these two figures are nearly identical, suggesting (unfortunately, without proof) that each knapper had one uniface in active use and one in reserve, which would imply a total of 6 to 8 level A or B knappers. Of course, this interpretation implies that all the unifaces were functionally equivalent.

Except in obvious cases, such as projectile points, the function of lithic tools is rarely directly interpretable. For Paiján unifaces, we can propose a few possibilities. They are usually associated with bifacial knapping workshops, although usually present only in small numbers. On the other hand, they are rarely found in campsites. This distribution could be due to the fact that, like bifaces, they are manufactured by soft-hammer percussion. However, except for the possible gray tuff uniface extensively knapped in concentration B, the knapping of unifaces resulted only in small series of flakes, at most a dozen, that refit onto each other. These invariably originate from a single edge of the tool. However, the unifaces in question are retouched over their entire perimeter. It is thus permissible to speak of partial rejuvenation of one edge in preparation for a cutting or scraping action. If this action is associated with knapping, and if, as we believe, the soft hammers used for knapping were made from *algarrobo* wood (*Prosopis pallida*), the unifaces could have been employed to reshape the wooden billets periodically, since bifacial knapping very quickly damages their surface. This reshaping, which rounded and smoothed the hammer face, was necessary to achieve precise percussion action. We could further speculate on the precise technical details, such as superficially burning the hammer face in conjunction with scraping and smoothing to remove rough and damaged spots. This interpretation supposes periodic round-trips to a central fire pit, which could have been superficial and is no longer visible. Hammer scraping and reshaping could be performed in varied locations: close to the fire pit; at the knapping locality itself; or somewhere in between. The same could be true for uniface rejuvenation, which probably involved use of the same hammer.

Unifaces are significantly represented in this relatively modest workshop. This fact must be considered in contrast to their weak representation in other workshops of the Pampa de los Fósiles zones that we have studied: Pampa de los Fósiles 13, unit 3, one uniface for 193 bifaces and points; unit 5, one uniface for 148 bifaces and points; unit 11, no unifaces for 120 bifaces and points (Chauchat et al. 1992:179–227). On the contrary, at Pampa de los Fósiles 27, which comprises four tightly spaced units, one of which is a small point knapping workshop (unit 2), there are 6 unifaces in unit 1, 2 in unit 3, and none in unit 4. However, the workshop is situated exactly between units 1 and 3; unit 4 is farther away (Chauchat et al. 1992:279–288). A similar situation is found in the Ascope zone, 30 km southeast of Pampa de los Fósiles on the margin of the Chicama Valley. We studied several sites there; one of the studies is still unpublished. These sites are unusual because bifacial tools and common tools are found together, accompanied by concentrations of micro-vertebrate remains (Chauchat et al. 1992:299–324). There is also a high proportion of unifaces, including a number of rough-outs or pieces in the process of manufacture. We interpreted these sites as uniface fabrication workshops because of the ready availability of good-quality gray tuff that can easily be extracted in place and in nearby alluvium and outcrops. Also present are unifaces reduced to the state of *limaces*, which were thus used and rejuvenated in place until abandoned. The uniface workshop function is therefore not the only explanation for their abundance at the Ascope sites. Soft-hammer maintenance in projectile point workshops thus undoubtedly constitutes a small part of uniface function.

Our experience in this region suggests that unifaces tend to be most numerous when a workshop and a living site coexist on the same surface. Therefore an alternative explanation might be that unifaces were utilized by knappers who made and rejuvenated them with techniques similar to those employed for the bifacial pieces, but for a function more related to subsistence activities. However, in the Paiján complex, points were knapped with the objective of hunting large fish, thus replacing the hunting of terrestrial game, which, if we have correctly interpreted the sexual division of labor (Testart 1986), was an activity reserved for adult males. Therefore it seems that at least part of the function of unifaces could have been preparing fish (scaling, eviscerating, and cutting) shared among the group. This interpretation would not eliminate the additional possibility of other functions, such as those discussed above. There is strong evidence of alternate sequences of utilization and rejuvenation in our group of workshops; thus it is probable that both operations were performed by the same persons, adult males.

Rare Materials

At the very beginning of this study we saw that, in addition to the pale rhyolite and green tuff utilized for fabricating projectile points and the fine-grained black quartzite and gray volcanic tuffs used for unifaces, there are a certain number of objects made from miscellaneous stones, some recognizable as common tools by comparison with those observed at Paiján campsites in the Cupisnique region. However, debitage of these various materials, and sometimes of raw materials not even recognized among the common tools, is also found among the raw materials collected in the workshop (Tables 10, 13, 16, 19, and 22). These materials cannot be assigned to any operation interpretable in terms of knapping or subsistence activity. In this section we briefly examine the spatial distribution of the main varieties of these materials, including a small amount of undetermined material that was nonetheless unambiguously knapped.

Brown rhyolite is mainly distributed in concentration B in two loose clusters, one in B2 toward the north short of B1, the other northwest of B5. There is another concentration a short distance away in A (Figure 60). Brown rhyolite is represented in concentration D by only five flakes in D4.

Andesite is a coarse-grained gray-green stone with white and black inclusions. Its distribution is practically the same as the

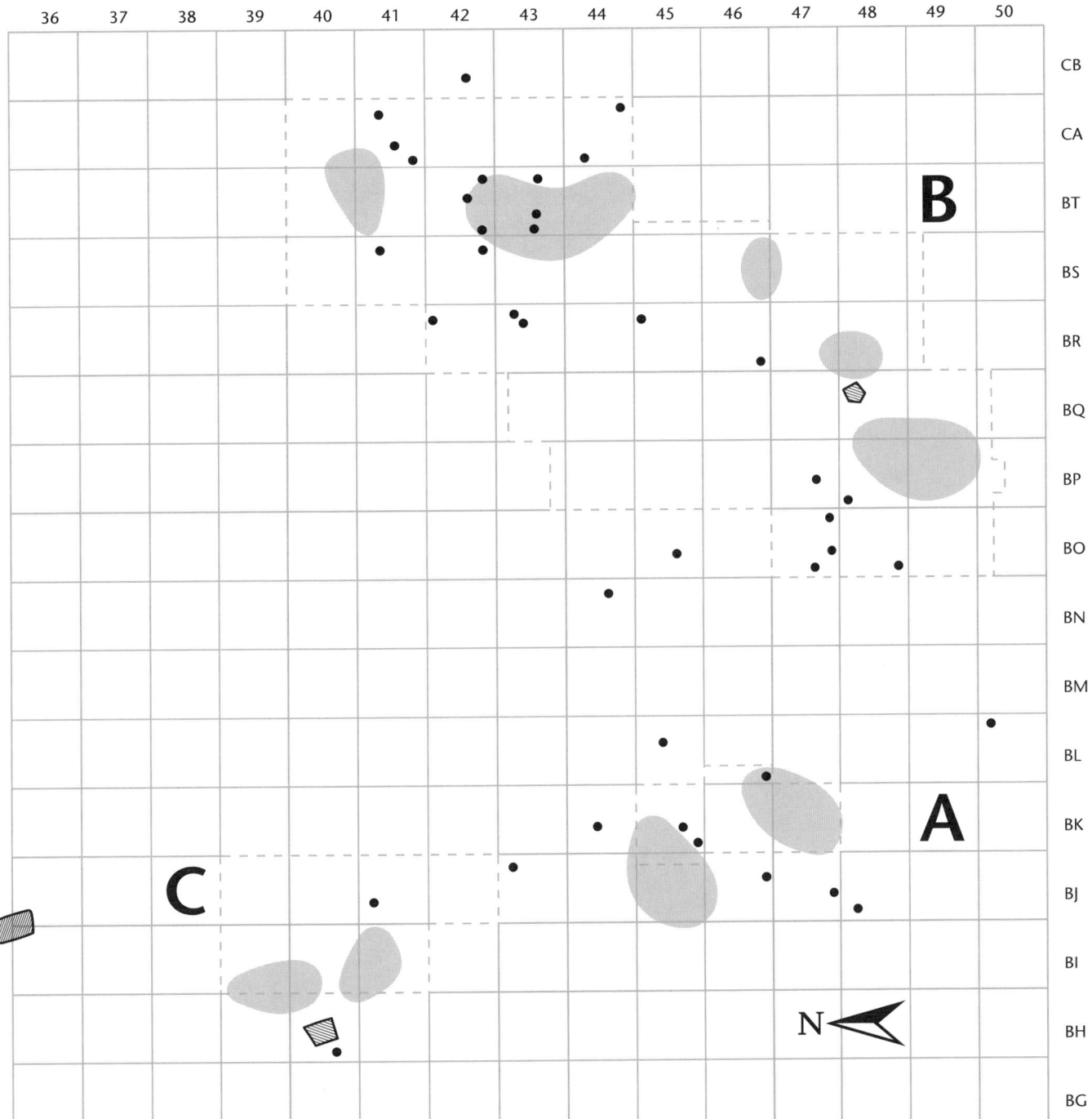

Figure 60. Spatial distribution of brown rhyolite debitage flakes.

brown rhyolite but with one difference, the absence of objects in the southern half of concentration B. On the other hand, a strong concentration present in B2 continues with trails in the northeast and southwest directions. In the latter direction the trail extends until concentration A, where a few flakes are present. There are only two flakes in C, but four more in D, including three clearly in D4.

The green stone is probably the same as the micro-diorite already identified in other sites of the Pampa de los Fósiles zone (Chauchat et al. 1992:74, no. 13). It is precisely concentrated in knapping locality B2. However, milky quartz and rock crystal extend over all of concentration B without any preferential clustering. Two rock crystal flakes were also collected in D.

There are also around 50 flakes of miscellaneous stones, most of which are undetermined. Generally these miscellaneous materials are present in B (with a concentration in B2) and in the southern half of the ellipse between B and A. A small minority of objects is found in concentration D.

Chapter 6
Conclusions

The study we have presented here primarily concerns the knapping of Paiján points, particularly in the Cupisnique region, where most of the studied Paiján sites are located, and the origin of the raw materials utilized in our experiments. Our results constitute an important step in solving the Paiján puzzle, for they contribute to reconstructing the way of life of the first inhabitants of the coast of Peru during the Pleistocene-Holocene transition.

Methodology

At the beginning of this study we described our research strategy for analyzing Paiján bifacial technology. In the first phase, having studied the morphology of projectile points found at archaeological workshops in the Cupisnique region, we documented a number of knapping experiments that explored the variability of the points, using the same tools and raw materials supposedly used by Paiján knappers (Pelegrin and Chauchat 1993).

In the second phase, which is presented here, we returned to an archaeological site, a Paiján point knapping workshop, and applied the information obtained from our experiments to interpret our findings. From the beginning we believed that this strategy could enable us to estimate the number of pieces produced (and thus disappeared from the archaeological record), with a margin of uncertainty of one to three pieces, which could be reduced to one to two pieces by more precisely analyzing the dimensions of knapping by-products.

With this objective in mind, we systematically drew upon the methodological and conceptual framework developed during the first phase of this research program (Pelegrin and Chauchat 1993) by:

a) dividing the knapping process into phases and identifying these phases on abandoned pieces and identified series of flakes.

b) distinguishing flakes characteristic of phase 2a in order to determine the nature of the original blank from which each piece was knapped; a relatively large number of large cortical flakes could indicate a block or plaque; depending on the total number of flakes, their association with one or more Kombewa flakes could indicate either several different blanks or one or more large cortical flake blanks.

d) estimating the dimensions of preforms, based on refits and the largest dimension attained by the knapping flakes, particularly during phase 2a; and comparing them with abandoned pieces, which we can suppose represent the same mental templates of the knappers. Indeed, within the same phase, the proportion of length to width is nearly stable; therefore short, medium, and long pieces, as well as intermediary values, can be distinguished.

d) evaluating the degree of expertise of the knapper based on abandoned pieces and refits.

Precisely distinguishing raw material varieties, which enabled us to identify individual blocks from which one or two pieces were manufactured, became a key element in this study that made it possible to refine our estimates of the number of knapped pieces. Identifying raw material varieties was also a valuable help in refitting series of flakes. Refitted flakes are the only direct evidence, albeit partial, of knapping sequences performed in the past; through them we can examine the actual work of the prehistoric knappers, rather than relying solely on experimentally obtained results, which are at best a close approximation. Besides helping us gauge the dimensions of the knapped piece, refits provide precise data for defining the knapping process used by the ancient craftsman. The original distribution of these refit flakes on the occupation surface fixes the context of this behavior in the topographic space of the workshop, rather than simply as a process that took place in an undetermined location. Spatial analysis of knapping waste products for each raw material variety is thus a second indispensable element in reconstituting and understanding the knapping processes that took place in the past.

All these interpretations carry a more or less significant degree of uncertainty. Nonetheless, they all contribute to a greater goal that is more difficult to achieve: determining how many pieces were knapped, by whom, and how much time was invested in these activities, thus helping us understand the lifeways of an important part of the Paiján social group, the knappers. We seek to understand their behavior, their degree of expertise, and perhaps their age class by examining the waste products of their knapping activities left on the ground for us to find 10,000 years later.

Obviously we could ask whether a finer and more precise study would have produced more reliable results and sounder conclusions. In particular, we could have recorded the knapping waste flakes of each raw material variety in greater detail. Although the locations of all flakes were recorded in small 25-by-25-cm squares, we made complete lists only of those flakes that were part of a refit series, not of each raw material variety. We could also suppose that a more intensive search for refits would have yielded more complete results. However, we must remember that since the knapping localities had been significantly disturbed and diffused as a result of their long exposure on the surface, more complete plans would not necessarily clarify the picture of the original occupation. Finally, the search for refits was an extremely long and tedious effort, and we realized we had reached the point of diminishing returns. Without question, all research leaves room for perfection; but only new attempts will show whether greater effort yields more reliable results.

It is also necessary to proceed with tempered optimism in applying these research procedures to different contexts. This study was made possible by a workshop surface where the whole of the site was visible to the naked eye; in the particular conditions of the Cupisnique region, numerous raw material varieties can be distinguished. The nature of this workshop, where knapping by-products were found in discrete concentrations, was another benefit.

There is no reason not to launch similar research programs in the future; properly structured, they can test reproducibility with a high level of confidence and yield concrete answers about bifacial technology. For future studies under conditions similar to ours, we recommend several modifications to analysis and recording procedures:

a) In the field, we realized that, at the scale employed, it was not necessary to record the exact location of every tool. The 25-by-25-cm grid we used when collecting objects proved to be adequate and saved a significant amount of time. On the other hand, it is absolutely necessary to separate objects found on the surface from those found during excavation. Whenever possible, it is also helpful to record the plan of superficial flake distributions before beginning to excavate.

b) In the laboratory, it is absolutely necessary to make complete lists of flakes for each raw material variety identified, not just for refitted flakes. This advice, confirmed by the procedure we practiced, means that all flakes must be labeled according to their location in the 25-by-25-cm grid and according to whether they were found on the surface or underground. An arbitrarily contrived system for labeling objects is useful, since it does not require a great deal of additional work beyond the intensive effort we just described. Flakes can then be entered into a computer database and manipulated in future analyses. Note that a long process of familiarizing oneself with the material is still absolutely necessary for learning precisely how to distinguish raw material varieties (unless this knowledge has already been learned through previous research). This familiarization poses certain physical requirements, such as a large table on which all the material can be displayed at once.

c) In analyzing refits, it is absolutely necessary to make every effort to refit small groups of flakes found at a distance from the majority of flakes of that particular raw material, as we did in our study, in order to determine if these flakes could represent a short knapping sequence that took place in another area.

d) All flakes isolated either spatially or in terms of raw material must be analyzed in order to determine if they constitute only knapping flakes from a reduction sequence or a type of *a posteriori* tool.

It is possible that these procedures will not yield benefits commensurate with the significant effort needed to implement them. However, the only way to know is to try.

Results of Knapping Activities

According to our analysis, in this workshop 12 to 22 Paiján points were successfully knapped, and another 13 to 17 were broken in the process of manufacture. In addition, three rough-outs were soon abandoned; two or three fragments collected away from the site were also rejected after a few blows, an activity that we attributed to children. When the knappers arrived, they carried with them a projectile point base that was probably still hafted, as well as two small fragments of finished points that may have been embedded in fish brought with them. On the whole, production at this site, which includes as many failed pieces as finished ones, cannot be considered very successful. The evidence bears witness to the difficulty of this work. However, these figures obscure our interpretation that apprentices were probably responsible for nearly all failed attempts at projectile point manufacture; expert adult knappers, on the other hand, produced functional projectile points almost every time they began the reduction process.

The knappers also had with them unifaces, ovate multipurpose scrapers that they used to scrape and smooth the faces of their wooden hammers and for subsistence activities. The edges of some of these scrapers were resharpened, and seven of them were abandoned when they became unusable. However, raw material found among the resharpening flakes indicates that six to eight other pieces were utilized at the site, then exported to continue their functional lives elsewhere. One of these pieces was in fact also counted as a projectile point because of its uncertain nature.

However, our experience with Paiján workshops demonstrates that this is an unusually large number of unifaces abandoned in a relatively small workshop. The fact that we normally find only one or two unifaces in much larger workshops containing several hundred abandoned pieces certainly indicates that unifaces were used here for functions other than maintaining wooden hammers. Another feature of this workshop not found at any other workshop in the Pampa de los Fósiles zone is the presence of food remains, which are undoubtedly related to the relative abundance of common tools. Both these traits are characteristic of Paiján campsites. However, these campsites are usually spatially separated from the workshops and unifaces are rare in them. The situation at Pampa de los Fósiles 14, unit 1, resembles that observed at Paiján sites in the Ascope region, 30 km to the southeast (Chauchat et al. 1993:299–324). There, campsites and workshops for knapping projectile points and unifaces are contiguous or even merge, suggesting that the numerous unifaces found were not only made but also used on site. Any further research concerning uniface functions should take these facts into account.

Occupation Duration and Group Composition

At Pampa de los Fósiles 14, unit 1, it appears there were four to six level A knappers, accompanied by one adolescent (level B) and at least one child, as well as possibly one or more adult females. This tally gives a total of six to nine adults and one child. If we compare these results with the quantity of unifaces utilized during the occupation, it seems that each knapper could have possessed an average of two unifaces, one of which was left at the site. According to our calculations, a duration of two or three days is thus a feasible estimate for the knapping operations, but we must undoubtedly add at least one full day for collecting raw materials and knapping rough-outs (*Chivateros* bifaces).

Integrating the food remains into this evaluation is somewhat difficult (see Appendix, next chapter). We could suppose that the lizards, birds, and terrestrial animals were strictly local resources, along with the snails that could have been collected on the rocky hillsides. However, the fish were brought by the group from the coast, unless perhaps some members made a special trip to procure fish while the others remained to continue knapping activities. However, this hypothesis is not very feasible, since it supposes a solution to the problem of procuring points, which is, in fact, what the knappers came to accomplish; and it implies a round trip of several days. Therefore it appears likely the group stopped in this area when returning from a fishing expedition to the coast and supplemented their store of seafood with local resources. Probably the fish were consumed first and the terrestrial resources afterwards. The five to seven fish brought from the shore constituted an appreciable source of animal protein if complemented with vegetable products. However, the fish certainly would not have been edible for more than a few days, even if the heads were removed. In any case it seems reasonable to conclude that the local animals, despite the small quantity of faunal remains found in the pit, substantially contributed to the subsistence of the group.

Circulation and Territory

Studies of the settlement patterns of Paiján human groups of the Cupisnique region were discussed in the conclusion of a recently published atlas of archaeological sites of this region (Chauchat et al. 1998). Unfortunately we have no knowledge of certain zones that could contribute to a more complete understanding of these settlement patterns: the marine shore, which was 10 to 15 km farther out than the modern shoreline when the sea level was around 60 m lower; the two zones currently under cultivation, in the Jequetepeque Valley to the north and the Chicama Valley to the south, where Holocene alluviation and agriculture have eliminated all traces of ancient habitation; or the mountainous zone, for which we still have only sporadic data concerning Paiján peopling. (For all the following discussion, refer to the regional map in Figure 3 and the map of surrounding sites in Figure 4.)

However, we know that Paiján groups frequented the plateaus and crests at an altitude of around 1800 m. We also know that they sometimes brought plain fragments of flint, which cannot exist in the volcanic geology of the coastal zone and which we have not found during our surveys in the alluvium. More intensive research on the western slope of the cordillera is definitely needed.

In contrast, the coastal plain appears to have been a zone of fast walking trips to and from the shore. In the area remaining today, which is 10 km wide and 25 km long between two cultivated valleys, we know of only four projectile point knapping workshops and not one campsite. It is likely that along the former coastline there existed numerous Paiján campsites and probable shell heaps. Shellfish are a resource that certainly would have been important locally. In the interior sites, marine shells, which have a significant dead weight, are rare.

Paiján settlements begin to be visible on the upper part of the coastal plain, 12 km from the modern shoreline. The sites are of a particular nature that is rare in the arid valleys; they consist essentially of knapping workshops, which benefit from the good quality volcanic and volcano-sedimentary rocks of the outcrops closest to the shore. Associated campsites are spatially separated and generally modest in size. This set of data suggests that a single important resource, lithic materials, was exploited during short occupations in the course of trips between the interior and the coast. This zone is where the Pampa de los Fósiles 14 site is located.

Surveys and excavations in the Cupisnique region show that the population was concentrated in the middle part of currently arid valleys that descend from the western slope, between 400 and 1000 m in altitude (Chauchat et al. 1998). Due to the succession of ecological zones in parallel altitudinal bands on the coast and cordillera, vegetation becomes significantly diverse and abundant in this zone, even though the shoreline is 20–50 km distant today and was 35–85 km distant 10,000 years ago. Beyond this distance, toward the interior, narrow canyons and steep slopes discourage human occupation, even though the passage into the upper zone is well proven. The high population density in this zone of arid valleys is indicated by the frequency of burials in Paiján campsites. Around 20 burials that were eroding out on the surface have been studied, but despite intensive searching we know of only four in the entire higher part of the coastal plain.

Information on the circulation of members of the group that occupied the workshop at Pampa de los Fósiles 14, unit 1, comes principally from our detailed knowledge of the original sources of various exotic materials present at the site.

The varieties of pale rhyolite are found at outcrops located not very far away. As we already described above, the outcrop most exploited here, found around 2 km to the east, is catalogued as site 125 (Chauchat et al. 1998:62). The outcrop that yields the *porosa-rosada* variety is located a little further away, 3 km to the southwest (unit 104 of site 12); it is possible that the *porosa-blanca* variety comes from a different nearby outcrop (unit 135 of the same site) at the same distance from the workshop (Chauchat et al. 1992:80; Chauchat et al. 1998:21–25). The origin of the *gris-fina* and *gris-violácea* varieties is unknown. Obviously they could come from a rhyolite outcrop farther away. There are two known in the north of the region, in the Quebrada de Cupisnique, and evidence found in the alluvium suggests that some must exist in the Quebrada Santa Maria, which we are not familiar with. However, we cannot totally eliminate the possibility that these two varieties also come from site 125, which has probably not been completely explored; it is very large, and lateral variations of material are evident.

As we have already stated, an outcrop of green tuff has yet to be definitively located. However, workshops containing a great majority of green and gray tuff, often in the form of large knapping flakes detached by soft-hammer percussion, are found at the foot of several small, rocky hills, 7–9 km to the north of our workshop (sites no. 33 and 129; Chauchat et al. 1998:37, 63). Moreover, these hills consist of stratified cinerites, or volcanic tuff. A few large flakes that suggested the beginnings of a quarry were found in the past on the steep flank of a hill overlooking site 33, but they could not be found again during a recent exploration. Knapping experiments with this material have always yielded unsatisfactory results. The pale gray tuff probably has the same origin. The other isolated varieties of tuff found as flakes at the workshop could have this same origin, but we should not forget that numerous varieties of this material are found in the alluvium and outcrops of the Quebrada de Cupisnique.

The black quartzite, which comes from the upstream area of the Quebrada de Cupisnique, is frequently found in its alluvium, probably as far as the coastline. In each case, whenever the nature of the original blank could be determined, it was found to be either a cobble or a flake detached from one. This material thus originates from a rather vast zone at least 10 km north of the site.

Rare materials, especially the andesite and brown rhyolite, as well as materials of which the common tools are made, could have come from sources immediately surrounding the site. The same is true for quartz, which is found as inclusions in granitic zones like the one at the foot of site 125.

The brown to reddish stones (quartzite?), which constitute the fragments of projectile points broken after utilization, are of unknown origin. They could have originated from the interior of the region, perhaps from the Quebrada de Cupisnique. However, the important fact that they were utilized indicates that these points and fragments arrived from the ocean shore, probably with the person or persons who brought back fish.

Finally, even if the remains of terrestrial fauna and bird bones found in the refuse pit proved to be strictly local (including the vizcacha, which has always lived in the vicinity), evidence of fish indicates that members of the group had very recently returned from the coast.

These data indicate origins that are spatially opposed and thus difficult to synthesize into a simple model. The preponderance of directions points to the Quebrada de Cupisnique as an origin; it is also the zone of the greatest density of sites. It is tempting to postulate a simple model according to which the small group of knappers of this workshop descended from the Quebrada and continued toward the south, where abundant good-quality materials for manufacturing points were to be found, before heading to the ocean for their fishing expedition. New unifaces would already have been made some time before in the Quebrada to replace others that were much reduced but still usable. On the way, one knapper stopped at the hillsides of volcanic tuff to collect 5–9 blocks of green and gray tuff, which he immediately transformed into rough-outs. The group then explored site 125 and obtained 20–30 bifaces that they carried to site 14, where they continued their knapping activities.

This model does not take into account the broken points or the presence of fish that came directly from the coast. Nor does it consider the pieces that originated from unit 104 of site 12, which, although a short distance away, is located in the direction opposite this route. We can be sure that the original departure point was the interior of the Quebrada, where we find the raw materials of the unifaces and perhaps of the reddish and dark quartzite points. However, after leaving the Quebrada, the group traveled to the shore and did not return to the interior until their stock of points was exhausted. To renew their stock they went to the Pampa de los Fósiles zone, which is closer than the interior of the Quebrada. On arriving in this zone, the group made a series of forays to several outcrops at various distances to gather raw material whose remains we have identified through our analyses. Since there were several knappers, it may be that they dispersed and thus did not all begin knapping at the same time.

However, following this hypothesis, it seems unlikely to us that one of the knappers made a special trip in a different direction (to the north instead of the east) to collect green tuff. It seems more feasible that in a nearby location they had already cached rough-outs made during an earlier trip. This behavior of storing and caching lithic artifacts manufactured elsewhere is described ethnoarchaeologically by Pétrequin and Pétrequin

Conclusions

(1993:146–147) for the rough-outs of adze blades in New Guinea (Irian Jaya).

Supplied with new points, the group then began their journey back toward the shore, which represents a full day's walking. The important aspect of these trips is the rapid shuttling between Pampa de los Fósiles, where lithic resources were available, and the coastline, where an important food resource could be procured. The group may have stayed for a time on the shore, depending on their stock of points, before again returning quickly to the raw material sources or to a base camp in the Quebrada de Cupisnique.

The availability of fresh water is the great unknown factor in our knowledge of the local environment during the Paiján period. We know it was present year-round in the middle part of the currently arid valleys (the *quebradas*), which nowadays benefit only from very temporary runoff, and we can suppose with high probability that seasonal water sources existed in the ravines around Pampa de los Fósiles after summer rains coming from the Andean *Sierra*, as is the case today farther toward the interior (Briceño 1995). However, closer to the coast, this resource was certainly always rare or difficult to access.

These data and inferences lead us to further postulate a model of seasonal nomadism between the main zones of the coast and the mountains. Within these large zones there could have been displacements of lesser amplitude, such as that observed between Pampa de los Fósiles and the shoreline. Even though it cannot be confirmed, similar journeys may have occurred between the lower zone of the *quebradas* of the interior, at 400–800 m altitude, and the higher zone above 1500 m, suggested by occasional flint remains found on the sites.

Alternatively, we could propose a different model that postulates the existence of two groups, one on the coast, the other in the interior. These groups would have exchanged a number of products, particularly ocean fish, whose remains are found in Paiján archaeological sites as far as the head of the Quebrada de Cupisnique, and lithic resources such as flint. No argument of lithic material provenience disproves this hypothesis: black quartzite could have come from the coastal part of the Cupisnique alluvium; finished projectile points of brown to reddish stone are of unknown origin and do not necessarily come from the interior, as we indicated above. In this second model, we must abandon the idea that the group of knappers originally came from the Quebrada de Cupisnique. Rather, we must suppose they lived on the coast and were in more or less frequent contact with other groups based in the middle part of the *quebrada*, with whom they exchanged these products.

In their current forms, both models suffer from too many suppositions and unknowns. However, they both conform to the history of all Andean societies until the present time (Murra 1972, 1975). The first model, which supposes a vast territory of exploitation including the ecological zones of the western slope of the Andes, corresponds to a foraging way of life consistent with what we know of Paleoindians and early-Archaic human groups elsewhere in America. The second model is more in accord with our understanding of how Archaic groups of the region adapted to an emerging food production economy by cultivating plants from the high Andes. Abundant and reliable archaeological data indicate that, in this later period, sedentary groups along the coastline specialized in exploiting marine resources coincident with the phenomena of Holocene aridification and the extension of coastal upwelling, which caused an explosion of the marine biomass. At the same time they benefited from primitive agriculture, which was practiced mainly in times of seasonal water runoff along the valley watercourses in the interior of the region and perhaps in the middle mountains, since the first experiments with cultivated plants appear to have taken place in the inter-Andean valleys at the beginning of the Holocene. Moseley (1992:22), for example, alludes to this idea when attributing this duality to hypothetical "maritime foundations of the Andean civilization"; he forgets the probable symbiosis that existed between these two specializations and the notable importance of cultivated plants in later pre-Ceramic coastal settlements (Bonavia et al. 1993, Chauchat and Bonavia 1998).

Acknowledgments

The long-term research project of which work on Pampa de los Fosíles 14 was a part was funded from 1978 to 1999 by the French Ministry of Foreign Affairs. Field investigations in 1988 were authorized by Resolución Suprema no. 188-88 ED from the Peruvian government. Field work and preparing the manuscript have benefited from help of a number of people who, hopefully, have been all mentioned in the text. Additionally, Georges Clément (C.N.R.S.) prepared the histograms of the counts of large flakes. The authors wish to thank Robson Bonnichsen, as well as Ruth Gruhn and two anonymous reviewers for their insightful comments and suggestions, and for accepting our manuscript for publication in the Peopling of the Americas series. We are also grateful to C&C Wordsmiths for their work in editing the text and preparing the text and illustrations for publication.

Projectile Point Technology and Economy　◫　*A Case Study from Paiján*

Appendix
Faunal Remains Found in the Pit near Concentration D
Prepared by Cesar Galvez, Hélène Martin, and Philippe Pannoux

A first list of the taxa represented in the pit of BI-BJ30 was compiled by C. Galvez a short time after its excavation. It separates the animal remains found in this refuse pit into broad categories. Particularly noted are the tooth of a large mammal (probable *Cervidae*); a probable fragment of a vizcacha (*Lagidium peruvianum*), a rodent larger than the habitual rats of the Peruvian desert (*Cricetidae*); and 15 half-mandibles or maxilla among the bones of *Teiidae* (lizards). Three otoliths were found among fish bones (Table 60). Galvez also reported the existence of terrestrial snails of the *Scutalus* and *Bostryx* genera, which were not counted.

The fish bones were then studied by P. Pannoux, who determined the species and minimum number of individuals (Table 61). Galvez identified fewer fish remains (41) than Pannoux (92, with 54 undetermined). The expertise of each researcher plays a role in these differences: Galvez did not recognize the head bones; Pannoux counts 322 total vertebrae, which implies the breaking of numerous pieces between the time of the two studies. Curiously, Pannoux does not mention the three otoliths indicated by Galvez.

In the study by Pannoux, *Micropogonias altipinnis* (Spanish *Corvina dorada*, a fish species typical of the tropical waters in far northern Peru) is represented by at least three individuals of medium size, probably around 50–70 cm long. One probably complete individual and at least two heads are present in this sample. This species, common in the middens of the Paijanense, signifies a climate (thus environment) different from today. Since the beginning of Holocene conditions, the coastal climate of Peru has been dominated by the influence of coastal upwelling of cold waters, resulting in a thermal inversion in low atmosphere and general aridity of the coastal zone. *M. altipinnis* is no longer found in the coastal middens during the late Preceramic period, beginning at 6000 yr B.P. (e.g., Pannoux 1991). The persistent appearance of this species in Paiján subsistence remains leads us to postulate a much lower aridity for this region of Peru due to seasonal tropical rains whose intensity is difficult to assess precisely. This interpretation implies that the coastal desert of Peru and Chile had a much smaller geographic extension than is extant today. On its northern margin, instead of extending to the north of Piura and toward the modern border of Ecuador, the desert would have been limited to the central coast of Peru and perhaps the southern part of the north coast. In the Cupisnique

Table 60. General composition of vertebrate remains in the pit of BI-BJ30 (count by Cesar Galvez).

Taxon	Count
reptiles (*Teiidae*)	41
fishes	41
birds	8
rodents	3
mammals	4
total	97
undetermined	115
total	212

Table 61. Composition of fish species in the pit of BI-BJ30 (determinations by Philippe Pannoux).

Taxon	Count	Min. number of individuals
Mugillidae		
Mugil sp.	13	1
Mugil cephalus	7	1
undet. Mugillidae	13	1
Sciaenidae		
Micropogonias sp.	8	2
Micropogonias altipinnis	9	1
Paralonchurus sp.	3	1
undet. Sciaenidae	1	
total	54	

region, where Pampa de los Fósiles 14 is located, the environment could have been at least similar to the Sahelian zone that we observe today in the extreme north around Piura.

The other two species, *Mugil cephalus* (mullet) and *Paralonchurus* sp. (Spanish *coco* or *suco*, of which there exist several species) are still present in the cold waters of the Peruvian coast. Mullet, represented by one or two specimens, is a coastal and estuarian water fish. *Suco* is represented by only two caudal vertebrae. These medium-sized fish are comparable in dimensions to *M. altipinnis* individuals.

The terrestrial and avian species present in this sample demonstrate the trapping skill of the Paijanenses. Lizards, of which at least 10 individuals were counted, are still consumed by the peasants of the north coast of Peru and are not particularly difficult to trap. The same cannot be said for birds or the vizcacha, a rabbit-sized rodent that is very timid and has crepuscular habits.

These food remains, to which we must add an imprecise quantity of landsnails and an unknown proportion of vegetable foods, attest to foraging activities during occupation of the site. The few common tools discussed earlier (Table 12, Figure 15) are also unquestionable evidence of activities besides lithic knapping. In other, much denser workshops in the vicinity, the absence of such remains strongly suggests the presence of a distinct campsite nearby. In contrast, at this relatively modest workshop the subsistence activities necessary to feed the hunters seem to have taken place on the same spot, implying the presence of at least part of their families.

The fragmentary character of some of the skeletons, such as the two heads of *Micropogonias*, the caudal vertebrae of *Paralonchurus*, and the existence of only one maxilla of vizcacha, can be attributed to several causes. First, small bone remains are exceedingly rare on the surface of Paiján sites, since they are inevitably destroyed by wind erosion; if small animals were consumed at the various concentrations of the workshop and their osseous remains left in place, they surely would have disappeared by now. It is also possible that the practice of sharing food by hunter-gatherer societies played a role; a portion of this food could have been exported for activities that took place away from the workshop or removed by temporary occupants of the site that did not belong to the group of knappers.

The presence of fish vertebrae and skulls suggests that fish were rapidly transported from the coast. Moreover, they show that these fish received no preparation other than simple evisceration, even though the coastline was several tens of kilometers away. Even for such minor conservation treatments as drying and smoking, we would normally expect that at least the head, if not the spinal column, would be removed after gutting the fish to assure thorough desiccation.

References Cited

Ardila Calderon, G.
    1991 The Peopling of Northern South America. In *Clovis: Origins and Adaptations*. R. Bonnichsen and K. L. Turnmire, eds., pp. 261–282. Center for the Study of the First Americans, Oregon State University, Corvallis.

Bell, R. E.
    1965 *Investigaciones arqueológicas en el sitio de El Inga, Ecuador*. Department of Anthropology, University of Oklahoma, Norman, Oklahoma. Editorial Casa de la Cultura Ecuatoriana, Quito.

Bird, J. B.
    1948 Preceramic Cultures in Chicama and Virú. In *A Reappraisal of Peruvian Archaeology*, ed. by W. C. Bennett, pp. 21–28. Memoirs of the Society for American Archaeology no. 4, Menasha.

Binford, L. R.
    1972 Model Building—Paradigms, and the Current State of Palaeolithic Research. In *An Archaeological Perspective*, pp. 244–294. Seminar Press, New York.

    1977 General introduction. In *For Theory Building in Archaeology: Essays on Faunal Remains, Aquatic Resources, Spatial Analysis, and Systemic Modeling*. L. R. Binford, ed. pp. 1–10. Academic Press, New York.

    1978 Dimensional Analysis of Behavior and Site Structure: Learning from an Eskimo Hunting Stand. *American Antiquity*, 43(3):330–361.

Binford, L. R., and S. R. Binford
    1966 A Preliminary Analysis of Functional Variability in the Mousterian of Levallois Facies. *American Anthropologist* 68(2), part 2, pp. 238–295. Recent studies in Palaeoanthropology, ed. by J. D. Clark and F. C. Howell.

Binford, S. R.
    1968 Variability and Change in the near Eastern Mousterian of Levallois Facies. In *New Perspectives in Archeology*, ed. by S. R. Binford and L. R. Binford, pp. 49–60. Aldine publishing Co., Chicago.

Bonavia, D.
    1979 Consideraciones sobre el complejo *Chivateros*. In *Arqueología Peruana; seminario sobre las investigaciones arqueológicas en el Perú, 1976*, Ramiro Matos compilador, pp. 65–74; Lima.

    1982 El complejo *Chivateros*: una aproximación tecnológica. *Revista del Museo Nacional*, tomo 46, pp. 19–37; Lima.

Bonavia, D., L. W. Johnson, E. J. Reitz, E. S. Wing, and G. H. Weir
    1993 Un sitio precerámico de Huarmey (PV35-6) antes de la introduccion del Maíz. *Bulletin de l' Iinstitut Français d'Etudes Andines,* 22 (2):409–442; Lima.

Bordes, F.
    1961 *Typologie du Paléolithique ancien et moyen*. 2 vol. Delmas, Bordeaux.

    1967 Considérations sur la typologie et les techniques dans le Paléolithique. *Quartär*, Band 18, pp. 25–55.

    1970 Reflexions sur l'outil au Paléolithique. *Bulletin de la Société Préhistorique Française* Tome 67, C.R.S.M. no. 7, pp. 199–202; Paris.

Briceño, J.
    1994 Investigaciones recientes sobre el Paleolítico superior en la parte media alta del valle de Chicama. *Investigar*, 1:5–18; Trujillo.

    1995 El recurso agua y el establecimiento de los cazadores recolectores en el valle de Chicama. *Revista del Museo de Arqueología, Antropología e Historia*, no. 5 (1994), pp. 143–157; Universidad Nacional de Trujillo.

    1997 La tradición de puntas de proyectil "cola de pescado" en Quebrada Santa María, y el problema del poblamiento temprano en los Andes Centrales. *Revista Arqueológica SIAN* no. 4, Noviembre, pp. 2–6; Trujillo.

Chauchat, C.
    1976 The Paiján Complex, Pampa de Cupisnique, Peru. *Ñawpa-Pacha* 13 (1975):85–96, Berkeley.

    1977 El Paijanense de Cupisnique; problemática y metodología de los sitios líticos de superficie. *Revista del Museo Nacional* 43, pp. 13–26; Lima.

    1978 Recherches préhistoriques sur la côte nord du Pérou. *Bulletin de la Société Préhistorique Française*, tome 75, no. 8, pp. 253–256; Paris.

    1979 Additional observations on the Paiján complex. *Ñawpa-Pacha* 16 (1978), pp. 51–64; Berkeley.

    1987 Niveau marin, écologie et climat sur la côte nord du Pérou à la transition Pléistocène-Holocène. *Bulletin de l' Institut Français d'Etudes Andines.*, 16(1-2):21–27; Lima.

1988 Early Hunter-gatherers on the Peruvian Coast. In *Peruvian Prehistory*, ed. by R. W. Keatinge, pp. 42–66. Cambridge University Press, Cambridge.

1990 Les Paijaniens, premiers chasseurs cueilleurs du versant pacifique des Andes. *Les dossiers d'Archéologie; no. 145: les Amériques de la Préhistoire aux Incas.* pp.42–47; Dijon.

1991 L'approche technologique dans une étude régionale: le Paijanien de la côte du Pérou. In: *25 ans d'études technologiques en Préhistoire ; bilan et perspectives.* APDCA, pp. 263–273. Juan-les-Pins. (Actes des XIèmes Rencontres internationales d'Archéologie et d'Histoire d'Antibes; 18–20 octobre 1990).

Chauchat, C. and D. Bonavia
1990 Presencia del Paijanense en el desierto de Ica. *Bulletin de l'Institut Français d'Etudes Andines,* 19 (2):399–412, Lima.

1998 Débuts de l'exploitation de la mer sur la côte du Pérou. In *Colloque "L'Homme préhistorique et la mer," 120 ème congrès CTHS, Aix en Provence, 1995.* pp. 427–436; Editions du Comité des Travaux Historiques et Scientifiques, Paris.

Chauchat, C. and J. Briceño
1998 Paiján and Fishtail Points from Quebrada Santa María, North Coast of Peru. *Current Research in the Pleistocene* 15:10–11. Center for the Study of the First Americans, Oregon State University, Corvallis.

Chauchat, C. and P-Y. Demars
1989 Structures de combustion et de chauffage dans le Paijanien de Cupisnique, côte nord du Pérou. *Nature et Fonction des Foyers Préhistoriques; Colloque de Nemours, 1987.* Mémoires du Musée de Préhistoire d'Ile de France, no. 2, pp.239–248; Nemours.

Chauchat, C. and J. Pelegrin
1994 Le premier peuplement de la côte désertique du Pérou. *Bulletin de la Société Préhistorique Française,* Tome 91, no. 4-5, pp. 275–280; Paris.

Chauchat, C., E. Wing, J-P. Lacombe, P-Y. Demars, S. Uceda, and C. Deza
1992 *Préhistoire de la Côte Nord du Pérou: le Paijanien de Cupisnique.* Les Cahiers du Quaternaire no. 18, C.N.R.S.-Editions, Paris.

Chauchat, C., C. Galvez, J. Briceño, and S. Uceda
1998 *Sitios Arqueológicos de la zona de Cupisnique y margen derecha del Valle de Chicama.* Patrimonio Arqueológico Zona Norte / 4; Travaux de l'Institut Francais d'Etudes Andines no. 113. Trujillo-Lima.

Chauchat, C. and J. Zevallos Quiñones
1980 Una Punta en Cola de Pescado Procedente de la Costa Norte del Perú *Ñawpa-Pacha* 17 (1979):143–146, Berkeley.

Crabtree, D. E.
1972 *An Introduction to Flintworking.* Occasional Papers of the Idaho State University Museum, no. 28, Pocatello.

Dibble, H. L.
1984 Interpreting Typological Variation of Middle Palaeolithic Scrapers: Function, Style or Sequence of Reduction? *Journal of Field Archaeology,* 11(4):431–436.

1987 The Interpretation of Middle Palaeolithic Scraper Morphology. *American Antiquity,* 52(1):109–117.

1988 Typological Aspects of Reduction and Intensity of Utilization of Lithic Resources in the French Mousterian. pp. 181–197. In: *Upper Pleistocene Prehistory of Western Eurasia*; H. Dibble and A. Montet-White eds. University Museum Monographs, no. 54, University of Pennsylvania, Philadelphia.

Gallay, A.
1991 *Itinéraires Ethnoarchéologiques I.* Documents du Département d'Anthropologie et d'Ecologie de l'Université de Genève, no. 18. p. 154; Geneva.

Hall, D. A.
1995 Stone Tool Tradition Endures Radical Environmental Change. *Mammoth Trumpet* 10-3:1, 4–11.

Inizan, M.-L., M. Reduron-Ballinger, H. Roche, and J. Tizier
1999 *Technology and Terminology of Knapped Stone,* followed by a multilingual vocabulary (Arabic, English, French, German, Greek, Italian, Portuguese, Spanish). Cercle de Recherches et d'Etudes Préhistoriques, Nanterre.

Kvamme, K. L.
1997 Patterns and Models of Debitage Dispersal in Percussion Flaking. *Lithic Technology,* 22(2):122–138.

Lanning, E. P.
1963 A Pre-agricultural Occupation on the Central Coast of Peru. *American Antiquity,* 28(3):360–371.

1970 Pleistocene Man in South America. *World Archaeology* 2:90–111. London.

Lanning, E. P. and E. Hammel
1961 Early Lithic Industries of Western South America. *American Antiquity,* 27(2):139–154.

Larco Hoyle, R.
1948 *Cronología Arqueológica de la Costa Norte del Perú.* Biblioteca del Museo de Arqueología Rafael Larco Herrera, Hacienda Chiclín, Trujillo.

Lavallée, D., M. Julien, J. Wheeler, and C. Karlin
1985 *Telarmachay: Chasseurs et Pasteurs Préhistoriques des Andes ,* 2 vol. Institut Francais des Etudes Andines. Editions Recherche sur les Civilisations, Paris.

Leroi-Gourhan, A.
1964–1965 *Le Geste et la Parole. I: Technique et Langage. II: La Mémoire et les Rythmes.* Albin-Michel, Paris.

Leroi-Gourhan, A. and M. Brezillon
1966 L'habitation Magdalénienne No. 1 de Pincevent, près Montereau (Seine et Marne). *Gallia-Préhistoire,* T. 9, fascicule 2, pp. 263–385, Editions du CNRS, Paris.

1972 *Fouilles de Pincevent. Essai d'analyse Ethnographique d'un Habitat Magdalénien (La section 36).* VIIème supplément à Gallia-Préhistoire, 2 vol. Editions du CNRS, Paris.

Lopez Castaño, C. E.
1990 Cazadores-recolectores tempranos en el Magdalena medio (Puerto Berrio, Antioquia). *Boletín de Arqueología.* Fundación de Investigaciones Arqueológicas Nacionales, año 5, no. 2, p. 11–29; Bogotá.

1995 Dispersión de Puntas de Proyectil Bifaciales en la Cuenca Media del Río Magdalena. In *Ambito y ocupaciones tempranas de la America Tropical,* pp. 73–82, Inés Cavelier y Santiago Mora, eds. Fundación Erigaie, Instituto Colombiano de Antropología, Santa Fé de Bogotá.

Lynch, T. F.
1989 Chobshi Cave in Retrospect. *Andean Past* 2:1–32. Latin American Studies Program, Dept. of Anthropology, Cornell University, Ithaca.

Lynch, T. F. and S. Pollock
1980 Chobshi Cave and Its Place in Andean and Ecuadorean Archeology. In *Anthropological Papers in Memory of Earl Swanson, Jr.,* pp. 19–40, Lucille B. Harten, C. N. Warren, Donald H. Tuohy, eds. Idaho Museum of Natural History, Pocatello.

1981 La Arqueología de la Cueva Negra de Chobshi. *Miscelanea Antropológica Ecuatoriana; Boletín de los Museos del Banco Central de Ecuador 1,* pp. 92–119; Quito.

Moseley, M. E.
1992 Maritime Foundations and Multilinear Evolution: Retrospect

References Cited

and Prospect. *Andean Past* 3:5–42. Latin American Studies Program, Dept. of Anthropology, Cornell University, Ithaca.

Murra, J. V.
    1972 El "Control Vertical" de un máximo de pisos ecológicos en la economía de las sociedades andinas. In *Visita de la provincia de León de Huánuco (1562), Iñigo Ortiz de Zuñiga, Visitador,* ed. J. V. Murra, T. 2, pp. 429–476. Universidad Nacional Hermilio Valdizán, Huánuco.

    1975 *Formaciones Económicas y Políticas del Mundo Andino.* Instituto de Estudios Peruanos, Lima.

Newcomer, M. H. and G. de G. Sieveking
    1980 Experimental Flake Scatter-Patterns: A New Interpretative Technique. *Journal of Field Archaeology* 7:345–352.

Ossa, P. P.
    1973 *A Survey of the Lithic Preceramic Occupation of the Moche Valley, North Coastal Peru; With an Overview of Some Problems in the Study of the Early Human Occupation of West Andean South America.* Unpublished Ph D. dissertation, Department of Anthropology, Harvard University, Cambridge, Mass.

    1976 A Fluted "Fishtail" Projectile Point from La Cumbre, Moche Valley, Peru. *Ñawpa-Pacha 13* (1975):97–98; Berkeley.

Ossa, P. P. and M. E. Moseley
    1972 La Cumbre, a Preliminary Report on Research into the Early Lithic Occupation of the Moche Valley, Peru. *Ñawpa-Pacha 9* (1971):1–16; Berkeley.

Owen, W. E.
    1938 The Kombewa Culture, Kenya Colony. *Man,* 38, 218:203–205.

Pannoux, P.
    1991 *Etude des dépôts d'ichtyofaunes des gisements précéramiques de Cerro El Calvario et Cerro Julia (Vallée de Casma - Pérou).* Mémoire non publié de D.E.A., Histoire de l'Art et Archéologie, option Préhistoire, Université Paul Valéry–Montpellier III.

Parenti, F.
    1993 *Le gisement quaternaire de la Toca do Boqueirão da Pedra Furada (Piauí, Brésil), dans le contexte de la Préhistoire américaine. Fouilles, stratigraphie, chronologie, évolution culturelle,* 4 vol. Thèse de Doctorat, Ecole des Hautes Etudes en Sciences Sociales, Paris.

Patterson, L. W.
    1997 Comments on Shott's Bifacial Reduction Debitage Analysis. *Lithic Technology* 22(2):184–187.

Patterson, T. C.
    1966 Early Cultural Remains on the Central Coast of Peru. *Ñawpa-Pacha* 4:145–153; Berkeley.

Pelegrin, J.
    1981 Experiments in Bifacial Work: About "laurel leaves." *Flintknappers Exchange* 4(1):4–7.

    1991 Aspects de Démarche Expérimentale en Technologie Lithique. In: *25 ans d'études technologiques en Préhistoire; bilan et perspectives,* pp. 57–63. APDCA, Juan-les-Pins: (Actes des XIèmes Rencontres internationales d'Archéologie et d'Histoire d'Antibes; 18–20 Octobre 1990).

    1995a Réflexions Méthodologiques sur l'étude de séries lithiques en contexte d'atelier ou de mine. *Les mines de silex au Néolithique en Europe: avancées récentes,* pp. 157–165, J. Pelegrin et A. Richard eds., Editions. du Comité des Travaux Historiques et Scientifiques, Paris. (Actes de la Table-Ronde internationale de Vesoul: "Les minières de silex néolithiques en Europe occidentale," 18–19 Octobre 1991).

    1995b *Technologie lithique: le Châtelperronien de Roc de Combe (Lot) et de La Côte (Dordogne).* Cahiers du Quaternaire no. 20, CNRS Editions, Paris.

Pelegrin, J. and C. Chauchat
    1993 Tecnología y función de las puntas de Paiján: el aporte de la experimentación. *Latin American Antiquity* 4(4): 367–382.

Petrequin, P. and A.-M. Petrequin
    1993 *Ecologie d'un outil: la hache de pierre en Irian Jaya (Indonésie).* Monographies du C.R.A. No. 12, CNRS éditions, Paris.

Pigeot, N.
    1987 *Magdaléniens d'Etiolles: économie de débitage et organisation sociale (l'unité d'habitation U5).* XXVème supplément à Gallia-Préhistoire, CNRS Editions, Paris

Roosevelt, A., et al.
    1996 Paleoindian Cave Dwellers in the Amazon: The Peopling of the Americas, *Science* 272:373–384.

Roux, V.
    1991 Peut on interpreter les activités techniques en termes de durée d'apprentissage? Apport de l'ethnologie et de la psychologie aux études technologiques. In *25 ans d'études technologiques en Préhistoire ; bilan et perspectives.* APDCA, pp. 47–56; Juan-les-Pins. (Actes des XIèmes Rencontres internationales d'Archéologie et d'Histoire d'Antibes; 18–20 Octobre 1990).

Shott, M. J.
    1996 Stage Versus Continuum in the Debris Assemblage from Production of a Fluted Biface. *Lithic Technology* 21(1):6–22.

    1997 On Apples and Oranges. *Lithic Technology* 22(2)188–189.

Testart, A.
    1986 *Essai sur les fondements de la division sexuelle du travail chez les chasseurs-cueilleurs.* Cahiers de l'Homme, Ethnologie-Géographie-Linguistique, Nouvelle Série 25; Editions de l'Ecole des Hautes Etudes en Sciences Sociales, Paris.

Tixier, J.
    1967 Procédés d'analyses et questions de terminologie concernant l'étude des ensembles industriels du Paléolithique récent et de l'Épipaléolithique dans l'Afrique du Nord-Ouest. In *Background to Evolution in Africa,* W. W. Bishop and J. Desmond Clark eds., pp. 771–820, Chicago University Press, Chicago. (Proceedings of a Symposium held at Burg Wartenstein, Austria, July–August 1965, Wenner-Gren Foundation).

    1978 *Méthode pour l'étude des outillages lithiques.* Unpublished ms. Notice sur les travaux scientifiques de Jacques Tixier, présentée en vue du grade de Docteur-ès-Lettres; Université Paris X.

    1980 Raccords et remontages. In *Préhistoire et technologie lithique, 11–13 Mai 1979,* pp.50–55. Publications de l'URA 28 ; cahier 1, Centre de Recherches Archéologiques. Centre Régional de Publication de Sophia-Antipolis, Editions du CNRS, Paris.

Tixier, J., F. Marmier, and G. Trecolle
    1976 *Le Campement Préhistorique de Bordj Mellala.* Editions du Cercle de Recherches et d'Etudes Préhistoriques, Paris.

Uceda, S.
    1986 *Le Paijanien de la région de Casma (Pérou): industrie lithique et relations avec les autres industries précéramiques.* Thèse de Doctorat; Université Bordeaux I.

    1992 La ocupación paijanense en la Region de Casma, Peru. *Ciencias Sociales; revista de la Facultad de Ciencias Sociales,* Vol. 2, Año 1992-1, pp. 1–78. Trujillo.

Uceda, S. and C. Deza
    1979 *Estudio de dos talleres líticos en superficie; un aporte metodológico.* Tesis de bachillerato, Universidad Nacional de Trujillo, Perú.

Whittaker, J. C.
   1994 *Flintknapping: Making and Understanding Stone Tools.* University of Texas Press; Austin.

Young D. E. and R. Bonnichsen
   1984 *Understanding Stone Tools: A Cognitive Approach.* Peopling of the Americas Process series, vol. 1; Center for the Study of The First Americans, University of Maine, Orono.

Young, D. E., R. Bonnichsen, D. Douglas, J. McMahon, and L. Swartz
   1994 Low Range Theory and Lithic Technology: Exploring the Cognitive Approach. In *Method and Theory for Investigating the Peopling of the Americas;* pp. 209–238, R. Bonnichsen and D. G. Steele eds. Center for the Study of the First Americans, Oregon State University, Corvallis.

Index

algarrobo (*Prosopis pallida*)   7, 17, 110
andesite   110, 116
biface   1–2, 6–9, 13–18, 20–23, 25, 33–38, 41–42, 45, 50–51, 54–55, 60, 64–66, 69–70, 72–73, 75, 77–80, 82–89, 92, 94, 96, 98–99, 103, 106, 109–110, 113–116, 129–130
bone   4, 30, 37, 40–41, 43, 116, 119–120
Bostryx   See snail
brown rhyolite   37–38, 41, 45–46, 50–51, 110–111, 116
Caverna de Pedra Pintada site   6
Cerro Chivateros site   1
Cerro Tres Puntas   1, 5, 29, 30, 35
chaîne opératoire   7, 14–16, 21–22, 25, 33–34, 37–38, 94, 96, 98, 129
Chobshi site   6
cobble   5, 7, 37, 39–41, 106, 116
coco   See *Paralonchurus*
cortex   7, 15–19, 21–23, 25, 27, 33, 45, 47, 50–51, 59–60, 62, 65, 67, 69–70, 72–74, 77, 80–81, 84–86
Corvina dorada   See *Micropogonias altipinnis*
Cupisnique   1–4, 10, 30, 35–38, 106, 110, 113–117, 119, 129–130
dacite   37
denticulate   37
discoid core   40
El Inga site   3, 6
Fell's Cave   3
fishtail point   3–6
foliate   6–9, 11, 14–15, 17–19, 24–25, 35, 37–38, 50, 54–55, 60, 65, 67, 72–74, 77, 79–82, 85, 87, 94, 96
gray tuff   See pale gray tuff
green tuff   33–34, 37–39, 41, 45–46, 48–51, 57, 80–89, 92, 96–99, 103, 108–110, 116
hammer   6–7, 14–18, 20–24, 30, 33, 50, 54, 72, 80, 92, 104, 106, 109–110, 114–115
hammerstone   37, 39–40
hearth   30, 32, 40, 55

knife   37–39, 77, 81, 85, 109
Kombewa flake   17–18, 22–23, 27, 33, 45, 47, 50–51, 59–60, 62, 65, 67, 69, 72–74, 77, 80–82, 84–86, 92
La Cumbre site   2, 4
Lagidium peruvianum   See *vizcacha*
limace   2, 103, 106, 109–110
lizard   36, 115, 119–120
Luz complex   1
Micropogonias altipinnis   119
Mugil cephalus   See mullet
mullet (*Mugil cephalus*)   119–120
Odocoileus virginianus   17
pale gray tuff   33, 37–38, 41, 45–46, 50–51, 88, 92–94, 97–99, 106–107, 109–110, 116
pale rhyolite   29–30, 33–34, 37–38, 41, 44–55, 57, 59–60, 62, 65, 67, 69, 72–74, 77, 80, 82, 85, 88, 92, 96, 110, 116
  arenosa   67–68, 70, 82, 86, 88, 91–92, 97–99
  colorada   72, 74, 78, 82, 84, 92, 97–99
  crema/rayada   74, 77, 84, 86, 88, 91–92, 98
  ferruginosa   59–64, 68, 82, 86, 88, 92, 96–99
  floreada   62–63, 65, 70, 74, 82, 88, 92, 97–99
  granito   73–74, 79, 82, 84, 86, 88, 91–92, 96–99
  gris-fina   72–73, 76, 82, 92, 94, 96–99, 116
  gris-violácea   73–74, 82, 84, 92, 94, 96–99, 116
  linea-azul   69, 86, 90
  linea-rosada   67, 69, 71, 82, 86, 88, 90, 92, 97–99
  linea-rosada/azul   67, 69, 71, 82, 86, 88, 90, 92, 97–99
  micro-puntillada   65–67, 70, 82, 86, 88, 91–92, 97–99
  morada   74, 77, 80–84, 92, 96–99
  naranjilla   60–62, 64, 77, 82, 92, 96–99
  porosa-blanca   69–70, 72, 99, 116
  porosa-rosada   69–70, 96, 99, 116
  puntillada   62–65, 70, 77, 82, 88, 92, 96–99
  rosada-verde   72, 75, 82, 98–99
  salmón   4, 69, 74, 77, 82, 92, 97–99
Pampa de los Fósiles   1, 4–11, 13–15, 17, 20, 23, 25, 29–30,

33, 35–38, 56, 59, 69, 80, 84–85, 92, 98, 103–104, 109–111, 115–117, 120, 129–130

Paralonchurus 119–120

pebble tool 2, 37, 39

Pedra Furada rockshelter 6

percussion 6–7, 16–17, 20–22, 33, 37–38, 41, 47, 54, 65, 67, 82, 94, 96, 103–104, 106, 109–110, 116

point 1–11, 13–15, 18–25, 29, 33–38, 40–42, 46, 48, 50, 54, 59–60, 62–63, 65, 67, 69–70, 73–74, 77, 79, 81–82, 85–88, 92, 94–100, 103–104, 106, 109–110, 113–117, 127, 129–130

Prosopis pallida See *algarrobo*

quarry 1–2, 5–9, 15–17, 22, 29, 37, 59, 62, 67, 69–73, 79–80, 92, 94, 96–98, 116

quartz 6, 37–38, 41, 45–46, 50–51, 111, 116

quartzite 7, 33, 37–39, 41, 45–46, 50–51, 88, 103, 106–110, 116–117

Quebrada de Cupisnique 36–38, 106, 116–117, 130

Quebrada Santa Maria site 10, 116

refits 7, 29, 33–34, 36, 38–41, 46, 54–55, 59–60, 62–88, 90, 94–96, 103–104, 106, 109–110, 114

resharpening 11, 34, 100, 105–109, 114

retouching 6–7, 9, 18–22, 33, 38–40, 43, 54–55, 65, 69, 81, 88, 94, 96, 100, 103–104, 106, 109–110

rhyolite 5–6, 13, 20–21, 29–30, 33–34, 37–39, 41, 44–55, 57, 59–62, 65–86, 88, 90–92, 96–98, 103, 109–111, 116

Scelidodon 5

scraper 37, 109, 114, 130

Scutalus See snail

sidescraper 2, 39

siret fracture 7

snail 36, 115, 119–120

suco See *Paralonchurus*

thinning 7, 17–18, 20–22, 24, 88, 97–98

tranchet 37, 39, 85

uniface 2, 30, 33–34, 37–38, 41–42, 87–88, 97–98, 100, 103–110, 114–116, 130

vizcacha (*Lagidium peruvianum*) 116, 119–120

volcanic tuff 37–38, 41, 48–49, 80, 82, 86–87, 94, 103, 108, 116

workshop 1–4, 6–7, 9–11, 13–17, 20, 22–25, 29–30, 32–33, 35–41, 46, 55–56, 59, 62, 71–72, 80, 85, 87–88, 92, 94, 96–98, 100, 103–104, 110, 113–116, 120, 129–131